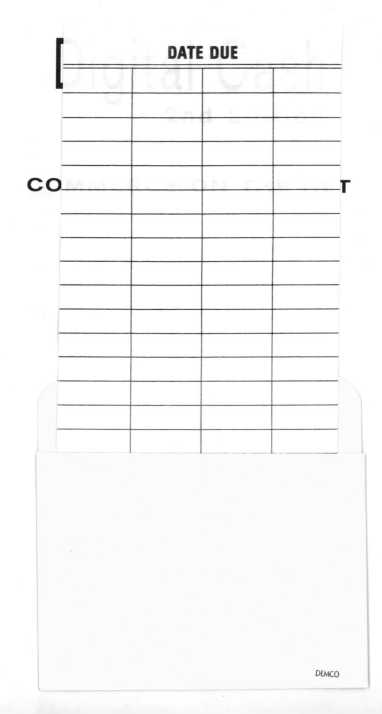

DATE DUE

Digital Cash
2nd Edition

COMMERCE ON THE NET

Peter Wayner

AP PROFESSIONAL
AP Professional is a division of Academic Press

Boston   San Diego   New York
London   Sydney   Tokyo   Toronto

United Kingdom Edition published by
ACADEMIC PRESS LIMITED
24–28 Oval Road, London NW1 7DX

ISBN 0-12-788772-5

Printed in the United States of America
97 98 99 00 CP 9 8 7 6 5 4 3 2 1

Contents

Contents

Contents   ix

Preface

The topic of this book, digital commerce, is one of the fast-moving areas of computer science research today. This means that the book, alas, will be obsolete or at least incomplete from the minute it is sent to the printer. I hope to maintain pointers to new information from my Web page, which is listed at the end of this section. Please feel free to contact me (`pcw@access.digex.net`) with new and updated information so I can post it to this page.

This book would be incomplete if it did not come with an acknowledgment of the indirect help I received from the people who contribute to the cypherpunk mailing list. Many of the members of this list started following the details of electronic money long before I became interested in the topic. Thank you to everyone on the list for providing such a strong group with an intense interest in mapping out the future.

I also owe special thanks to several members in specific. Both Tim May and Hal Finney offered deeper help when I needed it. Bruce Schneier provided both important details and an electronic copy of the bibliography from his book. Bodo Moeller and Rob Slade offered very helpful suggestions for correcting errors in the first edition.

Tom Vartanian, Bob Ledig, Dave Banisar, and Stewart Baker deserve thanks for submitting to the questions I asked them for the interviews.

Jeff Pepper, Mike Williams, Chuck Glaser, Gael Tannenbaum, and Cindy Kogut at AP PROFESSIONAL helped me through many details and provided the support that writers need.

Finally, I want to thank everyone in my family for their strong support.

Peter Wayner
Baltimore, MD
`http://access.digex.net:/~pcw/pcwpage.html`

Book Notes

The copy for this book was typeset using the LaTeX typesetting software. Several important breaks were made with standard conventions in order to remove some ambiguities. The period mark is normally included inside the quotation marks like this "That's my answer. No. Period." This can cause ambiguities when computer terms are included in quotation marks because computers often use periods to convey some meaning. For this reason, my electronic mail address is "pcw@access.digex.com". The periods and commas are left outside of all quotes to prevent confusion.

Chapter 1

Introduction

Money is a great invention that makes much of modern life possible. A society just can't support so many people working in so many different endeavors without a standard way to trade goods and services. Barter begins to fail and some central, most-desired item starts to assume the role of a currency. Even in prisons where the wardens often try to control behavior by controlling the money supply, surrogate currencies like cigarettes evolve to fill the vacuum. Money is distilled work. It lets us bottle up our work, save it, invest it, or trade it for someone else's work.

The Internet and all of the network culture is reaching that point where everyone is clambering for a way to exchange money. The Net evolved as a generous place where people freely gave away information, in part because there was no simple way to charge for it. You could ship a megabyte across the country in a flash, but you couldn't move a penny. People shared with the hope that someone would share with them. Now, people want to do more.

Free information is nice, but there are many cases where people are willing to pay for more. They may want, for instance, to trade some physical good that can't be spun out of raw imagination like most of the information on the network. The Net is just another convenient way to place an order and complete a transaction. There is a pizza delivery service on the network that lets people order and pay the cash on delivery. If some electronic money transfer would work, the drivers would not need to carry cash, saving them the danger of robbery and the annoyance of false orders.

There are many advantages to digital orders and digital shopping malls. They allow people to get up-to-date information that they really want. There is no need to flood the paper mail system with printed catalogs. Both printing costs and postage charges disappear. If a company wants to launch a sale, it can change the current catalog available on-line immediately. Close-out sales, narrowly targeted marketing, and flexible catalogs tailored to past orders become possible instantaneously.

Beyond the world of real goods, people are also willing to pay for information. The morning newspaper is worth something in part because the paper's staff spends plenty of time sifting through the raw data coming from the world and then presenting it well. This takes time and effort, and someone must pay for the food on the writer's table. In the future, electronic news services should continue to supply the network with information that is clean, accurate, and sorted for relevance. There needs to be a way for people to stick electronic coins in an electronic newspaper machine to receive the data.

There is also no doubt that even more original sales techniques could emerge if some quick and digital means of exchange were possible. A novelist might post the first chapter of a book for free and charge for the remainder. If people like it and become hooked, the book might sell. This can be done with conventional paper or credit card transactions, but the delay of delivery is often imposing. A quick, digital transaction would solve all of this and deliver the rest of the book before the reader's desire cooled.

The digital market has great potential because the transactions might grow increasingly small if the costs drop. What if someone discovered a way to cheat on a popular game like SimCity? Would you pay $1.00 for a tidbit of knowledge that would let you add a million dollars into your city's treasury and pay for a vast expansion of the city? Would you pay $.10? Now, most people don't charge for such small transactions because the accounting and transaction costs are too high. But digital money has the possibility to make much of this incidental. People with insight might make a decent amount of money selling these tips to a world that is willing to pay a trifle for them. You only need to sell 100,000 trifles at $.10 apiece to make $10,000. If there are one billion people on the Net, that is only one out of 10,000. Digital transactions on the network have the chance to make all of this possible.

We are about to step into a different realm. Some of the uses of digital money won't be much of a change. We'll still buy things in much the same way that we buy them today—the Net will just serve as the transaction ether. Other uses, though, may turn out to be surprising if the low cost of digital transaction makes new markets possible. Small bits of information and products will travel in new markets created by lower transaction costs. Only time will tell what will emerge when fast, digital transactions become possible over the network.

What Can Emerge

The regular world already supports many different forms of payment. There is cash, the bank check, the cashier's check, the traveler's check, the credit card, and the bank wire. All of these are denominated in a government's currency. There are also gold coins, gems, and other valuable items that often act as money in more circumspect situations. In larger transactions, U.S. Treasury bonds often serve as cash that is backed by full faith and credit of the U.S. government. In other cases, the bonds of local governments and large companies also serve as cash for large transactions. The stock of companies is also used for transactions because the stock market often allows us to value these companies effectively. When the employees of the companies receive stock options as compensation, the derivative securities are used to make payments. The list can be expanded even further if you relax the definition of what constitutes a payment.

Most of these forms of payment are already computerized. Pieces of paper are still used in many transactions, but computers back up most of the details and keep everything straight. What more can be done? Why can't these current instruments and their electronic systems be changed to serve the wider network? Isn't this a matter for the programmers to work out the details? Yes, all of the old methods will be carried over onto the network, but it is not as simple as creating some PC software that allows anyone with a modem or an Internet connection to charge someone's credit card. Fraud is already a big problem with credit cards. Removing physical signatures and phone calls will only add more problems. To paraphrase a *New Yorker* cartoon, on the Internet, no one knows if you're really the dog who owns the credit card.

This book is really about creating and maintaining authentic, online reputations of people who have been and will be responsible for their debts. It is about signing documents without paper or pen, proving that you are who say you are without a laminated driver's license, and transferring money without transferring something physical. Each of these techniques can be accomplished using some intriguing mathematical algorithms.

The algorithms designed to maintain secrecy and authenticity make it simple to create completely digital analogs of all of the forms of payment. Digital cashier's checks, traveler's checks, and credit card transactions just need digital signatures. If more complicated algorithms are used, then even anonymous digital cash can be created that prevents people from tracking who spends what where.

When digital cash is available, then truly digital transactions will be possible. Although the topic of this book is digital money, there is no reason why the algorithms can't be used in many other contexts. Some of the manifestations could be:

Private Cash System A bank, corporation or person, for that matter, could begin to issue private, anonymous digital notes to the world and stand behind them. Solid companies with good reputations for managing large amounts of money could succeed. In the past, many banks issued private bank notes in this way before the job was undertaken by the government. This is the most extreme use of the algorithms in the book.

Digital Clearinghouses Some companies on the network offer Net citizens the chance to convert bits into cash from the real world. They do this by billing the payer and then transferring the money into the seller's bank account. This technology will continue to be quite important in the near future because cyberspace is still a small, small fraction of the real world. There isn't that much that people are willing to pay for in cyberspace. This book will describe the systems of several companies on the market already.

Digital Coupons Coupons are like cash, but they come with many restrictions. In some cases, the companies use the coupons as advertisement and print as many as possible. If the companies want to limit the flow of coupons, they can use the algorithms described in here to constrain them.

Anonymous Auction Houses Many auctions are still conducted in lush settings of the premier auction houses like Sotheby's. Getting people together in a social setting is a valuable tool. But many markets are too thin to support this behavior. Better auctions can be run with this technology if there is no need to gather all of the interested people in one room in New York City.

Help Coupons Many manufacturers now charge for technical help. Some try to alleviate the pain of buying a new product by giving free help for a set period of time. Another solution might be to dispense digital help coupons that offered a fixed amount of free help.

These are just some of the systems that are possible using the basic protocols described in this book. They can be extended to cover many situations and may even create new markets that no one has imagined yet.

Technical Challenges

Creating truly digital money has a number of technical challenges. System designers are facing them with a variety of different solutions. The commercial systems actually working in the world today involve a number of compromises where the company chose to avoid one feature in order to reduce the complexity of their system. Some of the challenges are:

How can counterfeiting be stopped? The biggest problem with any digital cash system is the ease of copying digital information. Any digital bank note can be copied ad infinitum. This is bound to lead to cheating.

Digital signatures are one method of guaranteeing responsibility. If they are created in the correct order, then culpability can be assigned and fraud can be contained. But even digital signatures can be copied.

The solution is to create complex audit mechanisms that will identify the people who are spending a packet of bits twice.

How much security is necessary? Credit cards aren't very secure. If you know the number, then you can charge away. As a result, credit card fraud is immense. The companies, though, apparently decided that it was better to make transactions very easy because this encouraged cardholders to spend away. The profits from widespread use more than pay for the cost of fraud.

Any designer of a digital money system faces the same abstract decision. Many mathematical algorithms can add more and more security, but using these algorithms often has costs. More complicated mathematics requires faster computers to solve the equations, which means that the central computers must be beefier and the local computers that might be mounted on the credit card must also be stronger. More complicated mathematical algorithms often require more data per transaction. Transferring and storing this data adds to the total cost as well. How much security is a tough question to answer.

How powerful is the attacker? The average guy can steal a credit card number or a PIN number. It doesn't take much work or intelligence. Printing dollar bills, though, is much harder. An ordinary printing press won't do. What type of attacker will a digital money system be willing to withstand? Will an eavesdropper who manages to listen in to a transaction be able to gain enough information to spend away? Will the eavesdropper need a degree in advanced mathematics to break the system?

Many systems assume that the connection between the central computer and the user is secure. This is often a mistake. People peering over the shoulders of pay phone users can snag PIN numbers and phone credit card numbers. The cellular phone industry assumed that only a few computer hackers would be able to snag the secret ID number that a cell phone would broadcast automatically. That was true at the beginning, but the knowledge spread quickly and now cell phone fraud is a huge problem for the industry.

Can a digital money system assume that none of the attackers went to college? Rarely. The unemployment rate of college graduates is significant. Education and technological information are widely available. Some of the digital cash systems described here require physical access to the communications channel to break. Others can't be broken by any publicly known method. Digital money designers need to weigh these tradeoffs.

How powerful is the customer? The average person can remember a few PIN numbers, but starts to get confused when numbers get long or complicated. Credit card systems give the consumer a credit card and the consumer only needs to be able to read and keep the card reasonably secure. But any simple low-tech breach of security will do them in.

Many of the complicated mathematical algorithms offer excellent opportunities for security, but none of them can be used by a human without a computer. This means that some portable, smart credit card must be developed to fully implement these algorithms. The card maintains the customer's account information and then does all of the necessary computations to complete the transaction. Are these extra computers worth the cost? Are they that much more flexible than a piece of plastic?

How flexible is the system? Computer systems fail. Telecommunications links can be broken. Sometimes, people want to trade money in the middle of a desert. The best digital cash system will allow people to cut deals wherever they please.

But flexibility can be complicated. One of the simplest systems requires a central bank computer to approve all transactions. If this computer is out of touch, no deals happen. More flexible, off-line systems require more complicated mathematics and computers and they may not be as secure. Assessing the flexibility of these systems is not a purely technical problem. Choosing the right level of flexibility requires a good understanding of how people behave around technology.

Who takes the risks? Credit card fraud is a major problem, but the individual card holders don't have much to worry about. U.S. law restricts the losses of individuals and forces the card companies to socialize the losses. The people who carry a balance from month to month and the merchants are the ones who pay higher fees to cover this fraud and bad debt.

Any digital monetary system must place the risk of failure upon someone. Who pays when the digital money is lost? If it's cash-like, then it may be gone for good. If it behaves like a credit card, then the central bank can stop the loss. Who pays for fraud? Is it the individual customer or the bank? The answers to all of these questions are different for each system. Some allow the banks to offer more protection. Others don't. In many cases, the tradeoff for protection is a loss of flexibility.

What records are kept? Recordkeeping and audit trails are often good. They help prevent loss and fraud. But they also cost money for storage and add complexity. Each system must create enough records to do the job without encumbering the users.

Records, though, can cause problems. There are many times when anonymity is desirable, and this is not just when people are undertaking questionable activities. Many business plans depend upon stealth, secrecy, and security. Companies keep future plans secret to preserve their investment in ideas and technology. Anonymity helps people compete effectively and this often helps keep markets free.

How does it mesh with the past? The world's economy already has two major means of creating electronic transactions. Credit cards and interbank wires both allow people to move money electronically fairly efficiently. They still have serious costs, though, that prevent them from being highly automated. Banks usually charge between $5.00 and $20.00 to make a wire transfer because their staff must do so much work to ensure that the money arrives in the right place. They charge much less for standard direct-deposit transactions that are programmed automatically. New debit cards that access your bank account through the ATM network have lowered the cost, but many customers find they're charged $.75 to make a transaction.

Credit card companies bill the business receiving the charge between .75% and 2.5% of the transaction cost. This pays for the computer networks. Many of the billing costs are covered by the high interest rates charged to the people who borrow the money temporarily. There are also many hidden costs. Fraud is such a major problem that credit card companies are beginning to refuse to pay the charges on merchants who don't check the signatures on cards. Many banks refuse to clear the credit card charges for small retailers that don't maintain a storefront merely because these fly-by-night home operations have created so much fraud in the past.

How can these past techniques fit in with the future? The best way to move forward is often to build upon the past. Banks and credit card companies have a huge collection of customers. Some new digital transaction systems will work best if they mesh with the past.

Any designer of a digital monetary system will try to answer all of these questions in the process of creating a system. In many cases, the best answers to the tradeoffs involved may not come from reason or logic. People are involved and they have very personal reactions to the process. A digital monetary system might be very technically secure and able to withstand any assault, but it will fail if people don't feel comfortable with it.

Political Challenges

Money is ultimately a political creation. It may seem to have a very fixed and permanent quality because it is counted and measured again and again, but its foundation lies upon people's faith in a particular system. Any digital monetary system must create its own foundation that is not incompatible with the rest of the world. Any designer must consider these questions:

Which government holds control? In the near future, all digital monetary systems will be grown from the conventional banking system and so will be subject to the local laws and regulations. These laws will probably require that the digital monetary system will bear a strong resemblance, at least legally, to the system of checks and credit cards. This may not be because these are superior, but because they stand the best chance of making it to market without stepping upon any laws.

In the more distant future, governments will probably lose control. The 50 states once were able to enforce strong control over the banks within their borders. Today, interstate banking is rapidly becoming the norm as the regulations disappear. The local politicians don't have the will or the ability to maintain power over banks that want to expand. This trend will only continue in the future as banks become more and more global. Already, the public has been treated to a long but confusing scandal about BCCI and its attempt to maintain control over a U.S. bank. There will continue to be very strong market forces that will push to dissolve these national borders.

Any digital cash system must, at least for the short term, answer to a certain government. In the long run, though, no one knows what will happen as the forces of globalization and technological development make it possible for worldwide commerce to work quickly. Digital cash systems that don't require the transfer of physical assets will speed this evolution when they become available to everyone.

Which currency will be standard? Most people may instinctively choose the dollar as the denomination of choice for digital money. After all, Hong Kong, Mexico, and Argentina chose to tie the value of their local currency to the U.S. dollar to provide stability. But as this book is being written, the financial markets are roiling. The value of the dollar is dropping as more and more people flee toward currencies that seem more stable. No one, though, is sure whether the smaller countries like Japan and Germany have economies that are large enough to support a world-standard currency.

At the beginning, any digital cash system will be tied to a single currency. But there is no reason why banks will not be able to offer complicated accounts that automatically invest portions of the deposits around the globe. This is already done by mutual funds. If these funds begin to offer digital drafts upon the account, then the strength of one government will begin to dissolve in the face of market discipline.

Who is accountable? In the past, banks often invested heavily in strong, stone or marble architecture because they wanted to project an image of stability and permanence. This contributed to the faith of the people who deposited their money in the banks. Marble columns, though, don't count for much in cyberspace when anyone with a raytracing graphics program can create a stunning façade.

Many of the current companies offering digital monetary systems are small companies. Who will be accountable if they fail? Will they find a place in the Federal Deposit Insurance Corporation program? Will the government back these transactions? Any creator of a digital monetary system will need to pay particular attention to creating a solid reputation and maintaining its ability to pay debts.

What about taxes? In the past, many taxes revolved around real property. This was largely because it was impossible to track something as fleeting as a financial transaction. Today, the U.S. government actively attempts to follow money by requiring that all transactions worth more than $10,000 be reported to the government. This allows them to successfully run a sales and income tax system that is built upon the ethereal flow of money instead of the solid world of real property.

Digital money will need to be integrated into the taxation system in some form or other because it seems unlikely that governments will return to taxes collected solely upon real property. In the beginning, taxing digital money flows will be straightforward for systems that simply extend basic banking. In the future, it may grow even more complex. *Fortune* magazine tells the story of a man who made a long series of complex mutual fund trades over the year and ended up with a $50,000 loss at the end of the year. Yet the IRS demanded over $200,000 in taxes because their accounting system taxed each trade differently. The total taxes due didn't reflect the fact that in the end, $50,000 was lost.

Any complicated form of digital money could run afoul of the tax laws in just the same way. These laws were drawn up years ago when securities and contracts were traded infrequently by most people. Today, electronics have made many complicated transactions possible, and this may overwhelm the tax system.

What about money laundering? One definition of money laundering is the process by which law breakers convert their cash to make it look as if it had been legitimately earned. So a cocaine dealer may also run a pizza shop where the cash from drug transactions is reported as sales of pizzas. To the public, the police, and the IRS, the drug dealer looks like the owner of a very successful pizza business.

Another definition of money laundering is exchanging money without telling the government about it. The problem with any attempts to monitor the flow of money throughout the economy is that money is so fungible. A pizza parlor may charge $25.00 for a pizza that might normally cost $5.00. Then it would make the unwritten pledge to exchange some coupon from the box for $20.00 worth of drugs.

Distinguishing between the legitimate sale of a $25.00 pizza and the fake sale is logically impossible in the free market. The pizza dealer may claim, with a straight face, that the pizza sauce is so special that it is worth so much more to the customers. Unless the police are able to uncover a drug transaction where the pizza box coupon is exchanged, there may be no simple way to prove "money laundering" in court.

Governments are increasingly trying to regulate the flow of money in the hopes that this will help them control the profit from crime. Digital transaction systems will be under heavy scrutiny to prove that they will not undermine the government's efforts.

The political considerations for setting up any digital cash system can be significant. The best solution will be to mimic the past because people feel most comfortable when this happens. The most radical systems, though, may encounter substantial resistance from governments when these systems offer threats to their power. Money is a distilled essence of work, and bottling it means power. Changing the form of money can threaten power, and all changes should take this into consideration.

How to Use This Book

This book contains a wide collection of information about exchanging money over the Internet. A large portion of it is technical and filled with algorithms that can accomplish different tasks. The details are very mathematical and intriguing, at least to those who like abstract math. Another large section is devoted to a survey of the different commercial systems available. These details are quite important to anyone who is trying to set up shop on the Internet. The final section is devoted to discussing the money of the past and guessing about the money of the future. It is intended to expand the discussion of what was and might be possible.

Many people will read this book for a variety of reasons. Here are some suggestions for the best way to get what you want from the book.

A Broad Overview

Many people are interested in the general topic of exchanging value on the network. Here is the best way to proceed:

1. Read the first chapter as an introduction.
2. Read Chapter 5 for an overview of the various commercial systems around. Read the chapters devoted to any system that seems particularly interesting.
3. Chapter 26 offers a short, historical summary of the history of money in the United States. This provides a good basis for understanding the past and learning from it.
4. Chapter 27 contains a number of predictions about the future and some directions for future creation.

A Programmer Designing a System

Some people will be implementing a digital monetary system. Here are some suggestions:

1. Read this chapter with attention to the tradeoffs that are enumerated.
2. Read Chapter 2 if you are not familiar with the various encryption algorithms.
3. Study Chapters 3 and 4 for details about how to design digital cash systems.
4. Study Chapter 5 for an overview of the various commercial systems. These will give you some indication of how others have negotiated the tradeoffs for creating a digital cash system.
5. Read the particular chapters of interest.
6. Read Chapter 25 to get a brief understanding of how digital cash systems can be broken.

7. Read Chapter 26 for insight into how money was created and used in the past.

8. Chapter 27 is filled with some blue-sky ideas about how future cash systems can be built.

A Future Internet Merchant

Many people are ready to dive into business and open up a storefront on the Internet. Here are some suggestions for gaining the information you will need to do this:

1. Read Chapter 1 with an eye toward understanding the tradeoffs of creating a digital cash system.

2. Study Chapter 5, which describes many of the different commercial cash systems already supplying merchants.

3. Read the particular chapters of interest. Some chapters include sections on setting up a Web page that accepts transactions.

Chapter 2

Cryptography

Introduction

Anyone who wants to accept a pile of bits that claims to be worth something will want some way to verify the bits. Any digital monetary system requires the equivalent of a signature that proves that someone is going to stand behind the value that is encoded in the pile of bits. On the face of it, this seems to be an impossible proposition. Bits are easily rearranged and the editing process never leaves any traces behind. There is no reason why someone can't copy the signature from one digital bill or check and paste it on a new version. Nor is there any reason why someone can't copy the bill completely and spend it twice. The standard procedures against counterfeiting physical money require unique marks or complicated industrial processes that can't be duplicated by the average criminal. None of these techniques works in the digital world.

The solution lies in mathematics. There are complicated mathematical functions known as *digital signatures* that can simulate every feature of manual signatures. These digital signatures can only be produced by someone who knows a secret key, yet they can be checked by anyone.[1] The mathematical foundations of these signatures seem to be strong enough to prevent anyone from forging the signature without

---

[1] The term 'digital signature' could apply to a signature involving fingers, but this meaning is not used here at all.

the secret key. There is no publicly known way to break the systems presented here.

Digital signatures are often created from several different algorithms or equations. The rest of this chapter presents a basic introduction to the most popular algorithms in use today. The chapter also includes a description of some of the other encryption algorithms that are useful in constructing digital cash systems. The basic algorithms that will serve as building blocks for the systems in this book are:

Private-Key Encryption These encryption systems scramble data so it can only be understood by someone who possesses a single, secret or private key. This key is a large number and the same key must be used to lock and unlock the data. Some of the most common private-key systems are the U.S. government's Data Encryption Standard (DES); triple-DES, which repeats DES three times for good measure; RC-4, a proprietary algorithm from RSA Data Security (Redwood City, CA); and IDEA, an algorithm from Europe.

Public-Key Encryption These algorithms scramble data with two different keys. One is used for locking and the other is used for unlocking. The one that does the locking can't be used to do the unlocking. These algorithms have many intriguing uses including allowing people to communicate without meeting to set up a secret key. Each publishes one of their two keys (the public key) and keeps the other secret. Each then uses the public key of the recipient to encrypt the message. Only the holder of the corresponding private key can decode the message.

Public-key algorithms can be used to create digital signatures. When someone sends a file, he or she encrypts the signature line with his or her secret key. Now anyone who knows the corresponding public key can decrypt this line and check to make sure it is real. Normally the public keys will be published in an electronic "phone book," but the public key can also be attached to the message so someone can verify the signature immediately.

The most common form of public-key encryption available is the Rivest, Shamir, and Adleman system known as RSA and marketed by RSA Data Security. There are many other systems like discrete log public-key encryption that are not as well known and thus more likely to contain flaws that might be uncovered by careful scrutiny.

Secure Hash Functions Hash functions take a large file and reduce
it to a relatively short number (128 to 512 bits) so that this short
number can be used as a surrogate for the long file. The secure
hash functions have two important features that make them usable.
First, all of the possible short numbers are equally likely to emerge
from the hash function. This guarantees that all possible 2^n n bit
numbers get used. Second, it should be impossible to recreate a file
that generates any particular number.

Secure hash functions are used as surrogates to make sure that
no one changes a file. If I sent a file to you, then we could both
compare the hash values of our files. If both files showed the same
hash value then it was almost certainly not changed. The secure
feature of the hash functions is intended to prevent someone from
fiddling with the files until two are found with the same hash
value.

Long files are often digitally signed by computing the secure hash
function of the file and then "encrypting" it with the secret key.[2]
Anyone can verify the signature by decrypting the signature with
the corresponding public key and also computing the hash function of the file. If they match, then the files are almost certainly the
same. This system is often used because hash functions are much
faster to compute than public-key encryption functions.

Some of the better-known hash algorithms are MD-5, an algorithm
developed by Ron Rivest, and the U.S. government's standard
Secure Hash Algorithm (SHA).

Signature-Only Public-Key Systems Standard public-key algorithms
can be used to encrypt information. There is nothing technically
wrong with this feature, but it tends to annoy some governments
that want to control the use of encryption. This is one of the reasons why people study public-key systems that can only be used
to authenticate a signature. These systems have many of the same
features that make digital signatures useful. Only someone who
knows the right secret key can generate a digital signature. Anyone
can verify that the signature is authentic without knowing that

---

[2]The RSA public-key algorithm has symmetry so the public and the secret key can
both be used for "encryption." Not all public-key algorithms have this feature. Others
don't have this feature. The technical details are beyond this book.

secret key. But the system can't be used to encrypt messages and keep them from the eyes and ears of the police.

In practice, there are many ways that clever people can manipulate signature-only systems to send secret messages. The U.S. government, though, continues to support the systems for what seems to be reasons of bureaucratic inertia. They are unwilling to recognize anything that compromises their ability to listen in to international traffic, and they cross their fingers and hope that most people will not manipulate the systems.

The best-known signature-only system is the U.S. government's standard known as the Digital Signature Algorithm (DSA).

Blinded Digital Signatures Would you sign a blank check? Would you sign something you haven't read? In some digital cash systems, it makes sense for a bank to validate something without knowing the exact contents. Blinded digital signature algorithms let the bank do this effectively. These algorithms are used in anonymous cash to prevent the bank from keeping track of the serial numbers of digital bills.

Secret Sharing There are many times when people would like to lock up some information in a way that n different people need to be available to open it up. Safe deposit boxes require two keys, for instance. The nuclear warheads owned by the United States require two different keys to be turned simultaneously. The simplest secret-sharing systems split up data into n parts and require all n parts to be available to reconstruct the information. The more complicated ones might allow the data to be reconstructed if only k parts were available where $k < n$.

Secret sharing is used in anonymous digital cash as part of the detection system to prevent double spending. In essence, a person's identity is split into two parts. If someone spends a digital cash bill twice, then there is enough information available to reconstruct the spender's identity.

Bit Commitment These protocols are used to lock up something in a way that can't be denied later. You might want to seal a prediction for the future so that people will be able to verify that you made it in the past. These algorithms are also used in anonymous digital cash to trace cheaters.

Zero-Knowledge Proofs The current selection of cellular phones place a call by sending this message to the base station: "I'm caller 4123421939. Bill this call to my account." Is it any wonder that criminals wait with radio antennas to suck this number off the airwaves and use it with abandon?

Digital monetary systems face the same problem. They must prove they are authentic without revealing their ID number. How can you prove that you're someone who's in the club without revealing your name? Zero-knowledge proofs are a neat solution for proving that you know something without revealing any information. This algorithm could be used for a digital cash card to prove it is authentic without revealing its serial number.

Each of these algorithms is used in some form of digital money. Different systems use different algorithms. In general, the more privacy and anonymity a system offers, the more different algorithms are used. Protecting privacy while catching double-spending cheaters requires complicated collections of these systems.

Private-Key Encryption

The oldest and best-known forms of encryption use private keys that are known to both the sender and the receiver. The cryptograms in newspapers are simple examples of encryption systems that use a scrambled alphabet as a key. Each "A" might be converted into a "Q", each "B" becomes a "T", etc. Modern, computerized encryption systems use long collections of bits as the key and can be used to encrypt any digital data.

The most common private-key algorithm used today is still the U.S. government's Data Encryption Standard (DES). This algorithm was developed by IBM in the 1970s and reviewed by the National Security Agency (Fort Meade, MD) before it was released to the public. The system was adopted by the National Institute of Standards and Technology as the standard for nonclassified U.S. government data in 1976.

DES was controversial from the beginning because many people were suspicious of the intentions of the National Security Agency. Many publicly wondered whether there was a hidden trapdoor or weakness inserted to make government eavesdropping easier. Both

IBM and the government denied the existence of any trapdoor, but they never placated conspiracy theorists because they refused to declassify the reasons behind the design of DES. Letting out the details of the system into the public domain was bad enough. Teaching the world the design rationale was even worse. Many paranoid whispers were finally quelled when Eli Biham and Adi Shamir published a paper that described a type of attack they called differential cryptanalysis. Many algorithms that copied DES's structure turned out to fall easily to this attack, but DES remained firm. IBM later confirmed that it knew about differential cryptanalysis when it designed DES and strengthened the cipher against it.[3]

The basic structure of DES is now well known and imitated. Data is encrypted in 64-bit blocks with a 56-bit long key. The algorithm encrypts the data by repeating a basic scrambling in 16 rounds. In each round, the 64 bits are split into two 32-bit halves called the left and right halves. One half is scrambled by combining it with parts of the key and then passing it through a random function called an *s-box*. Then the left half is used to modify the right half.

DES gathers its strength as the basic scrambling step is repeated 16 times. The cipher gets most of its strength from the composition of the s-box, and this was the part of the design that was classified. One pass through the s-box is simple to break, but 16 passes remains computationally infeasible. Biham and Shamir showed that it was important that any biases caused by one pass through an s-box should be balanced by a different bias in the next pass. Sixteen passes is enough to thoroughly scramble the data.

That is a high-level abstraction of the DES algorithm. Here is a precise description that can be used to program it:

1. First, the 64 bits are passed through a function called the initial permutation. The order of the bits are rearranged. The first bit, for instance, is placed in the 58th bit slot. The second bit is placed in the 50th slot, and so forth. Figure 2.1 shows the complete permutation.

---

[3]Details can be found in [BS91a, BS91b, BS93a, BS93b]. Differential cryptanalysis of other ciphers is described in [BS91c, BS92]. Later work showed that Biham and Shamir were able to break DES if they had access to a large number of chosen plaintext pairs. That is, the attacker chooses a string and forces the system to encrypt it. The number of required plaintexts is much too large to be practical in many cases.

58 50 42 34 26 18 10 2 60 52 44 36 28 20 12 4 62 54 46 38 30 22 14 6 64 56
48 40 32 24 16 8 57 49 41 33 25 17 9 1 59 51 43 35 27 19 11 3 61 53 45 37
29 21 13 5 63 55 47 39 31 23 15 7

Figure 2.1. The initial permutation for DES. The 64-bit block of data is re-arranged using this table. The first bit becomes the 58th bit, the second bit becomes the 50th bit, and so forth.

Note that the bits with the same level of significance from each byte are lined up next to each other. The eighth bits from each byte end up in the first byte. These bits are often zero in data like ASCII text.

2. The 16 rounds begin. Let L_0 and R_0 stand for the left and right 32-bit halves formed by splitting up the 64 bits. Let L_i and R_i stand for the value of these halves after round i.

3. The values of L_i and R_i depend only upon the values of L_{i-1} and R_{i-1}. L_i is set to R_{i-1}. R_i is computed as $L_{i-1} \oplus P(S(K_i \oplus E(R_{i-1})))$. The function P is a 32-bit permutation, S is the s-box that takes 48 bits of input and scrambles it to produce 32 bits, and E is an expansion function that takes 32 bits and returns 48 bits. K_i is the key used in the ith round. The symbol $\oplus$ represents the exclusive-or function. The detailed steps of this process are:

   (a) At the beginning of round i, the right half, R_{i-1}, is passed through the expansion function E. This converts the 32 bits into a 48-bit set by duplicating some of the bits. The pattern is given in Figure 2.2.

   (b) The key for round i, K_i, is XORed with the result of $E(R_{i-1})$. This key contains 48 bits of the 56 bits of key material.

   (c) The result is passed through the s-box, S. In practice, the actual description of DES splits the s-box into eight parts, $S_1 \ldots S_8$. Each of these s-boxes accepts 6 bits as input and returns 4 bits. All eight of them combined convert the 48 bits of $K_i \oplus E(R_{i-1})$ into 32 bits. Notice how the 6 bits of input line up with the pattern in the E function described in Figure 2.2. Each block of

32 1 2 3 4 5 4 5 6 7 8 9 8 9 10 11 12 13 12 13 14 15 16 17 16 17 18 19 20 21
20 21 22 23 24 25 24 25 26 27 28 29 28 29 30 31 32 1

Figure 2.2. The expansion function, E, used in each of DES's 16 rounds. This converts 32 bits of input into 48 bits of output by duplicating some bits. For instance, bit 32 of the input ends up as both the first bit of the output and the 47th bit. The first bit of the input ends up as the second and the 48th.

$000000 \rightarrow 1110$	$000001 \rightarrow 0100$	$000010 \rightarrow 1101$	$000011 \rightarrow 0001$
$000100 \rightarrow 0010$	$000101 \rightarrow 1110$	$000110 \rightarrow 1011$	$000111 \rightarrow 1000$
$001000 \rightarrow 0011$	$001001 \rightarrow 1010$	$001010 \rightarrow 0110$	$001011 \rightarrow 1100$
$001100 \rightarrow 0101$	$001101 \rightarrow 1001$	$001110 \rightarrow 0000$	$001111 \rightarrow 0111$
$010000 \rightarrow 0000$	$010001 \rightarrow 1111$	$010010 \rightarrow 0111$	$010011 \rightarrow 0100$
$010100 \rightarrow 1110$	$010101 \rightarrow 0010$	$010110 \rightarrow 1101$	$010111 \rightarrow 0001$
$011000 \rightarrow 1010$	$011001 \rightarrow 0110$	$011010 \rightarrow 1100$	$011011 \rightarrow 1011$
$011100 \rightarrow 1001$	$011101 \rightarrow 0101$	$011110 \rightarrow 0011$	$011111 \rightarrow 1000$
$100000 \rightarrow 0100$	$100001 \rightarrow 0001$	$100010 \rightarrow 1110$	$100011 \rightarrow 1000$
$100100 \rightarrow 1101$	$100101 \rightarrow 0110$	$100110 \rightarrow 0010$	$100111 \rightarrow 1011$
$101000 \rightarrow 1111$	$101001 \rightarrow 1100$	$101010 \rightarrow 1001$	$101011 \rightarrow 0111$
$101100 \rightarrow 0011$	$101101 \rightarrow 1010$	$101110 \rightarrow 0101$	$101111 \rightarrow 0000$
$110000 \rightarrow 1111$	$110001 \rightarrow 1100$	$110010 \rightarrow 1000$	$110011 \rightarrow 0010$
$110100 \rightarrow 0100$	$110101 \rightarrow 1001$	$110110 \rightarrow 0001$	$110111 \rightarrow 0111$
$111000 \rightarrow 0101$	$111001 \rightarrow 1011$	$111010 \rightarrow 0011$	$111011 \rightarrow 1110$
$111100 \rightarrow 1010$	$111101 \rightarrow 0000$	$111110 \rightarrow 0110$	$111111 \rightarrow 1101$

Figure 2.3. This table shows how the first DES s-box converts 6-bit values into 4-bit ones. Note that a change in one input bit will generally change two output bits. The function is also nonlinear and difficult to approximate with linear functions.

4 bits is being scrambled in with two of its immediate neighbors. Figure 2.3 shows the first of the eight s-boxes.

(d) Some extra scrambling is added with another permutation P that is described in Figure 2.4.

(e) Finally, the result of $P(S(K_i \oplus E(R_{i-1})))$ is XORed with L_{i-1}.

4. After all 16 rounds are completed, an inverse of the initial permutation shown in Figure 2.1 is created. That means that bit 58 is returned to bit 1, bit 50 is returned to bit 2, etc.

The only step left to describe is the key scheduling algorithm. There are 56 bits of key material used in DES, but only 48 bits are used in each round. The steps for producing $K_1 \ldots K_{16}$ are as follows:

16 7 20 21 29 12 28 17 1 15 23 26 5 18 31 10 2 8 24 14 32 27 3 9 19 13 30 6 22 11 4 25

Figure 2.4. The P function used in each of the 16 rounds of DES. Bit 1 is moved to bit 16, bit 2 is moved to bit 7, and so forth.

57 49 41 33 25 17 9 1 58 50 42 34 26 18 10 2 59 51 43 35 27 19 11 3 60 52
44 36 63 55 47 39 31 23 15 7 62 54 46 38 30 22 14 6 61 53 45 37 29 21 13 5
28 20 12 4

Figure 2.5. The key transformation used to convert 64 bits of a password into 56 bits of key material by both scrambling the data and ignoring the eighth bit.

1. Initially the key may contain 64 bits. The eighth bit is ignored because it is often a zero in ASCII text. The rest of the bits are scrambled with a key transformation given in Figure 2.5. Call the result k_0.
2. The 48 key bits for each round are selected using the function described in Figure 2.6. Call this function KS.
3. Each K_i will be produced by computing $KS(k_i)$. Each k_i is produced by splitting the 56 bits of k_{i-1} into two 28-bit halves and rotating each half by s_i bits, where s_i is given in Figure 2.8.

The 16 rounds of DES are shown in a more schematic form in Figure 2.7. This figure and the text up to this point describe just how to encrypt data using DES. Decryption isn't any different. The algorithm was designed, quite cleverly, to use the same steps to encrypt and decrypt the data. The only difference is that the keys must be used in reverse order.

Many of the other private-key systems available today use a structure similar to DES. They rely upon a basic mixing step and repeat this a number of times. Ideally, the mixing steps will scramble the block of data in such a way that all parts of the block will affect all others. Some of the other systems include IDEA, Blowfish, Skipjack, and Khufu.

Although this section focused on DES, this algorithm is rapidly losing its dominance. The 56-bit key is widely considered to be too short, and some attacks have succeeded in finding minor weaknesses in the armor. Many people are using either triple-DES or one of the

14 17 11 24 1 5 3 28 15 6 21 10 23 19 12 4 26 8 16 7 27 20 13 2 41 52 31 37
47 55 30 40 51 45 33 48 44 49 39 56 34 53 46 42 50 36 29 32

Figure 2.6. The key selection function. This description is different than the other permutations given in other figures. Here, the 14th bit of the input is selected to be the first bit of the output. Bit 17 comes second. Bits like 9, 18, 22, 25, 35, 38, 43, and 54 are left out.

$$L_0 \qquad\qquad R_0$$
$$L_1 = R_0 \qquad R_1 = L_0 + f(R_0, K_1)$$
$$L_2 = R_1 \qquad R_2 = L_1 + f(R_1, K_2)$$
$$L_3 = R_2 \qquad R_3 = L_2 + f(R_2, K_3)$$
$$L_4 = R_3 \qquad R_4 = L_3 + f(R_3, K_4)$$
$$L_5 = R_4 \qquad R_5 = L_4 + f(R_4, K_5)$$
$$L_6 = R_5 \qquad R_6 = L_5 + f(R_5, K_6)$$
$$L_7 = R_6 \qquad R_7 = L_6 + f(R_6, K_7)$$
$$L_8 = R_7 \qquad R_8 = L_7 + f(R_7, K_8)$$
$$L_9 = R_8 \qquad R_9 = L_8 + f(R_8, K_9)$$
$$L_{10} = R_9 \qquad R_{10} = L_9 + f(R_9, K_{10})$$
$$L_{11} = R_{10} \qquad R_{11} = L_{10} + f(R_{10}, K_{11})$$
$$L_{12} = R_{11} \qquad R_{12} = L_{11} + f(R_{11}, K_{12})$$
$$L_{13} = R_{12} \qquad R_{13} = L_{12} + f(R_{12}, K_{13})$$
$$L_{14} = R_{13} \qquad R_{14} = L_{13} + f(R_{13}, K_{14})$$
$$L_{15} = R_{14} \qquad R_{15} = L_{14} + f(R_{14}, K_{15})$$
$$L_{16} = R_{15} \qquad R_{16} = L_{15} + f(R_{15}, K_{16})$$

Figure 2.7. This figure shows how 16 rounds encrypt the two 32-bit halves of the message L_0 and R_0. Initially, L_0 and R_0 are assembled using the initial permutation. At the end, they are disassembled using the inverse of this permutation. The function f is just shorthand for $P(S(K_i \oplus E(R_{i-1})))$.

other variants. Triple-DES uses three rounds of DES and three different keys.

Public-Key Encryption

Public-key encryption systems have two keys. One locks up the data and the other unlocks it. The important feature is that the key that locks the data *can't* unlock it. Only the other key can do this. This allows the owner of the system to publish one key and keep the other one secret. If someone wants to send a message that can't be read by anyone else, he or she looks up the public key of a person and uses it to encrypt the message. Only the person with that key can use it to decrypt the message.

1 1 2 2 2 2 2 2 1 2 2 2 2 2 2 1

Figure 2.8. The 16 values of s_i used in the key scheduling algorithm.

The owner of a pair of keys can generate digital signatures by encrypting a message with the secret key. Now anyone can decrypt the message using the published key and know that it could only have come from the person who possessed the secret key.

The most popular form of public-key encryption today is the RSA system developed by Ron Rivest, Adi Shamir, and Len Adleman. The trio developed the system when all three were at the Massachusetts Institute of Technology, and the university patented the system in their names. Currently, the Public-Key Partners in Sunnyvale, California, controls the licensing agreements.

There are other public-key systems, but they are not as widely used. For this reason, they are outside the scope of the book. Interested readers should explore Schneier's *Applied Cryptography* [Sch94] or Koblitz's *A Course in Number Theory and Cryptography* [Kob87].

While these algorithms are outside the scope of the book, they are still quite useful. Some of the basic digital cash algorithms use discrete log signatures instead of RSA signatures. Some argue, for instance, that these signatures may be more secure because they are not subject to a new factoring algorithm. This contention, however, is only a conjecture and has no solid theoretical foundation.

In any case, the world would benefit if the companies designing these systems would develop more than one algorithm. The RSA standard is good, but it is the equivalent of putting all of our eggs in one basket. A wider range of choices would allow the world to switch to a new system in an emergency caused by a sudden mathematical revelation.

RSA

The RSA public-key encryption system relies upon the mathematics of modulo arithmetic. Both encryption and decryption are completed by raising numbers to a power modulo, a number that is the product of two large primes. The two primes are kept secret. The system can be broken if the two primes are recovered by factoring, a process that has proven to be extremely difficult. No one has described any reliable way to attack the RSA system to this day, and many people are known to have tried.

Here is a short paragraph introducing modulo arithmetic for those who have never encountered it. In modulo arithmetic a number, say, p, is just like in regular arithmetic except that the system only allows numbers between 0 and $p - 1$. If the value runs over the top of p, then the values begin again at zero. For example, $4 + 5 \bmod 7 = 2$, $4 * 5 \bmod 7 = 6$, and $2 + 3 \bmod 7 = 5$. The circular nature of the domain led some to call this *clock arithmetic* because the hour of the day works as if it were calculated modulo twelve with an extra 1 added to screw up a perfect analogy.

To encode a message using RSA, a user needs to create a public and a secret key. In this system they are chosen through several steps:

1. First, two large primes, p and q, are chosen. These are usually in the range of 200 to 1000 bits today. The numbers are chosen at random and then tested to see if they are prime using tests like the ones described in [SS78, APR83, BBC$^+$88, DLP93].

2. The primes are multiplied together to yield $n = pq$. This is often at least 512 bits in practice, but it is determined by the size of p and q. 1024-bit keys are not uncommon and should become standard. Many are switching to 2048-bit keys in the face of recent attacks on shorter keys. The longer the key, though, the slower the encryption and the stronger the system.

3. The secret key e is chosen. The greatest common denominator of e and $(p - 1)(q - 1)$ must be 1.

4. The public key, d, is the inverse of $e \bmod (p - 1)(q - 1)$. The inverse can be calculated using Euclid's algorithm.

5. The factors p and q are now discarded or erased. The public key is the pair of values n and d. The secret key is the pair of values n and e.

Encryption is simple. A message is converted into a number less than n that will be called m. This can be done by any number of methods, but the simplest way is to concatenate the bytes until you have a number that is just smaller than n. If the message is longer, then the encryption must be done in blocks. m is encrypted by computing $m^d \bmod n$. This message is decrypted by computing $(m^d \bmod n)^e \bmod n$.

The decryption process works because:

$$(m^d \bmod n)^e \bmod n = m^{d^e} \bmod n$$
$$= m^{de} \bmod n$$
$$= m \bmod n.$$

One fact is left out of this chain: $m^{\psi(n)} \bmod n = 1$. $\psi(n)$ is the Euler Totient function and it counts the number of values less than n that are also relatively prime to n. $\psi(pq) = \psi(p)\psi(q) = (p-1)(q-1)$.

Encrypting could be a lengthy process if raising m to a power d required multiplying m with itself d times. A simpler algorithm can generate the same result and requires one step for every bit in d. The steps are:

1. Start with m and d. Let i be a counter that is set to 1. i will march through the bits starting with the least significant bit. Let *Ans* be the answer and initialize it to be 1. Repeat this loop until i has counted through all of the bits in d:

    (a) If bit i of d is set to 1, then set *Ans* to be $(Ans \times m) \bmod n$.

    (b) Set m to be $m^2 \bmod n$.

    (c) Increment i.

2. *Ans* now holds the value of $m^d \bmod n$.

The same algorithm can be used for decryption. The basic algorithm works quickly and efficiently, but it is not as fast as DES. For this reason, many people use RSA to encrypt a private key that will be used to encrypt the rest of the message.

The algorithm by itself is only a small part of a successful system for validating signatures. One major problem is providing people with a way to be sure that a published key is accurate. This problem can lead to eavesdropping and compromised traffic. The danger is simple to illustrate. Imagine that you create secret e_1 and publish d_1. An interloper with access to the public directory of keys creates key e_2 and substitutes d_2 for your key. If someone sends you a message, he or she mistakenly encrypts it with d_2, which allows the attacker to decrypt it with e_2. The attacker can read the message, modify it if desired and then re-encrypt it with d_1 before passing it on to you. When you receive it, you decrypt it with e_1 without realizing something went wrong.

The problem of authenticating keys is common and well studied. There are two major approaches. One involves a central authority like the Department of Motor Vehicles or a private company set up to be a trusted party. If you use Apple's newest versions of the system software, you can create your own digital signature application that will sign your files. In order to activate the software, though, you must take three copies of photo identification to a notary public who validates your form.

Apple processes the form and sends you your signing software on a disk. This software will now sign files by attaching four new values to the file. The first is the digital signature of the file computed using RSA. The second is your name. The third is a copy of your public key that anyone will be able to use to validate the signature of the file. The fourth is a signature of your public key created with Apple's pair of keys. This signature says that Apple vouches that the public key is the true key associated with the person who brought three forms of identification to the notary public.

When you ask your Apple system software to check the signature on a file it will first check to see if the public key attached to the file is authentic. The Apple system software has the public key used by Apple embedded in it. It uses this public key to check the public key of the signer. If this is valid, then it proceeds to see if the signature of the file can be checked with the signer's public key. If everything checks, then it signals success by displaying the name of the signer in a dialog box on the screen.

This model for validating digital signatures could also work well for digital cash or cashier's checks that are created by a bank. The bank could build its public key into the software that validated a bank draft and also sign the public key of a client. This would allow people to trust the signature of a client because they know that the client's public key was signed by the bank.

Another popular method of validating public keys is used by the PGP software first developed by Phil Zimmerman. This software uses a "web of trust" to bind all of the public keys. So, I might receive a public key from Alice and it comes with signatures of Bob, Carol, and Dave attesting to its authenticity. I don't know Alice, but I do know Bob. I just happen to have a copy of his public key right on my disk and Bob himself handed it to me. Knowing this, I can verify Bob's signature and this proves that Alice's public key is authentic.

The verification forms a web if you happen to traverse several of these connections before you find someone whom you "know." It's just one big web of connections. The old urban legend states that the chain of connections between any two people is no more than five links. When PGP becomes the standard for communication in this world (as it looks like it might), we will be able to implicitly measure this web of connections and see whether the story is true.

Signature-Only Systems

Public-key systems that only generate signatures began to appear with the work of T. El Gamal [ElG85a, ElG85b]. The system was novel because it created a signature for a document that could be checked, but it seemed that there was no way to encrypt information. The system worked by creating an entire class of numbers that could serve as the signature. Creating the signature was a one-to-many function, that is, a function that could have many different correct answers. Checking to see if the signature was correct was accomplished by testing to see if the signature was in the correct class of values.

The signature-only feature attracted the attention of the National Institute of Standards and Technology (NIST), which seems hesitant to advance the cause of nonclassified encryption if it can avoid doing so. A signature-only system would allow it to help the public authenticate documents without giving anyone new tools for thwarting law enforcement. They announced the Digital Signature Standard (DSS) in 1991 with the hope that this would rapidly take over the industry. Any software using the DSS could be exported, while any software using RSA would face a lengthy approval process that may or may not have resulted in an export license.

Two major problems appeared: patents and new ideas. Public Key Partners, the holding firm for the patents used by closely related RSA Data Security, quickly announced that they felt that the new DSS used technology that was covered by their earlier patents. Anyone using the system would owe them royalties. The government and RSA entered into seemingly endless negotiations that still haven't yielded any solution at this writing. This patent issue seems to be enough to scare any public group from using the technology.

Another major problem, though, was new discoveries. Gus Simmons, a scientist who worked for the U.S. government at the Sandia National Labs, discovered that it was possible to send messages through the DSS. This seems intuitively possible if you consider the fact that there is an entire class of numbers that serves as the signature. You could send a message through your choice of which number served as the signature.

Simmon's paper [Sim93] followed up earlier work from the 1980s that discovered these subliminal channels in other signature schemes like El Gamal's [Sim84, Sim85, Sim86]. He basically stated that a signature system had two channels: one overt and one that he called subliminal. The subliminal one could be used to pass messages if necessary. He graded the ability of the different signature schemes to pass information, and the DSS ranked at the top. It is my guess that this is a rough measure of the security of the system.

These subliminal channels did not seem to daunt NIST, perhaps because they are tricky to use and they might not carry enough information. It would look suspicious if there were ten different, but still consistent, signatures attached to a message. The extra nine would indicate that there wasn't enough room to hold the secret information in the first.

The DSS algorithm is described here because we may reach a point in time when the patent issues are resolved and the algorithm is free for use and export. If that happens, the algorithm would be ideal for many digital cash schemes that require signatures but not encryption. Some people may choose to use this system for its presumable exportability and resolve the patent issue simply by purchasing a license from RSA Data Security.

There are two parts to the Digital Signature Standard: the Digital Signature Algorithm (DSA) and the Secure Hash Algorithm (SHA). The DSA is based upon the El Gamal signature system [ElG85a, ElG85b] and newer work by C. Schnorr [Sch90, Sch91a, Sch91b]. All of these systems rely for their security on a problem known as the *discrete log*. This means that given a message m and a value a, it is easy to compute $m^a \bmod p$ where p is a prime number. If you are given another value n, it is difficult and certainly infeasible to discover a value of a such that $m^a \bmod p = n$. That is, it is hard to take the discrete log of n.

Any one-way function is fodder for an encryption algorithm. In this case, the one-way nature hides the signature process. The DSA begins with:

- p—a prime number between 512 and 1024 bits long. NIST suggests increasing the lengths in quantified amounts to affect the security. Longer primes mean that it would take longer to break the system. Anyone who wants to rely on signatures long into the future should choose longer values. Signatures with a value that will expire soon, though, should consider using shorter values of p because they require less time.

- q—a 160-bit prime factor of $p - 1$.

- $g = h^{\frac{p-1}{q}} \bmod p$ such that $h \leq p - 1$ and $h^{\frac{p-1}{q}} \bmod p > 1$.

- x is any number $< q$.

- $y = g^x \bmod p$

To sign a message,

1. The sender uses the Secure Hash Algorithm to compute the hash value of the message, $H(m)$. He also selects a random number k. (This random number selection is the basis for sending messages through a subliminal channel.)

2. The sender computes $r = (g^k \bmod p) \bmod q$ and $s = (k^{-1}(H(m) + xr)) \bmod q$. r and s constitute the signature and they should be attached to the message in a universal file format.

The signature is verified by computing:

1. $w = s^{-1} \bmod q$

2. $u1 = (H(m) \times w) \bmod q$

3. $u2 = (r \times w) \bmod q$

4. $v = ((g^{u1} \times y^{u2}) \bmod p) \bmod q$

5. If $v = r$ then the signatures match and the document is verified.

The easiest way to understand how the subliminal channels exist is to look at the random number selection process. If you wanted to send a one-bit message (odd or even), you could simply keep choosing random numbers and computing the signature until you came up with a signature that was either odd or even. The recipient could simply look at the signature and check to see whether it was odd or even to get the message.

Discrete Log Signature Schemes

There are several other signature schemes available, but one of the more significant is one that uses the strength of the discrete log problem. This is used as the basis for one digital cash system outlined in Chapter 3. That is, no one knows an efficient way to reverse the computation g^a mod p if p is a large prime, g is a generator, and a is an integer. Reversing the computation means receiving g^a mod p and determining a.

Although it is difficult to be precise in these matters, some cryptographers consider the discrete log problem to be more secure than RSA. The argument goes that RSA is vulnerable to both factoring attacks and ones that can be used to determine the discrete log. A new factoring algorithm could discover the two prime factors p and q that make up the modulus used in RSA and this would lead to an easy way to compute the decryption key. RSA could also submit to the same algorithm that broke a discrete log problem if this algorithm was not confined to prime moduli. This is quite possible.

An easy way to understand the discrete log signature is to look at an interactive version of it. This means that anyone who wants to check a signature generated in this way must interact with the owner of the signature. This is not optimal, but it can be modified to free it from this restriction and make it noninteractive.

Here are the steps:

1. If you have a document with hash m, you can sign it by computing m^x mod p. x is the secret key. The signature consists of m^x mod p as well as a generator g, p, and g^x mod p. These values can either be listed in a public-key directory or distributed with the signature.

2. Someone receives your message and wants to verify the signature. You create a random number w and use this to calculate g^w mod p and m^w mod p. You keep the w secret.

3. The person verifying the signature generates another random number c and sends it to you. This procedure imitates a zero-knowledge proof system constructed using discrete logs.

4. You send back the value $r = cx + w$. An attacker or eavesdropper can't use this information to determine x because a new version of w is created with each verification.

5. The person verifying the signature computes $g^r \bmod p$ and compares it with $(g^x)^c \times (g^w) \bmod p$. They should be the same. So should $m^r \bmod p$ and $(m^x)^c \times (m^w) \bmod p$.

The system works because only the owner of x can generate r such that $g^r \bmod p$ matches $(g^x)^c \times (g^w) \bmod p$ and $m^r \bmod p$ matches $(m^x)^c \times (m^w) \bmod p$. The system prevents anyone from discovering x because it is presumed to be hard to invert $m^x \bmod p$.

The system can be made noninteractive and more practical by using a cryptographically secure hash function. A hash of many of the principle values serves the same purpose as the random number c. The basic principles standing behind a secure hash practically guarantee that no one will be able to control the value of the c.

The modified steps are:

1. Given a document with hash value m, you sign it by computing $m^x \bmod p$. You also select a random number w and bind up $m^w \bmod p$ and $g^w \bmod p$ and g with the signature.

2. Instead of waiting for someone to verify the signature, you select a c by using a cryptographically secure hash function to hash up the values of $m^w \bmod p$, $m^x \bmod p$, and $g^w \bmod p$ arranged in a standard format. You cannot control the outcome of this step, so anyone verifying the signature can be sure they aren't being cheated.

3. You attach the four numbers r, $m^x \bmod p$, $g^w \bmod p$, and $m^w \bmod p$ as the signature. The value r comes from $r = cx + w$.

4. Any challenger can check this signature by computing c by hashing the four numbers m, $m^x \bmod p$, $g^w \bmod p$, and $m^w \bmod p$ and then computing $(g^x)^c \times (g^w) \bmod p$ and $(m^x)^c \times (m^w) \bmod p$.

This algorithm shows how secure hash functions can take the place of random numbers supplied by a challenger. Normally, the challenger must make the choice in order to keep someone honest. A prearranged and practically uninvertable process like the hash function can act as a good surrogate. Other one-way functions would also suffice.

Blinded Digital Signatures

You may not like signing a blank sheet of paper, but many digital cash schemes require banks to do the equivalent of this. They must be able to attach their signature to a bundle of bits despite the fact that the owner of the bundle doesn't want them to keep track of the bits. The solution to the conundrum is the blinded digital signature, which was invented and patented by David Chaum [Cha83, Cha85, Cha88b, Cha88a].

Imagine that a bank uses the RSA system to sign its bank checks. Ordinarily, it would use some hash function, $H(m)$, to compute the hash of the bundle of bits representing the note m and then it would compute $H(m)^d \bmod n$ using its secret key d and n. The problem is that the bank could keep a record of m and match it to your name. When a merchant returned with the digital note m to deposit it in an account, the bank would know where you spent your money.

You can get the bank to sign something without knowing what it is by using a *blinding factor*. That is, you ask the bank to sign $H(m)k^e \bmod n$ where k is a random number ($1 \leq k \leq n$) and e is the published key of the bank. You send the bank the value:

$$r = H(m)k^e \bmod n.$$

The bank signs this by computing:

$$r^d = (H(m)k^e)^d \bmod n.$$

The bank could try to keep a record of this transaction, but you thwart this by removing the blinding factor by computing:

$$t = r^d k^{-1} \bmod n = m^d \bmod n.$$

This solution works because $(k^e)^d \bmod n = k^{de} \bmod n = k$.

Naturally, this is only half of the solution. The bank won't want to sign a blank sheet of paper because it won't know whether r came from a \$100 bill or a \$1,000,000 bill. The solution, which is covered in detail in Chapter 4, is to present the bank with a handful of notes. It chooses one at random and sets it aside. Then it asks you for the unblinding factor for the rest so it can check them. If they all check out, it returns the one it set aside for you to use.

Hash Algorithms

The main purpose of a hash algorithm is to come up with a relatively short number that could be used as a surrogate for a large file. These are quite useful because you can then use a signature algorithm to sign the surrogate instead of the whole file, saving plenty of time.

A secondary use of hash functions is to provide a random number for two people separated by time or space in an indisputable way. The discrete log signature system described earlier uses a cryptographically secure hash function to come up with a random roll of the dice that will be the same for both the signer and the verifier. In essence, the function is meant to be so complicated that neither the signer nor the verifier can control the output of the function by twiddling with the input. This means it can be used as effective replacement for dice.

The algorithms presented here are *cryptographically secure* hash functions that make it infeasible for someone to tamper with the file in any way without the tampering changing the final hash value. A good way to see the need for this is to examine a non-cryptographically secure hash function known as the *checksum*. This procedure is still used widely in many file transfer protocols to determine whether an error occurred. Someone sending a file would add up all of the bytes of data and append this sum to the end of the file. The person at the other end would do the same thing. Since there are 8 bits in the checksum byte, then there are 256 possible values and a 1/256 chance that a random error will leave the checksum unchanged. A 32-bit checksum has a 1 in over 6 billion chance of an error going undetected.

These checksums may be quite effective against random error, but they fall quickly to malicious attack. Consider a simple file that is just the value of a money transfer: $100095. If the checksum is just computed on the digits modulo 10, then the checksum is:

$$1 + 0 + 0 + 0 + 9 + 5 = 15 \bmod 10 = 5.$$

This can be manipulated by simply rearranging the digits. A malicious attacker could convert the value of the transfer to be $951000 without changing the checksum. It can also be changed by adding some in some place while taking away in another. $960000 has the same checksum. Or it could be changed by adding extra values that sum to 10, which disappears in the modulo arithmetic. $969911 has the same checksum.

A cryptographically secure hash function is very similar to encryption. In fact, a simple hash function can be built out of a secure encryption function, $f(k, B)$, that takes a key, k, and a block of data B. For the sake of simplicity, let k, B, and the output of f have the same number of bits. If the file to be hashed consists of the blocks of data,

$B_1, B_2, B_3 \ldots B_i$, then a hash value could be computed as:

$$f(B_i, f(B_{i-1}, \ldots, f(B_2, f(B_1, R)) \ldots)).$$

The final answer serves as the hash value for the entire file. The value of R is a random vector that is part of the hash value standard [Win84a, Win84b].

It should be straightforward to see that it is hard to tamper with a hash value that comes out of this function. For instance, imagine that you want to change the first block of data, B_1, for whatever nefarious purpose you might have. The hash value will remain unchanged if you can find another value, say $\hat{B}_1$, such that $f(\hat{B}_1, R) = f(B_1, R)$. But f needs to encrypt and decrypt information successfully, which means that there should be one and only one encrypted block of data for each unencrypted block. This means that there is no other $\hat{B}_1$.

One solution is to find a $\hat{B}_2$ that balances the changes made in $\hat{B}_1$ so that $f(B_2, f(B_1, R)) = f(\hat{B}_2, f(\hat{B}_1, R))$. That means you are looking for a particular key $\hat{B}_2$ that encrypts $f(\hat{B}_1, R)$ into $f(B_2, f(B_1, R))$. Finding the key that converts one block into another is breaking the encryption with a known-plaintext attack. Most good encryption systems, including DES, resist this type of attack. Breaking the hash function would be equivalent to breaking the encryption.

MD-4, MD-5, and the SHA

Many hash functions are based on the same process as the chain of encryption functions, although they are optimized to make the process more efficient. The best-known hash functions now are MD-4 and MD-5, which were created by Ron Rivest [Kal92, Riv91, Riv92]. The structure of MD-4 was borrowed and modified by the National Institute of Standards and Technology when it created the Secure Hash Algorithm that is used with the Digital Signature Standard [Rob94, NIS92].

MD-5 processes data in 512-bit blocks and produces a 128-bit hash value. This is more efficient than using encryption functions like DES which have a block size and a key size that are close to each other. The last block of the file is often not a full 512 bits, so padding is added in the form of a single bit 1, a flexible amount of 0 bits, and then a 64-bit number representing the number of bits in the file. The extra 0 bits are added until the last block is 512 bits long. The 512-bit block is broken up into sixteen 32-bit blocks, $M_0 \ldots M_{15}$.

There are four 32-bit variables, A, B, C, and D, that are permuted in four major rounds by each of the sixteen blocks. When this is completed for all 512-bit blocks in the file, then the four values, A, B, C, and D, are appended to create the 128-bit hash value.

The four values are permuted by four different mixing functions. Round one consists of using the first function, called FF, to mix A, B, C, and D with the sixteen different values of M_0 through M_{15}. Round two has the same structure, but it uses a different function GG. Round three uses HH and four uses II.

These scrambling procedure can be summarized in equations as:

$$FF(a, b, c, d, j, s, t) = a := a + (F(b, c, d) + M_j + t) << s$$

$$GG(a, b, c, d, j, s, t) = a := a + (G(b, c, d) + M_j + t) << s$$

$$HH(a, b, c, d, j, s, t) = a := a + (H(b, c, d) + M_j + t) << s$$

$$II(a, b, c, d, j, s, t) = a := a + (I(b, c, d) + M_j + t) << s$$

The "$<<$" stands for left shift.

The basic scrambling functions, F, G, H, and I, are:

$$F(X, Y, Z) = (X \otimes Y) \oplus ((notX)andZ)$$

$$G(X, Y, Z) = (X \otimes Z) \oplus (Y \otimes (notZ))$$

$$H(X, Y, Z) = X \odot Y \odot Z$$

$$I(X, Y, Z) = Y \odot (X \oplus (notZ))$$

Here, $\otimes$ stands for a bitwise AND, $\oplus$ stands for a a bitwise OR, and $\odot$ stands for a bitwise XOR. Three of the basic functions that serve as this foundation are nonlinear. When they are used repeatedly, they scramble the data.

The entire hashing process can be summarized as follows:

1. The file is broken into 512-bit blocks and padded.
2. The four variables, A, B, C, and D, are set to 67452301, efcdab89, 98badcfe, and 10325476, respectively.
3. Each 512-bit block is processed in turn with these four rounds:

   (a) A copy of A, B, C, and D is made. Call them $\bar{A}, \bar{B}, \bar{C}$, and $\bar{D}$.

   (b) In round one, the function FF is used to operate on $\bar{A}, \bar{B}, \bar{C}$, and $\bar{D}$ sixteen times. In each of these instances, a different part of the 512-bit block, M_i, is used along with a different constant t and shift value s.

(c) In round two, the function GG is used 16 times in the same manner.

(d) In round three, the function HH is used 16 times in the same manner.

(e) In round four, the function II is used 16 times in the same manner.

(f) Finally, the values of $\bar{A}, \bar{B}, \bar{C},$ and $\bar{D}$ are added back into $A, B, C,$ and D.

4. $A, B, C,$ and D are concatenated to produce the hash value.

The values of t were chosen using a sine function. The values of s were chosen to maximize diffusion.

SHA, the Secure Hash Algorithm

The SHA is based upon MD-4, which is a shorter version of MD-5. The function produces, though, a 160-bit hash value. This is ideal because the DSS uses a 160-bit modulus and this allows the hash value to use all of it. Although some of the details behind the design of the DSS are classified, it is possible to guess that the National Security Agency felt that a 128-bit modulus was too short.

The major similarities and differences between the MD-5 and the SHA are:

- The SHA still processes information in 512-bit blocks. The padding is accomplished in the same manner.

- There are five variables, $A, B, C, D,$ and E, not four, that are used to accumulate the final hash value.

- There are four rounds, but in each round the functions are applied 20 times instead of 16. There are still sixteen 32-bit values in the 512-bit block being processed, but some are reused. This allows each of the five values, $A, B, C, D,$ and E, to get modified four times.

- The scrambling functions used are:

$$F(X, Y, Z) = (X \otimes Y) \oplus ((not X) and Z)$$

$$G(X, Y, Z) = X \odot Y \odot Z$$

$$H(X, Y, Z) = (X \otimes Y) \oplus (X \otimes Z) \oplus (Y \otimes Z)$$

$$I(X, Y, Z) = X \odot Y \odot Z$$

In this case, the same function is used in both the second and the fourth rounds. $\otimes$ stands for a bitwise AND, $\oplus$ stands for a bitwise OR, and $\odot$ stands for a bitwise XOR.

- In MD-5 the same sixteen 32-bit blocks are used. In the SHA, new versions are created for each of the 80 different rounds using an error-correcting code-like scheme. If the sixteen blocks are $M_0 \ldots M_{15}$, then the 80 modified blocks are $\bar{M}_0 \ldots \bar{M}_{79}$. For i between 0 and 15, $\bar{M}_i = M_i$. For i between 16 and 79, $\bar{M} = M_{i-3} \odot M_{i-8} \odot M_{i-14} \odot M_{i-16}$.

- The functions $FF, GG, HH,$ and II are much more complicated. The first, $FF(A, B, C, D, E)$, consists of these six steps:

1. $t = (A << 5) + F(B, C, D) + E + \bar{M}_i + 5A827999$
2. $E = D$
3. $D = C$
4. $C = B << 30$
5. $B = A$
6. $A = t$

- The function GG is the same, but it uses G instead of F and 6ED9EBA1 for the additive constant. The function HH uses H and 8F1BBCDC and the function II uses I and CA62C1D1.

The SHA may be the best hash function that is publicly available. The National Security Agency was involved in its design. While it is clear that the agency has a mission to listen in throughout the world, there is no reason why this mission would have encouraged it to weaken the SHA. The algorithm is only used to authenticate files.

Secret Sharing

There are many times when it helps to split up a secret among a number of different people. Only if all n parts are rejoined can the secret be reconstructed.

The simplest way to split up a secret is with the XOR function. If the secret will have k bits and it will be split into n parts, then create $n - 1$ random k-bit numbers, $s_1, s_2, s_3 \ldots s_{n-1}$. If the secret is S, then set $s_n = s_1 \odot s_2 \odot \cdots \odot s_{n-1}$. "$\odot$" is a bitwise XOR function. The numbers $s_1 \ldots s_n$ are the n parts of the secret, S.

This system for splitting the secret does not give a holder of one part any information about the entire secret. A simple but ineffective variant of this scheme is to simply divide the secret S into k/n bit parts. The problem with this approach is that each person knows some of the secret's bits. Let's say that the secret is a 56-bit DES key to a valuable file and this secret is shared by seven people who each hold one of the bytes. If two collaborate, then there are only 40 unknown bits of the key left. It may be possible to check all of these keys with a brute-force attack.

More complicated schemes allow a secret to be reconstructed if only m of the n total parts are available. A simple way to see how this is done is to imagine the secret as a point in m-dimensional space. Each part is constructed by creating an $m - 1$ dimensional hyperplane that contains the point. If m hyperplanes are available, then the intersection of them must be the point. It is necessary to take additional steps to ensure that the hyperplanes do not contain any degenerate cases that might cause the final intersection to be more than a point.

Bit Commitment

The bit-commitment protocol was developed to prevent people from changing answers. For instance, let's say that you wanted to prove that you were clairvoyant. You might encrypt your predictions in a file and give it to a friend. When the year is up, you would give the friend the key, he or she would decrypt it, and know you were not lying.

Here's the problem. Let's say you are predicting that O.J. Simpson is acquitted.[4] What if there are two different keys k_1 and k_2 such that $f(acquitted, k_1) = f(guilty, k_2)$? Then you could send $f(acquitted, k_1)$ to your friend. If Simpson is acquitted, then you follow up with k_1 proving you knew he was going to be acquitted. But if he is found guilty, then you send k_2.

Bit-commitment protocols are designed to prevent this deception from taking place. The simplest protocol uses a long, prearranged value, V, provided by the skeptical party. Since this protocol is often used in some of the more exotic forms of digital cash, this long value might be the bank's name in ASCII. The prediction, M, is encrypted with k to produce $f(VM, k)$. Here VM stands for concatenating the two messages.

Zero-Knowledge Proofs

The classic failure in many security systems comes when the attacker learns the password. He or she may gather this by chicanery, eavesdropping, leaning over a shoulder, or pure guesswork, but in any case the knowledge of the password is sufficient to break the system. Ultimately, this means that passwords are not very good choices to protect smart cards that must be used in potentially rough circumstances. Most cash machine cards are protected by PIN numbers, and this often does a good enough job preventing fraud, but there is nothing to stop bank employees or others with access to the internal machine from gaining access to the PIN. It is generally in the bank's interest, however, to prevent this from happening.

The problem is compounded when you use a bank card at a merchant and type your PIN into the merchant's computer. While most merchants are honest, there is little to prevent the merchant from eavesdropping on the PIN transmission and using this information to bill your account twice. Many people have noticed errors in their credit card transactions. I've been billed twice for the same transaction in several cases. In two cases, the merchants who did it claimed it was a mistake, but I know that they were some of the more disreputable people I've met. I've never noticed it happening with better compa-

---

[4]This is being written while the trial is in progress and it is entirely conceivable that you might be reading it in final bound form while the trial is still continuing.

nies. Today, it is easy for me to keep track of the times I use my cash card because I don't use it more than ten times a month. But if I used a cash card for all transactions, I'm afraid that double billing could easily go undetected.

So, is it possible to design a cash card that doesn't reveal its secret PIN number to a merchant? Yes. The electronics are beyond the scope of this chapter, but the mathematics are pure cryptography. The solution is the zero-knowledge proof. The phrase "zero knowledge" in the name means that any eavesdropper will gain zero knowledge even if he can overhear the entire conversation.

Although this sounds epistemologically suspicious, the structure of the system is not new. Many people may know it as a *challenge and response* protocol in which one side comes up with a question and the other side offers the correct answer. Its most obvious use is in the movies when ghosts come back and need to prove they're who they say they are. They're able to answer questions that only the dead person could.

In a more mathematical approach, the challenge and response might use random vectors. One of the more popular firewall systems installed on the Internet now is the Skey system. The host system sends the user a challenge string like "IDS00423". The user types this string and their password into a small program running on their local computer. This is hashed using MD-5 and then the 128-bit hash is sent back along the network. If someone was eavesdropping, then he would only get to pick up the hash value, not the password itself. This hash value would be useless because the host would issue a new challenge string to the next person who tried to log in. In this case, it might be "IDS00422".

The problem of measuring knowledge is a complicated and thorny theoretical issue. There is little doubt that the audience gains plenty of information in the first example of the ghost who comes back from the dead. They could get those particular questions correct in the future. The second example of the challenge and response question is more secure. If the host computer never reuses the challenge string, then the knowledge of the hash that the eavesdropper picked up can never be used in the future. Yes, he learned knowledge, but he did not gather any useful knowledge.

The first zero-knowledge paper written by Shafi Goldwasser, Silvio Micali and Charles Rackoff [GMR82] created quite a stir. The National

Security Agency tried to suppress the information from being published, but ultimately could not because the authors were not United States citizens. Much of the theoretical work that has followed this paper is beyond the scope of this book. The authors of these papers are concerned with understanding what happens as the power of the computers involved is modified.

A Discrete Log Zero-Knowledge System

Here is a straighforward zero-knowledge proof system that might be usable in a smart card. It is due to D. Chaum, J.H. Evertse, and J. van de Graff [CEvdG88]. In this case, you choose a large prime number, p, as well as three large numbers A, B, and x such that $A^x = B \bmod p$. In this case, $A^x \bmod p$ can be used as a digital signature of A if the value of x is kept secret. It is considered computationally infeasible to find this x given just A, B, and p.

Let's say that you want to prove that you created a particular signature. You might want to do this to prove you did, in fact, sign something or you might want to prevent someone from spoofing you. Challenge and response protocols can reveal information. I might say, "Prove you're authentic by signing this random string V." You could sign away and compute $V^x \bmod p$ and I could verify your signature. This would prove you were authentic, but it would reveal information to me. What if V were a blinded version of a blank check? I now have your signature on it. You can't just apply your digital signature to anything.

A simple zero-knowledge protocol (ZKP) reads like this:

1. You know x. The values of A, B and p are public. You want to prove that you know x such that $A^x = B \bmod p$ without revealing x.

2. You choose a random number, $r < p$, and send me $h = A^r$.

3. I send you a random bit, b.

4. You send back $s = r + bx \bmod p - 1$.

5. I compute $A^s \bmod p$. This should equal $hB^b \bmod p$. If it does not, then it is obvious that you don't know x.

One pass of this procedure shows that there is a 50% chance that you know x. If the procedure is repeated n times and you successfully generate consistent values for h and s, then there is only 1 chance out of 2^n that you're guessing correctly.

A Graph-Based ZKP

A *graph* in computer science is an abstract way to express relationships between objects. A typical graph consists of *nodes* that represent the objects and *edges* or *arcs* that represent the connections. One typical question is whether a graph can be *colored* by choosing a color for each node so that no two nodes that are connected by an edge have the same color. This is easy to do if there are n nodes and n colors, but the challenge is to prove that it can be done with a smaller number of colors. The famous proof that showed that all maps could be colored with only four colors was done using graphs to represent the countries on the maps. The countries were nodes and there was an edge between them if they were adjacent on the map. The proof showed that all of these planar graphs could be colored with no more than four colors.

It turns out that coloring a graph can be a difficult challenge. Even determining whether a particular graph can be colored with k colors is an NP-complete problem [GJ79]. The protocol here lets you prove you know how to color a graph with k colors without revealing any information about the coloring process to the questioner. At the end, the questioner will have no better idea how to create the coloring than at the beginning.

Begin with a graph containing nodes

$$\{v_1, v_2, \ldots, v_n\}$$

and edges

$$\{e_1, e_2, \ldots, e_m\}.$$

You know a way to assign colors from $\{c_1, c_2, \ldots, c_k\}$ to these nodes with a color function $c(v_i)$ that returns the color of that node. You can do it so that $c(v_i) \neq c(v_j)$ for all pairs of v_i and v_j with an edge between them. Now, you want to prove that you can do it successfully without giving me details.

Here are the steps of the protocol that will be repeated until everyone is happy:

1. I produce a random string S.

2. You permute the coloring of the graph by exchanging all reds for blues, all blues for yellows, and so on. This will allow you to reveal two nodes and their colors without revealing the overall coloring scheme. This permutation should be random.

3. You append the random string S to the color of each node $c(v_i)$ and encrypt it with a random key you select, k_i. Now send all n encrypted packets, $f(Sc(v_i), k_i)$, to me.

4. I choose an edge at random and ask for the keys to the nodes v_a and v_b at the ends of it. The random choice prevents you from anticipating what I will say.

5. You send me k_a and k_b.

6. I decrypt the right packets and discover the colors. If they don't match, then I know that your coloring is successful for this edge. The string S was used as a form of bit commitment to prevent you from fooling me by discovering a pair of keys k_1 and k_2 so that $f(c_1, k_1) = f(c_2, k_2)$.

After one pass of this protocol, I'm sure that you know how to color a graph so that one particular edge is handled correctly. I can satisfy myself that you can handle the whole graph successfully by repeating this process again and again. It is important for me to randomly choose the edge each time because it prevents you from anticipating my move and getting that edge correct.

You must change the permutation of the colors after each pass because this prevents me from accumulating any information about the way that the graph can be colored. I might learn that two nodes are colored blue and orange in one pass, but this information can't be combined with the information that two other nodes are colored red and orange in another pass. The rearrangement of the colors through the permutation prevents any knowledge from accumulating.

This graph coloring example is an excellent example of a *cut and choose* protocol. One side cuts up the information and the other chooses to examine one small bit. This technique is also used extensively in digital cash. Someone seeking to create anonymous digital cash would create n drafts and ask the bank to sign them. The bank would open up $n-1$ of the drafts and check to see that they were for the right amount.

The last one would be signed unchecked. This prevents someone from cheating the bank and also prevents the bank from keeping a record of the one draft that becomes active.

Kerberos

One of the big problems in cryptography is key management. If you want to hold a conversation with someone that you've never met before, it is hard to set up a key that both of you can use to create a secure channel. An even greater problem is knowing that you're really talking to Bob Smith instead of someone who is simply intercepting the messages and pretending to be Bob Smith. Public-key cryptosystems offer one solution to the problem, and many of the digital cash systems in this book rely upon public-key pairs that are certified by a central authority. The SSL low-level encryption standard used for secure HTML connections is one example (see Chapter 7).

The same key management problem can be attacked with private keys. *Kerberos* is one of the most popular models to emerge in common use. It was first developed at MIT where it kept many workstations on campus secure. This model using private keys is also used occasionally in digital cash systems like the NetCheque product described in Chapter 9.

In a Kerberos secured network, one machine known as the Kerberos server is responsible for keeping a list of everyone's password and everyone's secret key. This server, which MIT placed in a locked, unmarked room, could use this secret information to establish connections between any two machines that may never have met each other. As long as this server remained secure, then the connections between two machines would stay secure.

Let's say that user A wants to establish a secure connection with user B with the help of the Kerberos server KS. This example is simplified to illustrate how the Kerberos server leverages its knowledge of the secret keys without compromising security. The steps are straightforward:

1. User A petitions KS for a *ticket* that would create a connection with B. Both KS and A know A's password but they don't want this to travel across the network. So A's computer keeps it in local memory. The request merely asks for a connection to B.

2. KS receives the request and creates a new random key, K_{AB}, that A and B will use to communicate. Then it takes this key and encrypts it into two different packets. The first uses the hash of A's password as the key. The second packet uses the hash of B's password as the key. KS sends both of these to A.

3. A receives the two packets. A can decrypt the packet encrypted with the hash of its password, but it can't decrypt the other packet. A's password never traveled over the network so no network eavesdropper could have gotten it. Now A knows K_{AB}.

4. A sends the second packet to B over the network. Only B could decrypt this packet because only B and KS know B's secret password. When B decrypts it, B knows K_{AB}. The connection is established.

That is the basic mechanism by which a Kerberos server can establish secret links between any of its clients. One of the important features of the system is that it also authenticates the two clients to each other. A knows that it could only be talking to B and B knows that it is A on the other end of the line. Or more correctly, the connection joins a person who knows A's password with a person who knows B's. The Kerberos server protocol wouldn't work in any other case.

There are many other details that are built into a working system. The tickets, for instance, come with expiration times. All of the clocks in the network are synchronized and a ticket may only be good for a few minutes. This prevents someone from reusing a ticket time and again. If one happens to be compromised, it won't be valid for very long.

Many Kerberos implementations also maintain multiple ticket servers. A client that wants to access a particular data server must first ask the Kerberos server for a secure link to a ticket server. Then, it asks this ticket server for a secure link to a data server. The same basic protocol is used in both cases.

Political Concerns

Although this chapter is about the technical details of encryption, there are many political facets to the debate. Governments in general and the U.S. government in particular like to control cryptography as much as possible. They feel that the technology is a dangerous tool in the hands of lawbreakers because it would allow them to communicate successfully without the risk of a police wiretap.

At this writing, the U.S. government is loosening its stranglehold on the export of encryption. The Department of State is demonstrating a willingness to allow software to leave the country with high-quality encryption algorithms *if* it is clear that the software can't be used to send secret messages. The Department of State recognizes that someone might be able to disassemble the code and rework it to encrypt arbitrary messages, but it understands that this would probably be more work than simply creating a new implementation from nothing. This more practical approach was demonstrated when the Department of State recently released the software of CyberCash for export.

Chapter 3

Cash Protocols

Anyone building a system for exchanging digital money must weigh the relative value of various features like security, anonymity, ease of use, and ease of processing. There are a variety of systems that satisfy each of these criteria in different ways. For the most part, security and anonymity oppose each other. More security means less anonymity and vice versa. Both can be satisfied if more complicated systems with more complicated protocols are created.

All of the protocols use the digital signature as the foundation. Banks, customers, and stores will use their digital signature to validate a transaction. The basic signatures are fine for non-anonymous transactions because they are easy to validate by looking up a name in a directory of public keys. Anonymous transactions require more complicated algorithms like secret sharing that are described in Chapter 2.

This chapter surveys several basic protocols that range from simple and non-anonymous to complex and anonymous. All of them are based upon the basic procedures that were developed by David Chaum [Cha83, Cha85] and elaborated upon by others.

Digital Checks

Much of the money that flows throughout this country flows through paper checks. They are simple to use and popular because they provide proof of a transaction. A canceled check not only shows that a person intended to pay a certain amount, but it shows that the other party accepted the payment. This proof of a transaction offers many legal guarantees.

It is only natural that electronic transactions should imitate the check. Already many banks offer electronic payment systems that allow you to move some of your money with their computer systems. These systems lack much of the flexibility of the check. For instance, in Baltimore you can arrange to pay your gas and electric bill electronically by sending your checking account number to the utility company. They will arrange for your bill to be deducted automatically from your account on a certain day each month. Giving control over your account to an outside entity is not that popular—even if the company offers a panic hot line that you can call to cancel the transaction.

Other electronic payment systems require you to know the account number to which the money is headed. This is not much of a chore if the destination account is a common one to which you make payments each month. Mortgage and credit card payments all head to the same account each month and your computer's financial package can remember this number for you. But all other transactions, including those between neighbors, gets complicated. Who can remember numbers? Paper checks shine in these situations.

Neither of these popular forms of electronic fund transfer does a good job of imitating the simplicity of a check. They are hard to create ex nihilo and they don't give you as much control as you might want. One solution is to offer digital checks secured by digital signatures. Such a check would consist of a block of data like this:

$$\text{Signed}_{owner}(\text{Bank Name, Owner's Name, Amount,}$$
$$\text{Destination Name})$$

The phrase "Signed$_{owner}$" means that the entire block would be signed by the owner's digital signature. The block of data containing the bank's name would probably also contain an electronic address where the draft could be presented for payment. The owner's name would also include the account information. When the recipient gets the check, he would take it down to the bank, which would verify the digital signature and then transfer the amount into his account. The entire transaction would mimic normal checks.

The system could offer proof that the check was cashed by returning the entire block signed by the recipient's digital signature. The bank receiving the check could add its signature and then the bank on which the check is drawn would add its signature before returning the check to the owner. The entire chain of signatures would look like a set of nesting Russian dolls:

$$\text{Signed}_{Owner's\ Bank}(\text{Signed}_{Recip's\ Bank}(\text{Signed}_{Recip}(\text{Signed}_{owner}(details))))$$

The chain of signatures could be used to track down errors in two ways. One, it would show that each person along the chain signed off on the transaction. Two, it would show the order of the transaction. Nesting the signatures in this way proves the order in which the signatures were applied.

Forcing the Recipient

A digital check can be strengthened by locking up the check so only the recipient can spend it. This can be done in a number of different ways. The simplest is to encrypt your entire message to that person, check and all. This might be done with a private-key encryption system or it could be done with a public-key system. A public-key system would be ideal because it would allow people who have never met before to exchange checks. Each reader, for instance, could simply mail a digital check to me and seal it with my public key. They would be able to look this up in a public-key directory without bothering me to establish a private key for our transaction. Another solution would be to encrypt part of the check with the recipient's public key. The amount and the account number would be good places to start. This encryption would also help reduce information leakage.

This illustrates one of the major problems with the U.S. government's policy of restricting encryption software from export. The policy permits authentication software like digital signatures but forbids encryption software that might be used to seal a bank draft so it can only be cashed by the rightful recipient. It is clear that a new class of encryption algorithms might be useful here. It might be possible to fiddle with the structure of the digital signature algorithms to produce an algorithm that:

1. Requires a secret key of the sender to generate a signature;
2. Probably requires the public key of the recipient to generate a signature;

3. Requires the secret key of the recipient to check a signature;

4. Probably requires the public key of the sender to check the signature;

5. Could not transfer a secret.

If such an algorithm existed, then it is possible that the U.S. government would permit software using it to travel outside of the U.S. borders and be widely distributed. It is not clear, however, whether such an algorithm could really exist. Gus Simmons showed that most of the popular digital signature-only systems still encode secrets in a separate channel [Sim85, Sim86, Sim93, Sim94].

Adding Additional Security

The digital checks described here are very simple. They consist of a block of data and a signature that guarantees that the data was generated by someone. The information in the block of data still flies in the clear. Is there any additional security that can be gained by sealing up this information? For instance, the account number flies in the clear. In the paper world, people must guard these numbers and try to prevent their disclosure because they often act like passwords. Someone who knows a checking account number could create a forged paper check with a magnetic ink typewriter.

How can this number be protected? Only the sender's bank needs to know the account number, so it can be sealed with a public-key algorithm of that bank. A private-key algorithm would not work in this case unless the bank was willing to maintain a different secret key for each customer. If the same private key was used to seal up the account numbers of all checks drafted on a bank's account, then any customer could unseal the account numbers. This illustrates just how public-key algorithms changed the face of cryptography by cutting down on the need for shared secret keys.

A bank would also want to add check numbers and time stamps to identify each digital check uniquely. Check numbers prevent multiple spending. The bank records the number of each check spent and does not accept another check with that number. This is crucial because copies of digital checks are very easy to make. The time stamps may not be absolutely necessary, but they add a measure of accountability.

Digital Cashier's Checks

Cashier's checks are a common way to guarantee larger sums of money. The bank produces a special check and places a hold on the money promised by the check. People are able to trust the cashier's check more than an ordinary bank draft because the bank has guaranteed that the funds are available. In practice, this guarantee is protected by the standard physical systems that are intended to prevent copying. A cashier's check looks more official and has its amounts imprinted upon it in an official-looking way.

Digital cashier's checks can be even more secure. Digital signatures can only be compromised if someone learns the signer's secret key. It is entirely possible that someone could produce a fairly official looking piece of paper with a bank's name on it without knowing what the bank's real checks looked like. People would probably be fooled.

A simple digital cashier's check might look like a regular check with the bank's signature instead of the owner's:

$$\text{Signed}_{Bank}(\text{Bank Name, Owner's Name, Amount,}$$
$$\text{Destination Name})$$

It would probably be produced by the owner sending a regular check to the bank and asking the bank to guarantee it. The bank could strip the owner's signature off of the check for efficiency or it could leave it in place for completeness. The cashier's check could then travel through the same check-processing software as a regular digital check.

Figure 3.1 shows an allegorical interpretation of a digital cashier's check. The First Cyber Bank's signature is like a seal guaranteeing the contents of the details inside the box. Figure 3.2 shows an enhanced version that hides extra information from prying eyes.

The structure of this system is hardly anonymous. The bank must keep a record of all checks that are issued and maintain a block on the accounts. When the checks arrive, the transactions are recorded and every bank along the path can know the identity of both halves of the transaction. This information can be quite valuable. Banks and credit card companies are already discovering the marketing value of this information.

Digital cashier's checks could be made more anonymous. If a customer requested a cashier's check, the bank could transfer the money

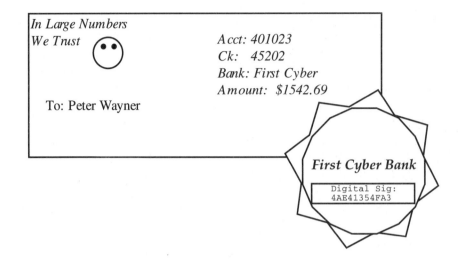

Figure 3.1. A basic digital cashier's check. The bank creates a digital signature for the note by hashing the recipient, the account number, the check number, and the amount, and then encrypting this value with its private key.

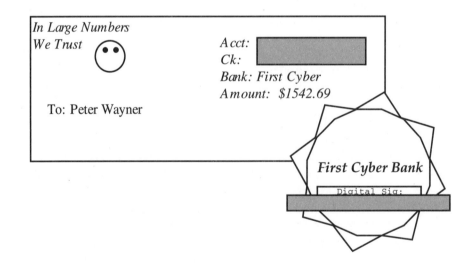

Figure 3.2. An enhanced digital cashier's check. The account and check number are encrypted with a secret key by the bank. Its signature is encrypted with the public key of the recipient so only the recipient can cash it.

into a bank account and write the draft against this account. This would hide the identity of the sender of the money from the recipient. The bank would still know both parties because it would create the check. The recipient's bank, however, would only know one half of the transaction.

The digital cashier's checks could not be made more anonymous if the bank would make out the cashier's check to "cash." A sender might decide to try to hide the destination of the funds by asking the bank to make out the cashier's check to "cash," effectively giving anyone the right to cash the check. The sender's bank would still be able to gather this information when the check was presented to it for cash. It would know the recipient's bank and it could use the check number to discover who ordered the cashier's check. The banks could collude if they needed to identify both halves of a transaction.

If a bank chose to issue cashier's checks made out to "cash" from a central account, then it would be minting a type of digital currency. The bits that made up this check could be passed around several times among different parties before it was presented for deposit at a particular bank. Bob might use it to pay Paul, who might use it to pay Harry, who would finally deposit it in a bank. This system is unlikely to succeed, however, because anyone along the chain could keep a copy of the cashier's check and then race to their bank to be the first to cash it. It is even more unlikely to succeed because crooks may be the first to use some anonymity to their purpose.

Simple Anonymous Cash

Drafting a check against an anonymous account owned by the bank is not enough to ensure anonymity because the bank can see who presents the check for payment. A true anonymous cash system can be built by preventing the bank from discovering any identifying information about a bill. The anonymity is preserved through the use of the blinded signatures described in Chapter 2 and a cut-and-choose protocol that is similar in structure to the zero-knowledge proofs described in Chapter 2. Combining these two procedures allows a customer to create a bank-certified check without letting the bank know what it is signing. If it doesn't know what it signed, then it can't recognize it when the check returns for payment.

The procedure is as follows:

1. A customer who wants a unit of anonymous cash creates k sample units and presents them to the bank. This unit would contain the name of the bank, the amount of value bound in the unit, and the underlying currency. There would be no mention of the account number or the name inside the unit.

2. Each unit is given a random serial number chosen from a large enough pool to virtually ensure that no other unit will get the same value. This serial number may be 64 bits long because the odds of a random number generating the same value twice are 1 in 2^{64}.

3. The data is bound in a standard format: $m_1 =$ (bank, amount, currency), ... $m_k =$ (bank, amount, serial number, currency).

4. The customer would blind the n units with random blinding factors $\{b_1 \ldots b_k\}$. That is, compute $m_1 b_1^e \ldots m_k b_k^e$ using the bank's public key e and the corresponding modulus.

5. The units are presented to the bank for signing. The blinding factors prevent the bank from checking the contents of the bills immediately.

6. The bank chooses $k - 1$ units to test. It requests the blinding factors for all but unit number i.

7. The customer gives the bank all the blinding factors except b_i. The selection process is illustrated in Figure 3.3.

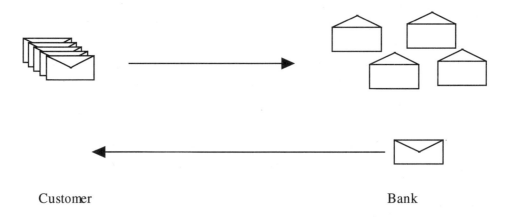

Customer   Bank

Figure 3.3. A customer who wants to create anonymous cash must create i sealed bills, shown here as envelopes. The bank opens up $i - 1$ "envelopes" to check for fraud and returns the last one.

8. The bank unblinds the $k - 1$ units and checks to make sure that the customer has not tried to cheat by bundling in some $200 notes instead of $100 notes. If there are any mistakes, the bank calls the customer and may start to press charges of bank fraud.

9. If there are no mistakes, the bank signs the one bill with its private key. This leaves $(m_i b_i^e)^d = m_i^d b_i$.

10. The customer unblinds this note by multiplying by the inverse, b_i^{-1}.

It should be obvious that the chances for fraud and the risks of getting caught are determined by k. But even if k is small and equal to 2, then the odds are still 1 to 1. If the punishment is serious enough, fraud should be nonexistent.

When the protocol is finished, the customer has a unit of anonymous digital cash. The customer can spend it anywhere, and the recipient can check the validity by checking the digital signature of the bank. If the signature is valid, then the bank will stand behind the draft. The recipient only needs to present it for deposit and the bank will credit the right account. The bank will not be able to match the transaction, however, because it will never see the identifying aspects of the bill. The entire transaction was blinded from it.

How does this system prevent fraud? The simplest fraud is for the unit to be presented for payment twice. When the bank receives a unit for payment, it records the serial number in a database. If the same serial number appears twice, then it knows that fraud is happening. It stops payment of the bill and begins to investigate. The bank doesn't know who is the cheater. It could be the first one to present a bill or it could be the second. The bank would know the identity of both and it could, presumably, discuss the matter. There would be no way to discover who did it.

How transferable is the cash? The units produced by this protocol can float around many times. But every time a copy is made, there is a greater chance that fraud could occur. The more people who know the bits, the more people who could be tempted to spend it dishonestly.

Traceable Anonymous Cash

The simple anonymous cash may be useful, but it still leaves a window for fraud. If double spending occurs, the bank cannot determine which of the two was the guilty party. A more robust system would allow the bank to catch the bad guy. This system can be created by using the secret-sharing techniques of Chapter 2 to seal the identity in a unit. If a unit is spent twice, then the information in both instances can be used to reveal the cheater.

Two cryptographic algorithms play a part in catching the cheater. The first, secret sharing, is only used in its simplest form. The identity of the cash creator is split into two halves, Id and $\bar{Id}$ so that $Id \odot \bar{Id}$ reveals the identity. The second is the bit-commitment encryption scheme that prevents someone from presenting a false key to unlock an identity half. Each of the halves of the identity of the person requesting the unit of cash will be sealed with a bit-commitment protocol so the half cannot be denied later.

The basic steps to the procedure are:

1. The customer requesting a unit of cash creates k sample units as before containing the bank's name, the amount of the draft, the underlying currency, and a unique serial number for the bill.

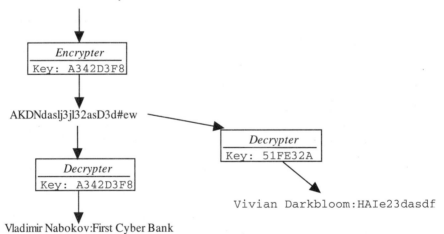

Figure 3.4. Vladimir Nabokov creates a bit-committed packet for some cash issued by "First Cyber Bank" by adding his name to the special phrase G and encrypting it. If he tries to deny this was created by him, he may find a key that, by some miracle, decrypted to the name "Vivian Darkbloom" and framed her. In this case, it is highly unlikely that the name of the bank would survive correctly.

2. The customer also takes j copies of his identity and splits them in half using the simple XOR secret-sharing system: $\{Id_1 \ldots Id_j\}$ and $\{I\bar{d}_1 \ldots I\bar{d}_j\}$. If anyone discovers both Id_i and $I\bar{d}_j$ he would know the identity of the customer creating the bill.

3. Each of the $2j$ identity halves in each of the k units is sealed up with its own bit-committed encryption key, $Key_{(a,b)}$. For instance, in unit m, the two halves of the identity, Id_i and $I\bar{d}_i$, are encrypted as $f(Id_iG, Key_{(2i,m)})$ and $f(I\bar{d}_iG, Key(2i + 1, m))$. The string G appended to the identity is a unique string that might be the name of the bank in ASCII. It is added to prevent someone from providing the wrong key later.

4. The k units are blinded using blinding factors $\{b_1 \ldots b_k\}$ and presented to the bank.

5. The bank selects one unit at random and asks to inspect the insides of the other $k - 1$ units. This means that the customer creating the unit provides all of the blinding factors and all of the keys for every bill except the selected one. The bank unblinds these bill and then decrypts the identity halves. If each pair of identity halves properly

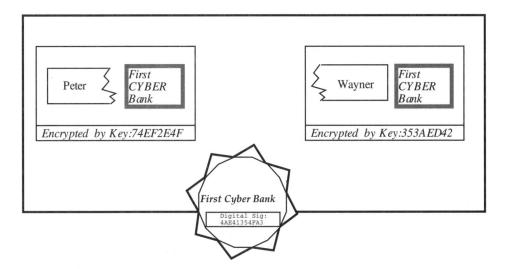

Figure 3.5. A schematic diagram of traceable anonymous digital cash. The identity is split between two puzzle pieces. Both are locked in a bit-committed box with the logo phrase of the bank. The entire package is signed by the bank with a blinded digital signature.

reveals the customer and each of the serial numbers is unique, then the bank is satisfied.

6. The bank signs the still secret unit and sends it back to the customer.

7. The customer unblinds the unit and uses it.

These bills are significantly larger that the simple anonymous cash because they contain the extra j copies of the identity bound within them. The structure of the units is still quite similar to the simple anonymous cash, so you can be certain that they will function in the same way. If a bank receives two bills for payment that have the same serial number, then it recognizes that fraud has occurred.

For the bank to catch double spenders, the people trading the bills must engage in a significantly more complicated transaction. Simple anonymous cash could be traded by copying it. This traceable variety must be traded with the protocol below, which is designed to reveal just enough of the identity to catch the cheater:

1. When a customer arrives at a store ready to spend some of the units created in this section, the shopkeeper flips a coin j times and gives the results to the customer as a j bit vector.

2. For each time the coin comes up heads in bit i of the vector, the customer reveals Id_i by producing $Key_{(2i,b)}$. For each time the coin flip comes up tails in bit i, the customer reveals $I\bar{d}_i$ by producing $Key_{(2i+1,b)}$. In the end, the customer has revealed j different halves of the transaction. But none of the two is from a matching pair so the identity hasn't been revealed.

3. The shopkeeper can check that the customer has presented the correct keys because the customer sealed them using a bit-commitment protocol. The special string G should appear at the end of each message.

4. The shopkeeper can check the validity of the bill by looking at the digital signature and checking to see that it is a valid bank signature.

5. The shopkeeper forwards the note to the bank including the vector of bits holding the coin flips and the individual keys.

This spending protocol forces the customer to reveal half of his identity j at different times. If two notes arrive with the same serial number, then this information will reveal the cheater. If the customer is

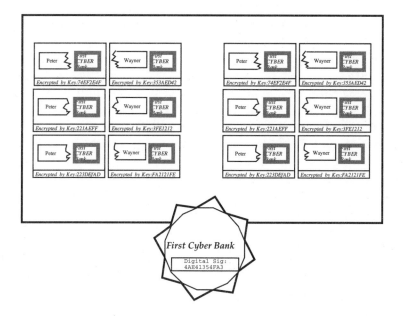

Figure 3.6. A true anonymous cash item will contain many bit-committed packets that split the identity into two halves. Here six packets ensure that a double-spending person will be able to be identified in all but 1 out of 2^6 cases on average.

the cheater who spends the bill twice, then there will be two different sets of identity halves. There is a good chance that one half in one note will match the other half in the other note and the identity will be revealed. In fact, the chance is only one out of 2^j that the customer would be asked to reveal the same halves in both of the transactions in which he tried to spend the same unit of cash. The two halves would be revealed and the cheating customer would be caught.

If the identities don't reveal the customer correctly, then the shopkeeper is the cheater. The shopkeeper doesn't know the values of the different keys and so can't decrypt a different set of pairs. The shopkeeper can only present the note twice for payment.

The digital cash produced by this system cannot be spent multiple times in a chain. It must be returned to the bank after each transaction because of the identity-revealing protocol. This effectively reduces the amount of anonymity available. The banks know who withdraws money and who deposits it, but they don't know how they trade it in between. The trades, however, are only one step away from the bank.

Cash without Choices

The last section described an anonymous cash system that bound up the identity of the cash's owner in a way that would only be revealed if he tried to cheat the system. This required an elaborate cut and choose protocol as well as j copies of the identity. The system can be quite inefficient. The creation process requires checking $k-1$ units and each unit is bloated by $2j$ halves of the identity.

A more efficient system was recently developed by Stefan Brands [Bra93, Bra94]. It relies on a modification of the discrete log signature system described in Chapter 2. This system avoids the process of creating many different potential notes by moving all of the verification to the spending phase. Anyone can create random notes, but only ones that are correctly formed can be spent.

This system has three major public numbers: a large prime p, a generator g, and an identity number for the bank d. Some banks may want to propagate several values of d that serve slightly different functions. One bank might specify several values of d that represent different sized bills. For this discussion, though, they'll all be d. Each customer receives an identification number, Id.

All bills must be in the form $d(g^{Id}) \bmod p$. The algorithms used for verification will not work if a customer presents the cash in the wrong form. They also guarantee to reveal the identity of the customer, Id, if the cash is spent twice. Before explaining how the verification and spending algorithms do this, it is necessary to describe how the cash is created. Here are the steps:

1. Someone who wants to create a note produces $d(g^{Id}) \bmod p$. The value of d should include both some information about the bank and a serial number for the bill. This can be done through a bit-commitment protocol that encrypts the string of the serial number followed by the bank's name.

2. The customer chooses a random number s and blinds the note by computing $d^s(g^{(s \times Id)}) \bmod p$.

3. The bank signs this using a discrete log signature scheme by computing $(d^s(g^{(s \times Id)}) \bmod p)^x \bmod q$ where x is the secret key of the bank and q is the prime modulus used in its signature scheme. The bank chooses a random number w and attaches $g^w \bmod q$ and

$(d^s(g^{(s \times Id)}) \bmod p)^w \bmod q$. Then it computes $r = cx + w$ and attaches it.

4. The bank returns the note and the customer unblinds it.

5. The customer encodes his identity by creating two numbers A and B such that

$$AB = d^s(g^{(s \times Id)}) \bmod p.$$

s is split into two parts x_1 and x_2 such that $x_1 + x_2 = s$. $s \times Id$ is split into two parts y_1 and y_2 such that $y_1 + y_2 = s \times Id$. These produce $A = d^{x_1}g^{y_1} \bmod p$ and $B = d^{x_2}g^{y_2} \bmod p$. These will be used in the spending algorithm.

The customer now has a note that was blindly signed by the bank. The bank did no checking up to now. There was no unpacking of a random selection of bills. The customer may have tried to cheat the bank, but this will become apparent in the signing process.

When the cash is spent, the algorithm must force the customer to reveal enough information to prevent double spending without forcing an honest customer to disclose his identity. The earlier version of anonymous cash described in this chapter hid the identity with a simple XOR version of secret sharing. This algorithm will hide the identity by drawing lines through a point in space. Each time the cash is spent, the customer will reveal the identity by giving one line that travels through the point representing the identity. If the cash is spent twice, the lines will intersect at this point, revealing all.

Here is the spending protocol that will force this disclosure and ensure that the cash was correctly formed:

1. The customer purchases something and offers up $d^s(g^{(s \times Id)}) \bmod p$, the bank's signature on that bill as well as A and B.

2. The store checks the signature and then challenges the spender with a random number c.

3. The customer returns $x_1 + cx_2$ and $y_1 + cy_2$. This is the information that could catch a double spender. If the bank get a second copy generated with a different value of c, then it can determine x_1, x_2, y_1, and y_2. This leads to s and $s \times Id$, which is enough to reveal Id.

4. This response is validated by the store by calculating:

$$A(B^c) \bmod p \quad \text{and} \quad d^{(x_1+cx_2)}g^{(y_1+cy_2)} \bmod p.$$

If these values are not equal, then the spender is trying to cheat by using fake values of A and B.

This protocol enforces the requirement on the form of the note. The bill must be correctly created in order for it to be split into the two halves, A and B, that are critical to the verification process.

Spenders can still cheat by using different versions of A and B each time they go to a store. The verification process will still work, but the two lines will not intersect at the right point to reveal the identity. This can be stopped if the bank uses a digital signature that also locks in the values of A and B. One solution is a variant of the discrete log signature from Chapter 2. The protocol goes like this:

1. The customer gives the blinded note to the bank for a signature, $m = d^s(g^{(s \times Id)}) \bmod p$.

2. The bank creates a random number w and computes $m^x \bmod q$, $m^w \bmod q$, and $g^w \bmod q$.

3. The customer presents a number c computed by hashing together m, $m^x \bmod q$, $g^w \bmod q$, $m^w \bmod q$, as well as the A and B that it will use to spend the cash later. This does not disclose A and B to the bank.

4. The bank computes $r = cx + w$, producing the signature consisting of the numbers $m^x \bmod q$, $m^w \bmod q$, $g^w \bmod q$, and r.

This signature can only be checked by someone who has the values of A and B. These are normally presented at spending time, so the store will be able to verify the cash by:

1. Determining c, the hash value of m, $m^x \bmod p$, $g^w \bmod p$, and $m^w \bmod p$ as well as A and B.

2. Checking to see if $m^r \bmod p$ is equal to $(m^x)^c \times (m^w) \bmod p$.

3. Making sure that $g^r \bmod p$ is equal to $(g^x)^c \times (g^w) \bmod p$.

This signature could not be changed by the customer because the customer doesn't know the values of x and w and could not determine them without taking the discrete logarithm of the values in the signature. The hash process forces the customer to choose A and B at the beginning and stick with these values. They can't be changed because the bank's signature would become invalid.

This system has several major advantages. There is no need to create k different notes that the bank will verify by taking apart $k - 1$ of them. The notes must be correctly formed or they can't be spent. If the A, B, and the shape of the note aren't chosen correctly, the signature of the bank won't check out and the cash will be obviously invalid.

The notes produced by this method are also significantly smaller. There is no need to keep many copies of the identity split into two. The customer must reveal half of the identity in the spending process and this can't be fudged. The signatures themselves are larger because they are discrete log signatures, but this is not as significant.

Chapter 4

Flexible Cash

The algorithms described in Chapter 3 can be used to build up fairly flexible digital cash systems. The notes created from the information in that chapter can circulate freely and be spent off-line, but they still have some limitations. The notes cannot be passed along between chains of people nor can they be split into smaller subparts in order to make change. Some of the latest digital cash systems offer solutions to these problems.

On an abstract level, there are three basic approaches that can be used to create reusable bills. The simplest is toying with the spending process so that each spender acts like a bank and the recipient acts like the original customer withdrawing cash. The recipient would create, say, 100 new bills and present them to the spender. The spender would open up 99 by demanding the blinding factors and verify that they correctly encoded the spender's identity, and then would apply a blind signature to this new bill. Each note would grow in the process and pick up enough information along the chain to identify each person who held the bill if they tried to cheat by spending it twice. Naturally, this growth in cash is a disadvantage, but it may be acceptable if each note may only pass through, say, 20 people.

The second basic solution is to fiddle with the identification process. In most cash systems, the identity of the miscreant is split into two parts and revealed if the cash is spent two times. Why not force the secret to be split into k parts and allow the cash holder to spend it $k - 1$ times? This would lower the interaction with the bank and make it easy to carry change. If you wanted to withdraw \$100, then you might withdraw one \$1 bill that reveals your identity if it is spent

101 times. Your electronic wallet only needs to carry one copy and you do not need to spend hours connected to your bank executing all of the blinded cut-and-choose protocols to get 100 bills.

The third approach is to split a unit of cash into multiple units by appending a fraction onto the serial number of the unit and sealing up the new bill with the signature of the spender. That is, if I wanted to spend a $1 from a $100 note, then I would add the fraction 1/100 in the spending process and seal up the identity. As I spent the other 99 fractions, I would append strings like 32/100 or 45/100. When the bank received the note, it would check its list of serial numbers and see whether a note and its fraction were spent twice. If I tried to pass off fraction 23/100 of bill with serial number 1412312 twice, then it would appear. The process of embedding the identity can be changed so that it can only be revealed when a particular fraction is spent twice.

These solutions all have one major drawback: they connect multiple transactions. For instance, if your electronic wallet contains a note that can be spent 100 times, then up to 100 stores will examine this bill and verify the bank's signature. This signature on the serial number will be the same in each case. You can't get a new signature unless you go back to the bank. This would allow some centralized computer to notice that some person, it won't know who, spent their $100 at a string of stores along Broadway. This process is still anonymous, but it connects too much.

Universal Electronic Cash

In 1991, Tatsuaki Okamoto and Kazua Ohta [OO92] offered a digital cash system that they termed "universal." This meant that the cash can 1) travel digitally, 2) resist forgery, 3) offer privacy, 4) work off-line, 5) be transferred to other people, and 6) be divided into change. The first four characteristics are solved by cash protocols described in Chapter 3. The last two characteristics are the most interesting ones considered in this chapter. Okamoto and Ohta point out that even normal paper cash can't satisfy the sixth characteristic by being divisible.[1]

---

[1]This was done frequently with gold coins, where people would make change by cutting the coin apart. It was also done by cheaters who would slice off a small part of a gold coin before spending it. The coins that were in circulation for a long time often appeared worn down to a significantly smaller diameter.

Quadratic Residue

This cash approach relies upon the *quadratic residue* problem for its secret sharing. As before, the authorities would be able to compute the identity of a cheater if they receive enough information but only if they receive enough. In this case, enough information will be hidden in the quadratic residue.

The quadratic residues of a set modulo n are the elements that have a square root in the set. That means for $n = 11$, 4 is a quadratic residue because $2^2 \bmod 11 = 4$. The number 5 is also a quadratic residue because $7^2 \bmod 11 = 5$. If n is a prime, then there are $(n-1)/2$ quadratic residues. In the case of $n = 11$, the residues are:

$$1^2 = 1 \bmod 11$$
$$2^2 = 4 \bmod 11$$
$$3^2 = 9 \bmod 11$$
$$4^2 = 5 \bmod 11$$
$$5^2 = 3 \bmod 11$$
$$6^2 = 3 \bmod 11$$
$$7^2 = 5 \bmod 11$$
$$8^2 = 9 \bmod 11$$
$$9^2 = 4 \bmod 11$$
$$10^2 = 1 \bmod 11$$

Note the pattern. Each quadratic residue has two square roots if n is prime. One of them is smaller than $n/2$. The other is larger. The notion of quadratic residues can be generalized a bit with a function known as the *Jacobi symbol*, $J(a, n)$. If n is a prime, then $J(a, n)$ is 1 if a is a quadratic residue of n and -1 if it isn't. So $J(4, 11) = 1$ and $J(6, 11) = -1$.

When n is not a prime, then $J(a, p_1^{\alpha_1} \ldots p_n^{\alpha_n}) = J(a, p_1)^{\alpha_1} \times \cdots \times J(a, p_n)^{\alpha_n}$. More interesting things begin to happen. Here is an example: modulo 15 where $p = 3$ and $q = 5$.

$1^2 = 1 \bmod pq$	$2^2 = 4 \bmod pq$	$3^2 = 9 \bmod pq$
$4^2 = 16 \bmod pq$	$5^2 = 4 \bmod pq$	$6^2 = 15 \bmod pq$
$7^2 = 7 \bmod pq$	$8^2 = 1 \bmod pq$	$9^2 = 18 \bmod pq$
$10^2 = 16 \bmod pq$	$11^2 = 16 \bmod pq$	$12^2 = 18 \bmod pq$
$13^2 = 1 \bmod pq$	$14^2 = 7 \bmod pq$	$15^2 = 15 \bmod pq$
$16^2 = 4 \bmod pq$	$17^2 = 16 \bmod pq$	$18^2 = 9 \bmod pq$
$19^2 = 4 \bmod pq$	$20^2 = 1 \bmod pq$	

There are two different types of squares here. The first and most important type of quadratic residues are those where there exists a square root, x, that does not give any direct clues to either p or q. To be more precise, this set includes all y such that there exists an x such that $x^2 = y \bmod pq$ and $gcd(x, pq) = 1$. For $pq = 35$, the set is $\{1, 4, 16\}$.

Each of these quadratic residues has four square roots. If both p and q are equal to 3 modulo 4, then pq is referred to as a *Blum integer*, named after Manuel Blum. The four roots can be divided into four different sets by examining the quadratic residues relative to p and q. For instance, the quadratic residue 16 has four square roots, 4, 10, 11, and 17. The sets are:

$Z^{pq}_{(1,1)}$ The values between 1 and pq that have $J(a, p) = 1$ and $J(a, q) = 1$. The root 4 of 16 is in this set because $J(4, 3) = J(4, 7) = 1$. (You can compute the Jacobi symbol of $J(x, y)$ when $x > y$ by first reducing $x \bmod y$.)

$Z^{pq}_{(1,-1)}$ The values between 1 and pq that have $J(a, p) = 1$ and $J(a, q) = -1$. The root 10 of 16 is in this set because $J(10, 3) = 1$ and $J(10, 7) = -1$.

$Z^{pq}_{(-1,1)}$ The values between 1 and pq that have $J(a, p) = -1$ and $J(a, q) = 1$. The root 10 of 16 is in this set because $J(11, 3) = -1$ and $J(11, 7) = 11$.

$Z^{pq}_{(-1,-1)}$ The values between 1 and pq that have $J(a, p) = -1$ and $J(a, q) = -1$. The root 17 of 16 is in this set because $J(17, 3) = -1$ and $J(17, 7) = -1$.

You can note several facts about the values in this set. Let $x_1 \in Z^{pq}_{(1,1)}, x_2 \in Z^{pq}_{(1,-1)}, x_3 \in Z^{pq}_{(-1,1)}$, and $x_4 \in Z^{pq}_{(-1,-1)}$ be all square roots of y modulo some Blum integer pq. Then $x_1 = -x_4$ and $x_2 = -x_3$. $J(x_1, pq) = J(x_4, pq) = 1$ and $J(x_2, pq) = J(x_3, pq) = -1$.

The important fact used here is that knowing a pair of roots is enough to factor pq if the roots are not negatives of each other. That is, not a pair like x_1 and x_4 but a pair like x_1 and x_3. For instance if $x_1^2 \bmod pq = x_3^2 \bmod pq$, then $x_1^2 - x_3^2 = 0 \bmod pq$ and $(x_1^2 - x_3^2) = (x_1 - x_3)(x_1 + x_3) = kpq$ for some integer k. This means either the greatest common denominator of kpq, $x_1 - x_3$, and pq is one of the prime factors p or q or the greatest common denominator of kpq, $x_1 + x_3$, and pq is one of them. The greatest common denominator is easy to compute quickly.

The second type of exact square includes either p or q as a factor. That is, y such that there exists an x such that $x^2 = y \bmod pq$ and $gcd(x, pq) \neq 1$. These are $\{7, 9, 15, 18\}$. This set is not as important because the size of this set shrinks as pq grows. The number of x that contain either p or q as a factor are $p + q - 2$. On the other hand, the number of x that are relatively prime to pq are $(p - 1)(q - 1)$. For this reason, we can safely ignore this set. All of the mathematics in this section revolves around factoring pq. If you happen to discover a number x that is not relatively prime to pq, then you can factor pq by computing the greatest common denominator.

Hierarchical Secrets

Splitting a unit of cash into change can be tricky. An earlier version required that you split a bill into equal units, which could quickly grow unwieldy. Imagine you want to use a $10,000 note to buy a piece of candy priced at $0.01. That would mean you would need to split off one millionth of the note. If you were required to split the note evenly, then you would be left with 999,999 tiny notes each worth $0.01. You wouldn't lose any money, but the lost efficiency could be staggering.

In this version of cash, Okamoto and Ohta use a hierarchical system to encode the identity of the customer. The hierarchical system allows the cash to be split a minimum number of times so the change is kept small. The hierarchy is arranged as a tree in such a way that two nodes in the tree will reveal the secret identity if one of the nodes is a direct descendant of the other. If the two nodes are siblings or from different branches of the tree, the information can't be combined to reveal the secret identity. Figure 4.1 shows a tree with three nodes labeled.

How can this be used to make change? Figure 4.2 shows a tree with dollar amounts in the nodes. Each node is also labeled with a unique address. The top node is 0. Its two descendants are 00 and 01. This scheme is applied recursively. If the entire note was worth $1,000, then descendants 00 and 01 would be worth $500. When you went to a store and wanted to spend $375, you might turn over subnotes 0000 and 001. That would leave you with notes 0001 and 01.

The goal is to find a way to hide the secret correctly. Spending notes 0000 and 001 shouldn't reveal the secret identity, but spending

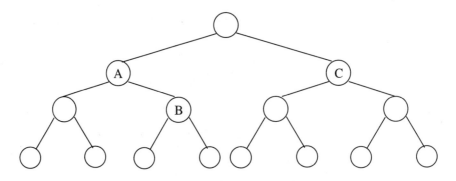

Figure 4.1. If nodes A and B are revealed, then the secret identity is blown because A and B are directly related. If A and C are revealed, then nothing can be recovered about the secret identity because A and C are from different branches. Exposing B and C will also reveal nothing.

0000 and 00 should. If this can be done, then it prevents someone from spending more than the value of the note while keeping change to a minimum.

Okamoto and Ohta discovered a simple way to use the quadratic residues to build up a heirarchy that allowed the right type of splitting. They used these properties of quadratic residues:

1. The square root of x modulo pq is easy to calculate if you know p and q, but hard if you only know the product pq.

2. The square of x modulo pq is easy to calculate for anyone.

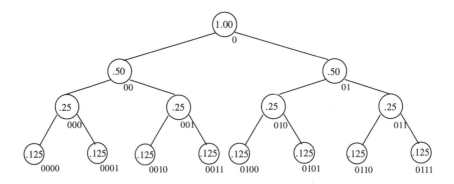

Figure 4.2. A hierarchical way to split a note into smaller and smaller bits. The numbers inside the nodes are the values and the binary numbers adjacent to the nodes are the addresses.

3. There are at least two distinct square roots of a number modulo pq and if you know two distinct values, you can factor pq.

4. The identity could be encoded so that it would be revealed if pq was factored.

To make this simple, consider the nodes 0, 00, 000, and 001. We're going to construct numbers, Γ_0, Γ_{00}, Γ_{000}, and Γ_{001}, that will allow someone to factor pq if they come across a pair in which one of the numbers is a direct descendant of another. Here are the steps:

1. Begin with an arbitrary number Γ and determine two distinct square roots from the different classes of quadratic residues. Set Γ_0 equal to one of them. Call Γ_{temp} the other one.

2. Find two distinct square roots of Γ_{temp}. Set Γ_{00} equal to one of them and set the other equal to Γ_{temp}. Set Γ_{01} equal to Γ_{00} times a factor Ω_0 that will be described later.

3. Repeat this last step recursively down the tree. Down the left branch, find new square roots of Γ_{temp} and down the right branch find new square roots of Γ_{temp} times the appropriate Ω factor.

When a customer spends a fraction of a bill, he must reveal the appropriate Γ value for that fraction. If the customer happens to try to cheat and spend two fractions incorrectly, then pq can be factored and the identity revealed and then reviled. Here's an example. Imagine that someone spends notes 0 and 000 and thus exposes Γ_0 and Γ_{000}. If $(\Gamma_{000}^2)^2$ is computed, it will be one square root of the initial value Γ. Γ_0 will be another distinct one and the user will be able to calculate the identity.

The Ω factor is included to allow the trees to branch and use different values for each branch without compromising the ability to recover the identity if there is fraudulent spending. Each of the Ω_i factors must be different, but they must be apparent to both the customer and the store verifying the transaction. The solution is to use a cryptographically secure hash function and hash up these three values in one concatenated data block: the entire bill, the value of i, and pq. So both the spender and the verifier could compute Ω_{00} if they wanted to do so. The verifier uses this ability to factor out the values of Ω when it is trying to compute the identity. If it is has the values Γ_0

and Γ_{01}, then it must compute Ω_0 and divide it out. This is simple to do because it is easy to take the inverse modulo pq.

The complicated algorithm for computing Ω factors is needed because it is not possible to use the same value at each level. If a constant value like 3 were used, then someone could discover $3^{1/2}$ by dividing, say, Γ_{01} by Γ_{00}. The verifier could also discover another value of $3^{1/2}$ if another pair like Γ_{1010} and Γ_{1011} were spent. In both cases, the customer would not be committing fraud by spending these values, but it could reveal two different square roots of 3.

Completing the Picture

The key insight of the Okamoto and Ohta cash system is the hierarchical structure that allows bills to be split into different parts while preventing fraud. The hierarchical structure described above doesn't defend against classic double spending. Okamoto and Ohta battle this using the classic solution of splitting the identity into two parts over n different times. When the note is spent, the store flips a coin n times and uses the result to open up n different halves of the identity. If the note is spent twice, the identity will probably be revealed. The combination of these two protocols provides all of the six features that Okamoto and Ohta feel are desirable for universal digital cash. The details of the algorithm are beyond the text of this book. Users interested in implementing it should explore the paper in depth.

Chapter 5

A Product Overview

At this moment in time, there are many different companies trying to position their system as the dominant way to transfer money across the Internet. The number of different approaches is surprising, especially given how simple regular money can be. The proposed systems offer a wide variety of answers to questions like "How much anonymity is good?", "How much flexibility is ideal?" and "How much security is necessary?" The world of Internet commerce is still in its infancy so there is no way to predict which system will emerge as the favorite. It is entirely possible that one great digital money transfer system will be created by selecting the best aspects of each of these systems.

This chapter will categorize the systems according to several important features like anonymity, connectivity, on- or off-line, or suitability for micropayments. Many of the systems will not fall neatly into tight groups and the differences will be explained as much as possible.

Finally, it is inevitable that some information will be left out of this collection. The domain is expanding quickly as many jump into the marketplace.

On- or Off-Line

Digital money systems that need the help of a distant computer throughout the transaction are said to be "on-line" cash systems. The transaction is monitored by this third party and it blesses it if everything is correct. Adding this third party to the transaction, though, takes communications resources, so many people are actively exploring "off-line" systems. These are ones that would allow people to meet on the street and transfer cash to each other even in the midst of a computer blackout. Clearly, "off-line" cash is better because it is more flexible and also because communications cost money. If it costs, for instance, $.02 to clear an on-line cash transaction through an acceptably fast digital network, then people won't want to use the system to buy penny candy. People might hesitate to pay this $.02 to transfer $.25, the current cost of the *Washington Post*.

One problem is there is no true off-line cash that can be traded ad infinitum without a third party acting as a referee. Paper money or gold coins can be traded for years without being deposited in a bank, but this is because they can't be counterfeited. Digital notes are easy to copy. The cryptographic algorithms described in this book can catch counterfeiters, but only when the money is processed through a bank.

This means that even off-line cash is still, in a sense, on-line. It just means that the interaction with the third party, the bank, can take place at a more leisurely pace. The people might meet on the street, do the deal and walk on. Any fraud would be detected later when the digital cash was deposited in the bank.

So the distinction between on-line and off-line is a bit unclear. It's really a distinction between now and later. The difference can add some crucial flexibility, but it may not be truly significant.

Here is a list of the major cash systems studied in this book and a rating of how much communication they require to complete a transaction and just when they must have it.

First Virtual The First Virtual system can operate with a wide range of connectivity. The system uses no cryptography, certificates, or digital signatures, so a merchant must have an on-line connection to verify that a particular account number offered by a customer is valid.

The rest of the transaction does not need as much connectivity. In the ideal system they imagine, someone will buy information or a product, offer his or her ID number, and get the information. The info broker would compose an e-mail message and send the request for the transaction into the FV central computers. When the buyer confirmed the transaction, then it would be billed to a credit card. In a sense, all of the confirmation and back-office transaction would happen "off-line" long after the goods traded hands. But in another sense, the transaction could be canceled or denied if the user decides not to confirm the trade.

In some ways, this is an acceptable balance for the information business. The merchant selling information does not lose any physical goods if someone refuses to pay. It just loses the sale. First Virtual is hoping that it will be able to police the people who abuse this right and stop them.

*i*KP IBM's *i*KP system requires complete on-line connectivity. The buyer's bank account information is encrypted at the transaction site and passed on by the merchant to the central clearing computer for authorization. No trade is possible off-line.

SSL and SHTTP These are not digital cash systems, per se, but they are ways for people to establish secure links for passing information. The amount of on-line versus off-line behavior depends upon the exchange system that travels through this secure channel. If a customer offers a credit card number, then this transaction might be considered off-line if the merchant does not clear it immediately with a bank. Stores can still accept credit cards without clearing them, but they risk losing payment if the card number is lost or stolen.

It is entirely possible that this secure channel could be used to exchange anonymous digital notes. The security is necessary to prevent an adversary from grabbing a copy of the note and spending it first.

NetCash and NetCheque NetCash requires a central computer to authenticate the coins and issue new replacements for the users. NetCheque requires a Kerberos system to establish signatures and this requires a central Kerberos server that generates Kerberos tickets. These Kerberos tickets are valid for a short period of time and this limits the amount of off-line behavior that is possible.

CyberCash This is also an on-line system that requires the bank to act as the third party to confirm or deny a transaction.

CheckFree CheckFree is a transaction processing system. It isn't well suited for face-to-face exchanges. Many transactions can be prescheduled, but this may require four days. This means that people can pay regular bills like the rent in an off-line fashion, but this is arguably not what most people mean when they talk about on-line versus off-line cash.

Open Market A completely on-line system that checks an account and charges it before transferring payment.

CAFE The CAFE system is designed to use electronic smart cards to process transactions. The transactions don't require the bank to mediate the trade because the cards are programmed to act as the bank's surrogate and not allow a bad transaction.

Many people have noticed that the European banks have pursued smart card technology more than American banks. This is because the European telecommunications system is much less amenable to on-line connections. The various natural borders and monopolistic practices have slowed the development of a pan-European clearance system. This could change in the near future.

DigiCash This requires an on-line connection to your DigiCash wallet. When you go to a store and buy something, the store asks the DigiCash computers to call up your wallet and get the payment. This is quite seamless for those on the Net, but it requires a more solid connection.

SET The credit card transactions may be either on-line or off-line. The merchant may choose not to clear a transaction if the amount is small and it is inconvenient. Also, the acquirer may choose not to block off the amount from credit limit if it is also small.

The SET system also includes a mechanism for processing many charges in a large batch. Some merchants may choose to use this level of clearance to save time and network expenses.

Millicent The Millicent system is an on-line system that has many of the advantages of an off-line system. Each vendor must maintain its own database of outstanding scrip and this must be on-line. But there is no need for the merchant to contact any central bank or database.

Citibank These smart cards can exchange money with each other without checking with a central database. The system forces each electronic note to be returned to the central bank by giving each note an expiration date. This may be done at any time and the system is designed to automatically refresh the money in a smart card whenever it gets a chance.

PayWord and MicroMint Both require a central database of unspent coins to prevent double spending. But the value of the coins is presumed to be fairly small so merchants may choose not to clear every coin immediately.

Encryption and Security

Security is one of the major components of any digital monetary system, but it is quite surprising how much many different systems are using. There are two major problems with security. First, encryption, the main engine for providing secrecy, is frowned upon by governments. Cryptographic systems that are used just for authentication, however, seem to meet the general acceptance of governments. Second, many of the major and most respected systems like RSA are patented and using them requires paying a royalty.

To some extent, the tension between the government and encryption systems is easing in this arena. The U.S. government, for instance, seems willing to approve the export of strong encryption algorithms as long as it is apparent that the encryption software can't be used for anything except protecting financial transactions.

First Virtual First Virtual uses no encryption and relies upon the security of the electronic mail system to keep transactions correct and accurate. The company argues as follows on a branch of its home page:[1]

> Encryption is almost always cumbersome and difficult. And it always adds an additional step, and something else to worry about. After all, even banks and armored cars are subject to robbery attempts, and sometimes those attempts succeed. Rather than use encryption, we decided to design a system in which it wouldn't be necessary.
>
> Encryption isn't necessary with FIRST VIRTUAL for a simple reason: when you use our system, sensitive information like your credit card number never has to travel over the Internet at all.

---

[1] http://www.fv.com/info/encryption.html

Transactions are all handled with your unique FIRST VIR-
TUAL account identifier, which may safely travel in ordinary
Internet Email. Even in the highly unlikely event that it were
intercepted, an unauthorized user couldn't use it for fraud.
He or she couldn't even use it to buy information over the
Internet fraudulently, because all transactions are confirmed
via Email before you're charged.

While it is correct that your credit card number never travels over
the Net, the company has only replaced it with its own billing
account name. This account name *does* travel over the Net and
may be stolen. First Virtual hopes to prevent misuse of this by
confirming the transaction with your account. This e-mail account,
it hopes, won't be compromised.

This argument is certainly fair. The current credit card system mails
statements with the account number through the postal service and
seems to sustain an acceptable amount of loss. It is anyone's guess
whether the electronic mail system is as secure as the paper mail
system.

*i*KP This system requires public-key encryption, which is generally
patent protected and export controlled. Although each customer
needs to be able to encrypt the details of his or her transactions,
the amount of encryption needed varies between the three different
levels of the protocol, 1KP, 2KP, and 3KP. In the lowest level, 1KP,
the customer only needs to encrypt information with the public
key of the bank. In 3KP, customers can add their own signatures
and offer their own certificates. Some combination of these should
be able to pass through the borders if it can be used only for
transactions.

SSL and SHTTP These systems offer high-caliber encryption connections that can carry arbitrary data. Although this flexibility is normally a sign of good software, it may cripple the use of the protocols for monetary transactions. Any current user must rely upon
export-grade encryption because the U.S. government won't allow arbitrarily secure encryption software to leave the country. So,
everyone is stuck with the least common denominator.

The users of SSL will probably be penalized because the system is
designed for arbitrary message traffic. The designers cannot argue
that the software won't be used to circumvent surveillance as the
developers of CyberCash were able to do.

NetCash and NetCheque All transactions would rely upon digital signatures for their accuracy.

CyberCash CyberCash relies heavily on encryption. In fact, at this writing, it has the distinction of being the first system to be exportable *and* as secure as desirable. The company writes, "CyberCash uses full 768 bit RSA as well as DES encryption of the messages. All transactions are authenticated with MD5 and 768 bit RSA signatures." The software can be exported to everywhere except Lybia, Syria, Cuba, North Korea, Sudan, Iraq, and Iran. This is because the software can't be used to keep secrets.

CheckFree No encryption is used here.

Open Market The Open Market system uses a flexible amount of encryption and leaves the amount at the discretion of the merchant.

CAFE Some of the most complicated algorithms are used with CAFE's smart cards. The cash that is created on the CAFE cards might be anonymous in some cases. The current versions being tested are not anonymous, but future versions might include this feature. The software, though, was developed in Europe, which means that it is not subject to the United States's restrictions on export.

DigiCash Again, a wide range of encryption is available, but it is not clear how much will be implemented in any final system. The current DigiCash system is merely experimental and includes nice blinded digital signatures for protecting the anonymity of the buyers. Everyone also gets RSA public-key pairs for creating digital signatures of his or her transactions.

SET SET uses the highest grade public- and private-key encryption available. The algorithms are carefully built and tuned to use the most efficient algorithm at each point. The client and server synchronize their lists of certificates, for instance, by comparing hash values. Each transaction, on the other hand, gets a full-fledged digital signature.

Millicent, PayWord, and MicroMint All of these systems use only cryptographically secure hash functions to speed processing. In some ways, this is just as secure. Only someone who knows the secret value can generate such a "signature." But this secret must be universally protected and must be known to check the signature.

Public-key algorithms have two keys and only the public one is needed to check a signature.

Cryptographically secure hash functions have none of the patent restrictions of public-key signatures. They are also less likely to encounter export restrictions from the U.S. government because they are used only for authentication.[2]

Citibank The smart cards from Citibank use the highest grade RSA digital signatures. This forces Citibank to use much stronger "smart cards," which are actually PCMCIA cards, because these are the only ones that can do the math quickly enough.

Certificates and Repudiation

Certificates are one way that people can add security to public-key systems by arranging for a central, trusted authority to verify and vouch for the public key of someone. This means that a store can start a transaction with a random customer and be certain of his or her identity when the customer presents a valid certificate.

The main advantage is that certificates prevent someone from denying a transaction later. The merchant could say, "I accepted a valid signature that was backed up by a valid certificate. Pay up." The courts should back this up if the system is designed correctly.

Naturally, the certificates can be compromised if someone gets a copy of the private key matching the public key endorsed by the certificate. Then such a person can masquerade as you. In many cases the private key will be bound up in a smart card and protected by a PIN. National Semiconductor makes at least two smart cards that do this and also provide public-key encryption.

One of the major problems with using certificates is that there is no infrastructure to speak of. Apple Computer distributes coupons for an RSA Digital Signature certificate bundled with the latest versions of their operating system. A user must visit a notary public and present three forms of identification. The form is notarized and sent in. Then a neat customized application program is returned on disk. This application will take any file and add a digital signature to it along with a copy of the certificate. Anyone using an Apple Macintosh can verify

---

[2]This is somewhat funny because any hash function can be converted into a cipher. If x is some random key, then the stream of values $y_1 = f(x), y_2 = f(y_1), \ldots$ can act like a one-time pad.

the signature. The RSA system probably makes a good model for other systems.

It is difficult to assess the need for repudiation. The banks need to solve this problem already with ATM machines, stolen checks, and credit cards. Although public-key certificates can be mathematically very convincing, they're not much more secure than ATM cards. People will need to store the corresponding private key in a file or a smart card and unlock it with a PIN. These smart cards would be moderately more secure than an ATM card because it would not be possible to simply create one from an account statement and knowledge of the PIN number. It is possible to forge an ATM card if you know the account number, which can be gained from the statement, and the PIN number, which can be picked up by looking over someone's shoulder. Finding the private key that matches the public one bound into a certificate is a hard problem that is currently intractable.

First Virtual No encryption means no certificates. First Virtual aims to stop repudiation through the social force of closing down the accounts of people who deny too many transactions. This promises to be a complicated process for them because they also encourage people to deny the charges if they're not satisfied with the material.

*i*KP This system is designed specifically to adapt to the changing availability of certificates. The lowest grade system, 1KP, only requires certificates for the bank. 2KP uses certificates for the merchants, and 3KP requires them for everyone. The designers of this system would clearly prefer 3KP but recognized that a public-key infrastructure would take time to establish. So they produced 1KP and 2KP as stepping stones that would enable others to follow.

SSL and SHTTP Certificates are used by SSL servers to establish their identity. Clients only recognize these certificates. There are no certificates used by clients.

NetCash and NetCheque The currency servers in the NetCash system use public-key certificates to vouch for their authority to issue digital coins. The user doesn't need certificates. In the NetCheque system, the Kerberos system is used to build authenticity. This doesn't use public keys for the certificates, but it has the same effect. The central Kerberos server must be on-line to generate a transaction key that is used between the two parties. This certifies them to each other because Kerberos sends the transaction key to each party encrypted with a different key known only to that party.

CyberCash No certificates per se are used at this time. But CyberCash creates public keys for each user that are stored on each machine. These keys are used solely by CyberCash, but they perform many of the same functions as certificates. Repudiation is just as difficult.

CheckFree No certificates are used at this time.

Open Market The Open Market system is designed for building a store. It can support multiple payment methods that might use certificates for repudiation.

SET This system will be the king of certificate users. SET will establish a hierarchy of certificate authorities that will cover everyone in the world. Each person will be authenticated according to card issues, brand, and perhaps even geopolitical authority. Everyone except the local Mafia kingpin, of course.

Millicent This system does not require public-key certificates, but it does require that each user has a "secret" value. This must be distributed via a secure channel and can't be generated locally like a public key.

Citibank Each smart card contains a certificate for the person. Each unit of cash is signed by a generating unit at the bank and it comes with the certificate of that cash generating unit. When two cards meet to exchange money, they use these certificates to authenticate themselves.

PayWord and MicroMint Neither requires certificates.

DigiCash No central certificate structure is used, but DigiCash effectively creates one when you register your initial key pair. This isn't published.

Anonymity

Anonymity is one of the most debated features for digital cash. Some see it as dangerous because it will protect criminals. Others see it as an essential component that we can use to preserve freedom.

The systems described here supply a wide variety of anonymity. Many offer next to none. Some protect the identity of the customer from the merchant but reveal the transaction to the bank. Only a few keep everyone in the dark.

There is some practical value in anonymity. If the identity of the customer, or at least the credit card number, is kept from the merchant, then the merchant can't go off and pretend to be the customer. This is significant because stores employ many clerks and some may gain access to customer records.

First Virtual No anonymity. The customer, the merchant, and the bank know everything. The merchant even knows the customer's secret account number, which is enough to initiate fraudulent transactions. The transactions, though, must be confirmed by e-mail, which should stop most bad merchants.

*i***KP** The identity of the customer is kept from the merchant. The bank, though, knows the identity of both parties. This anonymity is the opposite of a standard cash transaction. Normally, the merchant can see the customer across the counter, but the bank can't track what happens to the cash that leaves its doors.

It is hard to be sure whether this offers much anonymity. Purchasing something at a store reveals something of your identity. The clerk knows your face and may ask for a name and address. Many stores try to get this information to build customer lists. Many customers must reveal their identities to get warranty protection.

SSL and SHTTP These systems set up secure channels with arbitrary clients. The amount of anonymity is independent of this system. There is no need for clients to identify themselves in the transaction. The channel could be used to pass digital cash. Or the final system using these systems might require plenty of identification.

NetCash and NetCheque NetCash offers the potential for anonymous transactions. Each coin is given a serial number, and the bank could easily track the serial numbers coming and leaving. Presumably, some currency servers could offer anonymity as an option. But people would need to trust that the currency server was telling the truth when it said that it kept no records.

CyberCash The system is just a front end for credit card and bank transactions. No information is kept from the bank.

CheckFree This is just a transaction processing system. No information is kept from the bank or the merchant.

Open Market No anonymity is currently part of the system. There is no reason why anonymous payment systems couldn't be added in the future.

CAFE The designers of this system understand the structure of digital cash and have the ability to include truly anonymous cash in a future version of the system. The current test version is not anonymous.

DigiCash This system also has the ability to support true anonymous cash. This system protects the information about which buyer went to which seller. The bank knows who withdraws money and who deposits it. It can't match them up.

Millicent This system does not offer much anonymity. Although the scrip is sold by a broker and redeemed by a different merchant, the broker can easily determine where the user is going to spend the scrip. Why? Because the scrip is all merchant dependent. You can spend it only in one place.

More general forms of scrip may emerge and if that happens, then the system will be able to offer a limited amount of anonymity.

Citibank The details of every transaction are recorded for the central bank's computers to display. When a note is returned, it carries with it a trail of every place it has gone. If the bank knows the name associated with each smart card, then it can trail the money. But if the cards are available anonymously, then the bank will be able to identify only cards, not people. This can still be powerful information.

PayWord and MicroMint No blinding is built into the vending process. If a bank sells coins from these systems, it can record the serial numbers and wait for their return.

SET This is a front end for a credit card company. All transactions are tied to your name. The system does offer some anonymity because it hides your name from the merchant. Some credit card clearing companies, however, may choose to return this information to their merchants as a service.

Chapter 6

First Virtual

The First Virtual Holding Company is one of the first companies to offer a working digital money transfer system created for the Internet. The system, which was crafted by the principals in the corporation, is a simple, e-mail based system that transfers money by passing e-mail messages. First Virtual maintains a central clearinghouse computer system that reads correctly formatted electronic mail messages and transfers the money correctly. The charges for the system are minimal. First Virtual also offers a related information shopping market.

The structure of the system is not surprising given the people involved in the project. The Green Commerce Model paper[1] that describes some of the philosophical foundations of the system was written by Lee H. Stein (`lstein@fv.com`), Einar A. Stefferud (`stef@nma.fv.com`), Nathaniel S. Borenstein (`nsb@nsb.fv.com`), and Marshall T. Rose (`mrose@dbc.fv.com`). This team is heavy with experience in developing Internet mail protocols. Nathaniel Borenstein, the chief scientist at First Virtual, was one of the principal authors of the MIME mail standard that codified how programmers could bundle many different types of information into a mail message. Together Borenstein and Marshall Rose created Safe-TCL, one of the first systems for free-roaming software agents. Their design was intended to allow people to send actual programs in order to enhance electronic mail. Einar Stefferud was one of the first to create a mailing list in the primal version of the Internet in 1975.

A transaction is straightforward. Both buyer and seller must have First Virtual accounts. The seller sends in a message to the First Vir-

---

[1]http://www.fv.com/tech/green-model.html

tual clearing computer that includes the two accounts, the transaction amount, and a description. First Virtual sends the buyer a confirmation request; when the buyer confirms the transaction, the money moves.

First Virtual is currently offering several different pieces of software that would allow someone to initiate a transaction. They've produced sample WWW pages and scripts that someone might use to begin a transaction. Modified FTP servers that ask for a First Virtual account before allowing the transfer of information are also available. Anyone seeking to sell information on the network can use this software or turn to First Virtual's InfoHaus. This Net site incorporates all of the First Virtual software so people can sell information without a sophisticated Net presence.

A Model Transaction

A First Virtual (FV) transaction includes several steps:

1. The buyer opens up a First Virtual account. This can be done by sending electronic mail to apply@card.com, telnetting to card.com or connecting with the WWW page http://www.fv.com/html/ setup.html. The buyer needs to be ready to provide a Visa or MasterCard charge number because all bills will be sent to the buyer as a charge against this card. The substeps are:

   (a) The potential buyer fills out a form including his or her name, address, e-mail address, and requested passcode. The e-mail address is used for confirmation messages. The passcode is used as the account name and password.

   (b) If the application is processed correctly, First Virtual's automatic software will send a confirmation note to the e-mail address contained in the application. This note will include a temporary account number and a toll-free telephone number.

   (c) The potential buyer calls First Virtual's computer at this toll-free number and inputs the temporary account number. Then the buyer inputs the credit card number. First Virtual chose to have credit card numbers travel by the phone network because it believed that a pure electronic mail solution would be too insecure. There are too many ways that people can eavesdrop on the Internet.

(d) First Virtual charges the account $2.00 as a new account fee. All charges will be aggregated and applied to the credit card.

2. A potential seller must first get a buyer's account. This account can be converted into two different types of seller's accounts. The first, known as a *pioneer seller*, can be opened when the potential seller mails a paper check to First Virtual for $10.00. The check is cashed as a new seller's account fee and the bank account number is recorded. When First Virtual wants to deliver money to the successful pioneer seller, it will send it electronically to this checking account.

   The pioneer seller account is intended for small, relatively unorganized businesses. There is no credit check, which forces First Virtual to withhold payment for at least 91 days until the purchaser actually pays the bill. Credit card fraud by dishonest merchants is a major problem and this is one defense against it.

   Larger or more organized businesses can receive the money within four days if they open an *express seller* account. This costs $350 for a credit check and it may not be open to many home businesses. Credit card companies often require that a business have a "storefront" to ensure that it has made some financial commitment to staying open.

3. When the seller attracts a buyer, they negotiate the price and then the buyer gives a copy of his or her account ID to the seller.

4. The seller sends a transfer request to First Virtual through a variety of ways. The simplest is an e-mail message that looks like this:

```
To: transfer@card.com
From: seller's e-mail account
Subject: (anythingyoulike)
BUYER: buyer's account code
SELLER: seller's account code
AMOUNT: numerical amount without symbols like $
CURRENCY: Currency ID. For U.S. Dollars, it is "USD"
DESCRIPTION: A description of the transaction for
later identification.
```

The message can also include several optional fields like "TRANSFER-TYPE:", which can be either "info-sale," "cost-recovery," "donation," or "usage-fee." The other optional fields are "TRANSFER-ID:", which can be set to any unique identifier that would help keep the records straight, as well as "DELIVERY-STATUS:", which can be set to either "Delivered" or "Pending."

The First Virtual computers receive this transaction request and begin processing. Alternatively, a seller can enter the transaction by telnetting to fv.com and entering the significant information at the prompts. The third choice is to use the Simple Green Commerce Protocol to build low-level TCP/IP scripts.

5. First Virtual sends a request for a confirmation to the purchaser's e-mail account. The purchaser can answer it with three different responses:

   YES All is well. No complaints. The buyer authorizes First Virtual to bill the credit card on file for the amount.

   NO The buyer is refusing to pay. This is a significant event and FV keeps records of this. If a purchaser does this too often, First Virtual might terminate an account. First Virtual will make this determination because it doesn't want people to take advantage of sellers by refusing payment.

   FRAUD The buyer never authorized the transaction and First Virtual should investigate.

6. If the seller requests it, First Virtual sends along a transfer notification or payment authorization signed with their PGP key. This digital signature is a good guarantee for those who ship hard goods. They can send the product knowing that the credit card company has approved the transaction.

   First Virtual is careful about generating a new PGP key each month and distributing "certificates" signed by their master key. If you want a copy of their master key, they will either send it by paper mail or fax it to you.

7. When it is clear that the buyer has actually paid the credit card company, First Virtual deposits the correct amount in the checking account of the seller after subtracting the fees. The cost of the transaction is $.29 plus 2% of the total amount.

   Pioneer sellers receive payment after about 91 days, while express sellers receive payment after four days.

The steps are straightforward and completely automated. Electronic mail messages are clearly being used as proxies for the paper normally used in business. Everyone trades electronic mail to accomplish the job.

One feature that is missing from this system is content encryption. This is a clear departure from conventional wisdom that encourages secrecy as protection. First Virtual replaces the security of algorithms like DES with a centralized transaction machine that confirms all transactions. If a buyer's electronic mail is secure, then anyone committing fraud will be stopped when the buyer refuses to confirm the transaction. Credit card account numbers and other information that can be used outside of the First Virtual system do not travel in the clear.

First Virtual started offering *transfer notification* with a digital signature. That is, First Virtual sends the seller a notice that the payment has gone through and signs it with its digital signature using the RSA algorithm and the PGP software.

This signature certainly qualifies as "encryption" in one sense of the word. But First Virtual still does not scramble the contents of the messages. These still travel in the clear, although the company may add additional layers when it becomes easy to do.

There are several major advantages of living without encrypted data. The first is that the company doesn't need to ask the U.S. government for permission to export any software from the country. This continues to be a severe restriction on business. The second is that First Virtual doesn't need to have complicated purchasing software available on many machines. A buyer only needs to get his or her account name to the seller. This could be done by speaking it over a telephone, sending it via e-mail, or by faxing it.

First Virtual doesn't lose much by sacrificing encryption. Although eavesdroppers might gather up an FV account code, they can't charge it effectively. This account code would already be spread about the network anyway. A buyer would be giving a copy of the account code to any seller in the course of the transaction. Anyone in these deals could reuse the account code in the same way that any clerk at a store could copy down your credit card number.

Clearly, First Virtual is also relying upon the strength of its institutional partners, the banks and the credit card companies. If fraud is discovered, then First Virtual is probably hoping to lean on these partners to solve the crime and stop it from happening in the future. If it transferred $1,000,000 to a seller's bank account and the seller cheated, then the bank is going to get drawn into the turmoil.

Trying Before Buying

The electronic mail confirmation by the purchaser is clearly intended to reduce fraud, but it also has a secondary feature. The Green Protocol encourages buyers to try the information out before they buy. That is, they can request a long file filled with information by supplying their First Virtual account. If they don't like the information, they can respond "No" when they get the request for confirmation.

This is a significant feature of the First Virtual approach. Many bookstores have found that shrink-wrapped books sell poorly. If a book is shrink-wrapped, the stores will often display an open copy alongside so the curious can flip through the book before buying it. There is no reason why people on the network would not want to do the same thing when they're consuming information.

There is an important difference in the electronic domain. A buyer in a bookstore who doesn't purchase a book walks out of the door without the information. Aside from anything memorized by the browser, there is no information that is transferred. A First Virtual information browser, however, still has a copy of the facts on the disk. Such browsers could and should erase their disks immediately, but it isn't clear that they will do so.

First Virtual argues that a failed transaction is no loss for the seller because no resources are consumed. This is essentially correct. Allowing customers to browse is just one of the costs of doing business and it is one that can encourage many more transactions. People feel more comfortable if they're not buying things sight unseen. The protocol doesn't need to be used in this manner. A company might want to hold delivery until the buyer confirms the transaction. This is also permitted by the protocol and it is clear that it might be useful in some cases when people might be tempted to refuse payment.

Some information sellers might be hesitant to use the First Virtual protocol because they're well aware of the low rate of compliance among shareware users. Many people use shareware without paying the fee. If they try the information and then refuse to buy it, then this same instinct could rob information brokers of a good living.

First Virtual will encourage compliance by keeping track of the people who say "No." This is clearly going to be a sensitive political topic for First Virtual. Someone who says "No" often may just be a compulsive browser who is careful with a dollar. Or it might be someone who is building up a digital library for free. It is not clear what standards First Virtual will use to judge people, but the fine print in their contract specifies that they withhold the right to make the decision themselves.

Possible Attacks

The simplest attack on the First Virtual system goes like this:

1. Attacker gains access to the electronic mail heading to someone's account.
2. Attacker opens a bank account with a fake name.
3. Attacker creates a seller's account and registers it with the bank account opened with this fake name.
4. Attacker grabs the buyer's account code by reading the mail.
5. The attacker starts a transaction between the buyer and his seller account.
6. The attacker intercepts the confirmation request and responds with a "Yes."
7. When the money is deposited in the checking account, the attacker withdraws it in cash and disappears.

This scheme has several advantages. The buyer would be billed by credit card, which means that the notification of the charge wouldn't arrive by mail for as much as a month. The attacker could even delay this if the attacker had access to a physical mailbox.

Who would pay? The fine print that the buyer agrees to abide by includes a clause that requires the buyer to ensure that the electronic mailbox is secure. This is clearly a problem in the system because many users are incapable of assessing the security of their electronic mail delivery system. Even technically adept users don't know much about the route that electronic mail takes on the way to their mailboxes. This is compounded by the fact that the people who maintain the computer systems in the chain are rarely hired as bonded people. Many colleges use different undergraduates each semester to perform important system maintenance chores. Anyone in the chain might be tempted to become an electronic bank robber.

The buyer, however, could fight the bill by protesting it to the credit card company. The card companies often deal with double charges and other computer glitches, so they are prepared to investigate problems like this. They could decide to wipe their hands of the matter and tell First Virtual to seek payment directly from the buyer. This would force FV to sue the buyer if it thought a fraud was taking place. In reality, they seem ready to wash their hands of the situation and tell the seller that there will be no money coming. The seller gets stuck with the risk.

At this point, it is clear that First Virtual will delay paying money to the seller for 91 days. This can be frustrating to the seller. This will stop large fraud because the alleged purchaser will probably catch the huge charge on his or her monthly bill. But if purchasers fail to scrutinize the charges or it is blended in with others, then they might miss the charge. This limits the amount of the attack at a great inconvenience to the seller—the party that is already absorbing plenty of the risk of nonpayment.

It is clear that the solution to the problem would probably be found by examining the reputations of the parties. If a seller was a well-respected information provider who rarely had trouble with false charges, then First Virtual would probably pursue the buyer. If the seller had disappeared, then it would be clear that fraud had occurred.

The nature of fraud in the First Virtual system will be interesting to track. In many ways, the First Virtual system is quite similar to a credit card system. The account code is like the credit card number and it is all that is necessary to start a transaction. First Virtual hopes that it will be able to use its control of the central system to keep fraud to a minimum. Many credit card companies have already realized that they can't defend themselves against malicious sellers so they refuse to process transactions for companies without a storefront. This is a significant problem for small, home-based businesses. They hope that stores with a physical location will be significantly less likely to cheat than the fly-by-night home-based operations. They will be much easier to catch.

It is clear that the nature of fraud will be governed significantly by the security of the electronic mail system. If an attacker finds an easy way to ensure that "Yes" confirmations will echo his or her transactions, then First Virtual may be in trouble.

Would encryption help? It would certainly protect innocent buyers who might be the target of attackers. A buyer might be required to apply a digital signature to a confirmation message. This would prevent someone from intercepting electronic mail and blithely responding "Yes" to the money transfer.

But there are limitations to this. People who use public UNIX systems, for instance, also leave their files containing keys in the hands of the system administrators. Digital signatures are more secure, but they're not perfect.

How to Set Up a First Virtual Storefront

Setting up a First Virtual storefront on the Net is simple. Your software must collect the First Virtual account number from the customer and then forward it to the First Virtual machines with your own account number. These machines will process the request, ask the customer for confirmation, and eventually transfer the money.

There are several different options you can use to accomplish this. The simplest is to use First Virtual's InfoHaus, which will allow you to add your own storefront. First Virtual built this software to encourage people to adopt its Green Protocol and offer information to the network. They hope that this will encourage more people to use their system.

You can also roll your own software for processing First Virtual payments on your own system. First Virtual offers several sample HTTP scripts and HTML pages for your information. Or you can digest the Green Protocol that describes the information trading and create your own software to do the job. The process is not hard because First Virtual uses electronic mail to do the work. Writing a shell script to send mail is not hard.

A final option is to buy a Web server that offers First Virtual's system already built in. WebSTAR, a product for the Macintosh that was previously known as MacHTTP, now includes the ability to access the First Virtual accounting system. The product is made by StarNine, a company in Berkeley, California, and is available separately or as part of an Apple software/hardware bundle known as the Apple Internet Server Solution.

Using the FV InfoHaus

The simplest method for most people is to contract directly with First Virtual to sell the information. They run the InfoHaus (`http://www.`

infohaus.com/) to sell digital information from a variety of different people. There are some who are selling short stories at $1.00 a pop, others who are selling Netcruising guides, and some who are offering business information. Many are essentially text based, but there is no reason why you can't use the system to distribute binary files like executables or images.

Setting up a storefront is easy. After you set up a First Virtual account, you need to give the InfoHaus the name of your store and a short description of it. You can accomplish this by telnetting to `telnet.infohaus.com` or sending e-mail to `mimeserver@ infohaus.com`. Connecting via telnet is somewhat easier because you are asked for the information by dialog. If you send the e-mail, it must be in this format:

```
To: mimeserver@infohaus.com
    From: pcw@access.digex.com
    Content-Type:application/fv-infohaus;
    transaction=newseller-request
    Doing-Business-As:Tongue Twisters
    Preferred-Currency:USD
    Account-ID:TT
    E-mail-Address:hyphen@at.dot.com
    Tongue Twisters sells New Age titles that will taunt
    the tongue and tangle the brain. Parse at your own
    risk!
```

The `Content-Type` is a MIME tag that identifies the entry for the First Virtual InfoHaus mailer. The entry for `Doing Business As` establishes a name for the business. This will be found in the first-level directory of the InfoHaus. The entry for `Preferred-Currency` is probably going to be set to US dollars. The `account-ID` is the First Virtual account that will receive the cash generated by the sales. The `E-mail-address` is used in case of problems. The rest of the message is a short description that First Virtual places next to the name of the business. It should do a good job of describing what's available and why people should investigate.

To add information you can either send the information via FTP or you can bundle it up with an electronic mail message again. Here's a sample e-mail version:

```
To: mimeserver@infohaus.com
   From:pcw@access.digex.com
   Subject:
   Content-Type:multipart/fv-infohaus;
   boundary=my-separator --my-separator
   Content-type:application/fv-infohaus;
   transaction=addition-request
   Doing-Business-As:Tongue Twisters
   Account-ID:TT
   Info-Name:Favorite-URL
   Price:0.50
   --my-separator
   Content-Type:text/plain
   This is a Universal Resource Locator designed
   to make people cry.
   --my-separator
   Content-Type:text/plain
   http://www.double-U.dot.com/H-tee-em-el/slash/capital/
       SLASH/MuyPaige.html --my-separator
```

The first subpart of this messages contains the storefront name as well as a name for the new entry and a price. The First Virtual system will automatically install this information in your storefront with this name and price. The entry is followed up by the two subparts. The first is given away to everyone for free. This might include a long sample of the work if the entry is something substantial like a novel. Or it might include some sample equations or promises about what the information might offer the reader. The second part includes the actual information for sale. In this case, it is the brutal Uniform Resource Locator (URL).

You can also add the information to your page using FTP. This is probably the best way to add binary information that might not be encoded as ASCII. Your first step is to upload the information to the directory /infohaus/incoming at ftp.infohaus.com. You should remember the name of the file that you deposit here. Then you register the file by logging into telnet.infohaus.com and answering the correct questions. The telnet server will ask your account name, the code, the price, and the name of the file you will be adding to the service. You specify the free or demonstration data by either giving the name of a file you added to the FTP server or typing in the data. Then you give the other information for which you are charging.

HTML and HTTP Storefronts

First Virtual offers a selection of different software packages that you might use to help set up a storefront. They are several sample HTTP pages and corresponding scripts that can be installed on a UNIX-based HTTP server. There are HTML forms that are read by the scripts and bundled into messages for the First Virtual server.

The entire process is not too complicated because the First Virtual server communicates with simple messages. No encryption or additional non-standard HTML hooks are required. You probably could generate many of the transaction messages with little trouble yourself if you are a reasonably competent programmer. The Green Commerce protocol document gives the exact details.

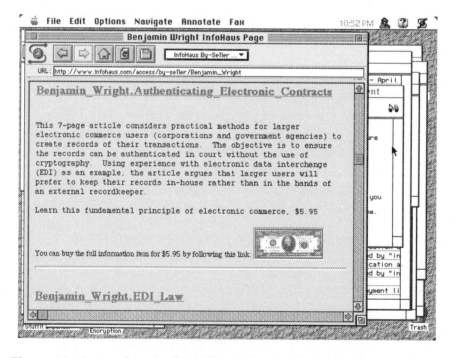

Figure 6.1. A sample page for selling information through First Virtual's InfoHaus. Clicking on the simulacrum of the cash starts the purchase process. Figure 6.2 shows what happens if you click on this button.

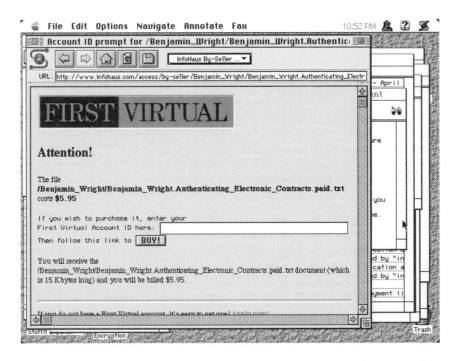

Figure 6.2. You fill out a form like this to purchase some information from First Virtual's InfoHaus.

Another solution is to use the bundled C API that First Virtual distributes to make it simple to write shell scripts. The code compiles with an ANSI-C compiler into the application `fv` and then accepts direction from command line arguments. This API makes it somewhat easier to charge people's First Virtual accounts by providing a simpler interface and supporting a complicated cost determination mechanism using *payment files*. These files contain information on how to price the data in different directories and the `fv` application automatically scans them to determine the cost of a particular file. This allows you plenty of flexibility to set prices.

The basic idea behind the payment files is to bundle information about pricing into payment files that affect both individual files and entire directories. The payment files are given names beginning with ".$" followed by the name of the file that it affects. The price of a file named "fred.txt" would be controlled by the *dot-dollar* file ".$fred.txt." The dot-dollar files can also affect entire directories. A file with the simple name ".$" would control the price of all of the files in the directory.

```
SERVER-IP: card.com
SERVER-EMAIL-ADDR: transfer@card.com
SELLER:FTP Test Seller
CURRENCY: USD US Dollars
DELIVERY-STATUS: Delivered
LOG-FILE:./xferlog.txt
TRANSFER-TYPE:
KILOBYTES: 0.10
EACH-FILE: 0.50
```

Figure 6.3. A sample dot-dollar file distributed by First Virtual with their API. The entries describe how to charge for a file and how much to charge.

If there are two files, ".$" and ".$fred.txt," then the file fred.txt would be controlled by the file created by concatenating the two together. This process is recursive, so the dot-dollar file for the information in "/pub/secret/top/snitch.txt" would be created by concatenating the files "/.$," "/pub/.$," "/pub/secret/.$," "/pub/secret/top/.$," and "/pub/secret/top/.$snitch.txt."

The payment file contains basic information about how to process the payment and how much to charge. The guidelines are placed in rows with data that follows. Figure 6.3 shows a simple dot-dollar file that is distributed by First Virtual with its API. The first entries describe which First Virtual server to contact for the charge; the rest describe how much to charge.

Here is a detailed description of all of the possible entries in a dot-dollar file:

SERVER-IP The server to contact via an IP-based packet protocol. This is usually `card.com`.

SERVER-EMAIL-ADDR This is an e-mail address to which to send e-mail-based transfer requests. It is usually `transfer@card.com`.

SERVER-EMAIL-PROGRAM Use this to specify another mail generating program if you don't like the standard sundial program that is normally installed in the `/usr/lib` directory.

FROMNAME From whom the e-mail messages will come.

SERVER-TRANSFER-PREFERENCE If it is 1, then try IP-based Simple Green Commerce Protocol then go to e-mail. If it is 2, then try e-mail before SGCP. If it is 65, then use only the SGCP. If it is 66, then only use e-mail.

NOTIFICATION-CC Send a copy of the transfer request to this address if necessary.

INFOHAUS-NAME A string describing what is going on and why the transfer is happening. This might be the store's name or it could be a longer description of the data.

SELLER Who gets the money.

SELLER-MAP A pointer to a file that contains a complete list of all the files and who gets paid for each of them. This is useful if an information server sells data provided by many different people. The FV API will scan this map file to determine who gets paid for the data in question.

SECURITY-REQUIREMENTS Apparently useless now.

TRANSFER-TYPE This can be either "info-sale," "cost-recovery," "donation," or "usage-fee."

DESCRIPTION A longer description appended to the transfer to allow people to audit the transaction later.

CURRENCY The underlying currency here.

LOG-FILE Where to record the transaction.

THIS-FILE If this is present, then the FV API charges the amount specified for the file.

PER-TRANSFER-REQUEST If this is present, then the FV API adds this charge for a transfer. This might be set to be $.29, which is the price that First Virtual charged for a transaction. If someone bought multiple files, this would only be added once.

PLUS-PERCENT If this is present then an additional amount is added by percentage. It could be used for sales tax or it could be used to recover the extra 2% that FV charges for a transaction. It is clear, though, that the mechanism is not sophisticated enough to distinguish between tax districts for the purpose of adding the right tax.

EACH-FILE If this is present, then every file would cost the same amount. This is usually used in directory-level dot-dollar files.

KILOBYTES If this is present, the cost is charged by the size of the data delivered.

CPU-SECONDS This seems to be included for future expansion of the system. The current version of the API won't charge by time.

CONNECT-SECONDS This also seems to be included for future expansion of the system. The current version of the API can't charge by time.

NO-CHARGE If this is present, then the data is gratis.

The scoping nature of the different dot-dollar files allows a fair amount of flexibility. You might include an EACH-FILE line in a directory-level dot-dollar file that set the default price at $2.00. A few particularly valuable files could get their own dot-dollar file that set a higher price of $5.00.

The program fv offers both primitive and sophisticated commands for people writing scripts to process sales. The primitive commands use the payment files. They are:

fv check *fvid* Determines whether a particular customer ID is valid. The First Virtual seller responds with: new, active, suspended, or unavailable.

fv checkat *server_addr fvid* Similar to check, but it ignores the SERVER information in the controlling dot-dollar file.

fv bill *buyer seller amount description* Sends a bill directly to the First Virtual server. If some argument is not specified, then the program computes it directly using a sophisticated scheme described later as a payment file.

fv costof *filename* Determines the cost of a file using the controlling dot-dollar file.

fv chargefor *filename fvid* Determines the cost and sends the bill.

There are several different examples of how to use the FV API in a shell script attached to an HTML page. The process is simple. You could do most of this yourself, but the FV API makes it simple to create a server that will expand and contract as more information is placed in directories. It is not necessary to price data directly. You can just add the files, and the dot-dollar files will process them correctly.

FTP Access

FTP is a popular low-level protocol that is disappearing as the Net becomes dominated by Web pages. First Virtual also offers various ways to modify an FTP server to charge for files that are downloaded by FTP. A user would send their account as the password and the bills would be calculated on the fly. It is fairly easy to use the FV API to extend an FTP server if you're a competent C programmer.

Final Assessment

The First Virtual system is one of the simplest approaches offered to people on the Net. The simplicity is the strongest point because it encourages many people to use the system without requiring fancy software or complicated encryption protocols. The protocols are not much different from the current credit card system and so it would not be surprising if the successes and failures of the credit card system are mirrored by this approach.

Risk The seller assumes much of the risk if the buyer decides to return the item. Risk is minimized to some extent by requiring confirmation.

The risk to the seller is reduced, to some extent, by the new digitally signed payment authorization. If the merchant received such a note, it has a legally binding document that proves that the credit card company authorized the transaction. After this, it is up to the merchant whether to give credit for a return.

Strengths The simple protocol can be used without approval by U.S. government or encryption patent holders. The protocol can also be used over the phone or fax.

Weaknesses A pioneer seller must wait at least 91 days for funds. Express sellers have a normal clearance time. While this may be inconvenient for pioneer sellers, it may be hard to do better than this in the marketplace. Merchant fraud is too big a potential problem.

The lack of encryption opens up the system to attacks by eavesdroppers. Someone who can forge and intercept electronic mail can attack the system.

The digital signatures on the authorization only partially solve this problem. The merchant knows that a transaction was complete, but the "buyer" may not know that someone has spent money in his or her name until the monthly credit card bill arrives.

Chapter 7

HTTP and Cash

The World Wide Web (WWW) is currently the most popular way for people to publish information over the Internet. Many businesses and people are exploring distributing their information encoded in the Hypertext Markup Language (HTML) and it is only natural that everyone will want to extend the protocol to send money across the Net. When this happens, digital monetary transfer will be easy enough for anyone to use.

In the simplest sense, anyone can use many of the basic form structures of HTML to exchange credit card numbers for purchases. A Web page might include a form and you would spend money by filling out the proper blanks with your credit card and expiration date. Some Web pages already use this method. This is perfectly acceptable, but it is insecure. Many people may be able to use this system already, but it is clear that it is not feasible in the long run. People can build automated programs that watch Net traffic for the credit card numbers. Fraud will grow if this low-tech way of sending information becomes common. One customer reports that most cellular phones only last 4 to 5 months in major cities before someone steals their secret identity number with a scanner. Then they're worthless.

Encryption is the obvious solution, and several companies are approaching the technology. One version, known as S-HTTP, comes from Enterprise Integration Technology, a Silicon Valley company devoted to developing standards and software for digital commerce. The company is one of the leaders of the nonprofit CommerceNet system and is working with RSA Data Security to develop actual software kits for developers through a company called Terisa Systems. Netscape is offering a protocol they call the Secure Socket Layer (SSL), which provides encryption for packets connected between standard Internet sockets.

At this point, the SSL software is well integrated into many Web servers and clients. Both Netscape and Microsoft support SSL links; this is the best definition of "established" that there is in the computer industry. The S-HTTP standard is less common and it is only left in this book for historical purposes. It also provides a good introduction for the section on UPP and JEPI. These systems are also extensions to HTTP designed to exchange money.

The encryption systems used in SSL and S-HTTP are not limited to safeguarding the exchange of money. The standards are composed of the basic cryptographic building blocks of encryption, digital signatures, and key exchange, and they can be used in many different ways. The digital signatures, for instance, might be required by everyone logging into a technical support Web page. A server might encrypt all of the information it sends out to safeguard against eavesdropping. Of course, the channels can also be used to authenticate credit card transactions.

The first part of this chapter will briefly describe S-HTTP and SSL. Although simply passing credit card numbers through a secure channel might not be very technically interesting, the technology is quite likely to play a major role in the Internet's economic landscape for a number of simple reasons. First, the technology is not complex if you understand the basics of encryption and digital signatures. These are just the beginning of more complicated digital cash systems. Second, the technology relies upon credit cards, a well-known and trusted form of monetary transfer. Third, the technology is sponsored by some of the biggest players in the Internet community. Finally, the technology is not limited to cash transfer. People can use it in many ways to provide secrecy.

The second part of the chapter will focus on the Universal Payment Protocol, an extension to HTTP that allows clients and servers to negotiate the best payment mechanism for completing the transaction. Another similar mechanism can be found in Chapter 19 describing the Millicent extensions to HTTP.

S-HTTP

S-HTTP (Secure Hypertext Transfer Protocol) is a simple extension to the normal HTTP that was first proposed in the Internet Draft in June of 1994 by Eric Rescorla and Allan Schiffman of Enterprise Integration Technology in Menlo Park, California. The latest version (1.1) emerged in December of 1994. Both of these drafts are available from the EIT Web server.

The S-HTTP standard allows the traffic to and from the server to be either encrypted, signed, or authenticated in any combination. At the beginning of each session, the client and the server choose the right combination of secrecy and security. A server might dispense information in encrypted form but only require the client to send the requests without encryption. Or the server might always send the information in the clear after it receives a signed message. Any combination of the nine different options (three for the server and three for the client) are possible. Naturally, using no security is also an option for servers that welcome requests from browsers that aren't configured for S-HTTP.

None of these features is limited to any particular algorithm, and the server and client can negotiate to find a mutually compatible set of algorithms that they both support. Many standard algorithms using RSA's public-key and shared-key algorithms are supported, but others may be implemented in the future. Some of the most important standards supported are PKCS-7, PEM, and PGP. Weaker versions that may be exported from the United States can also be included.

The negotiation is carried on through the encapsulated messages that begin an HTTP negotiation. Extra lines indicating the preferences of both the server and the client are embedded in this block of data. The format of the lines expresses all of the possibilities that a side will accept. The structure of these lines is specified by this grammar:

```
<Line>:=<Field>':'<Key-val>(';'<Key- val>)*
<Key-val>:=<Key>'='<Value>(','<Value>)*
<Key>:=<Mode>'-'<Action>
<Mode>:='orig'|'recv'
<Action>:='optional'|'required'|'refused'
```

An example of a properly constructed line is:

SHTTP-Symmetric-Content-Algorithms:recv-optional

= DES-CBC,RC4

which specifies the symmetric content algorithms used to encrypt the data in the message. This tells the other party that it can use either the DES-CBC or the RC-4 algorithm to encrypt the bulk data of a message. Another example is:

SHTTP-Symmetric-Content-Algorithms:orig-required=RC4

which says that this side will only ship data encrypted by RC-4. After both sides ship their specifications, both sides must choose the most secure option agreeable to all.

Both sides of an S-HTTP transaction must negotiate many different details beyond the encryption algorithm used to transfer the bulk of the data. Some of the different fields permitted in the <Field> response are:

SHTTP-Privacy-Domains This specifies a general class of algorithms that covers all encryption and data packaging. These domains include PKCS-7, PEM, or PGP, and they specify how data is encrypted and how the encrypted data is packaged for all to see.

SHTTP-Certificate-Types The certificates describe who guarantees a particular key. In many cases, the format of the certificate will be defined by the SHTTP-Privacy-Domain and it will be the same, but there is no reason why it can't be different. The S-HTTP standard includes the possibility that someone might generate or accept a certificate in a different format outside of these greater domains.

SHTTP-Key-Exchange-Algorithms These define how the key covering the data will be sent. Some values include RSA, Outband, Inband, and Krb. RSA is used when the data is enclosed with an RSA envelope that includes the key. Outband is used when the two parties might agree upon a key ahead of time. Inband and Krb are used when the key is negotiated or generated directly for this message.

SHTTP-Signature-Algorithms Both RSA and NIST-DSS are standard signature algorithms. Others may appear. The key length should be specified if either party requires a particular level of security.

RSA[100-1000] would mean an RSA algorithm using a key of between 100 to 1,000 digits.

SHTTP-Message-Digest-Algorithms The hash algorithm used to create the message digest.

SHTTP-Symmetric-Content-Algorithms This is the algorithm that will be used to encrypt the information being transferred. Some values include IDEA, RC-4, and several different varieties of DES that were either strengthened through triple encryption or weakened by limiting the key length.

SHTTP-Symmetric-Header-Algorithms The algorithms used to encrypt the header information in case it is different than the content.

SHTTP-Privacy-Enhancements These can include sign, encrypt or auth. Someone who wants everything might specify that SHTTP-Privacy-Enhancements for the orig and the recv be required to include all three.

Your-Key-Pattern The pattern of the keys. The details are beyond the scope of this book. See the standard.

Here is an example of a perfectly acceptable block from the Internet Draft:

```
SHTTP-Privacy-Domains:recv-optional=PEM,PKCS-7;
       orig-required=PKCS-7
SHTTP-Certificate-Types:recv-optional=X.509,PKCS-6;
       orig-required=X.509
SHTTP-Key-Exchange-Algorithms:recv-required=RSA;
       orig-optional=Inband,RSA
SHTTP-Signature-Algorithms:orig-required=RSA;
       recv-required=RSA
SHTTP-Privacy-Enhancements:orig-required=sign;
       orig-optional=encrypt
```

The side that sends this block will use PKCS-7 to send data, but is willing to accept it in either PKCS-7 or PEM. This side will provide X.509 certificates, but it will accept either X.509 or PKCS-6. The side can exchange the key in RSA or Inband, but it will only accept keys via

RSA enveloping. It will hold both sides of the communication to RSA signatures, but encryption is optional. This level of security would be appropriate for an information server that wanted to provide authentic data that was guaranteed by a signature. These might include a bond rating agency like Moody's that moved into the electronic domain by examining banks and their electronic currency. It would issue its opinion of the bank and guarantee it with a signature. It wouldn't require encryption, though, unless the other party wanted it. A protocol for exchanging digital cash might look like this:

```
SHTTP-Privacy-Domains:recv-optional=PEM,PKCS-7;
    orig-required=PKCS-7

SHTTP-Certificate-Types:recv-optional=X.509,PKCS-6;
    orig-required=X.509
SHTTP-Key-Exchange-Algorithms:recv-required=RSA;
    orig-optional=Inband,RSA
SHTTP-Signature-Algorithms:orig-required=RSA;
    recv-required=RSA
SHTTP-Privacy-Enhancements:orig-required=sign,encrypt;
    recv-required=sign,encrypt
```

Here both sides of the exchange will sign and encrypt the transaction. The side transmitting the credit card number should definitely send the numbers encrypted. The other side may not need to send any confirmation in encrypted form. In that case, the seller might offer this version that only binds the shopper:

```
SHTTP-Privacy-Enhancements:orig-optional=sign,encrypt;
    recv-required=sign,encrypt
```

The negotiation structure like this offers the flexibility that will allow the S-HTTP protocol to be used for a number of different jobs that require basic encryption solutions. To some extent, the wide flexibility to protect raw information does not lie outside of cash. As information becomes more and more important, it may take more and more of the place of other backings for currency. Hot tips that are signed by knowledgeable inside authorities could be worth much more than something that just has the full faith and credit of a government.

SSL

The Secure Sockets Layer (SSL) is a basic encryption system developed by Netscape. The software is designed to exist somewhat transparently just above TCP/IP. Any application, be it a Netscape browser, a Telnet terminal program, or a newsreader, can initiate a TCP/IP connection using SSL and the software will ensure that the data travels encrypted. Netscape is currently shipping a browser that includes a fairly crippled version of the software that can be exported from the United States. In the future, it hopes to distribute a highly secure version for use within the United States.

The place for SSL is different than that of S-HTTP. SSL is a low-level protocol that negotiates a security level when a channel is opened and then becomes transparent to the users. The channel is encrypted, but the applications don't know it is there. S-HTTP is integrated into the HTTP language and the negotiations about security are carried on through the attributes and the header attached to each page. It is possible to implement an S-HTTP that uses SSL to do the encryption work and it is entirely likely that Netscape and others may do this.

SSL uses this protocol to establish a secure socket-level connection. First, the client and the server agree on a cipher and a key. Then they optionally authenticate the client. The exchange looks like this in more detail:

CLIENT-HELLO This is the first message that a client sends asking to start up a connection with a server. It contains three different bits of information: the types of ciphers the client knows how to understand, any session ID number that might be left over from a broken connection, and some random data that it issues to the server as a challenge.

SERVER-HELLO The server responds with two different types of messages. If the server recognizes the old session ID that the client sent along, then it acknowledges this in the message so the connection can begin again. The only difference is that a new set of keys is selected using the old master keys established when the connection began.

If this is a new connection or the server doesn't recognize the old session ID, then a new connection is established. The server sends back a certificate with its public key that has been authenticated by a certificate authority, the list of ciphers that it supports, and a randomly chosen connection number. The challenge data sent in the CLIENT- HELLO message is not returned yet. It will be sent back when the server is verified.

CLIENT-MASTER-KEY The client finalizes the key selection process with this message. The packet contains the client's choice for the cipher that will be used to do the bulk encryption. The key information is transmitted in three blocks. One block contains any extra arguments that must be agreed upon for some ciphers. For instance, DES with Cipher Block Chaining requires an initial vector that starts off the chaining process.

The key is sent in two portions: the clear portion and the secret portion. If a key for a cipher is n bits long, then the first $n - k$ bits are shipped in the clear so anyone can read them and the other k bits are shipped encrypted with the server's public key. This segregation was created to satisfy the export restrictions of the United States government, which seems willing to approve many ciphers as long as the bit length is limited. At this writing, k is usually 40 bits. This may change in the future when faster computers make it possible to attack these short keys quickly. RSA Data Security's RC-4 can easily be exported if the key length is limited to 40 bits. Netscape uses RC-4 with $n = 128$ and $k = 40$. It hopes to distribute versions with $k = 128$.

CLIENT-FINISH The client indicates it is finished with its part of the authentication. It just contains the session ID encrypted with the current key.

SERVER-VERIFY When the server receives the master key in the CLIENT-MASTER-KEY message, it decrypts the secret portion using the hidden portion of the public key it sent along in the original certificate. This gives the server the master key used for the session. To verify this, it encrypts the challenge data sent in the CLIENT-HELLO message using the master key.

When the client receives this message, it decrypts the result and compares it. If everything matches, then a trusted link between the client and an authenticated server is established.

REQUEST-CERTIFICATE This is an optional message that a server may choose to send if it wants to establish the identity of a client.

In this case, it sends some challenge data and the type of authentication requested. In the current version of the SSL specification, only RSA encryption with an MD-5 digest is supported.

CLIENT-CERTIFICATE If the server asks the client for proof of who it is, then the client answers with this message containing a certificate and an encrypted version of the challenge data. At this writing, the SSL specs only support X.509 type certificates.

SERVER-FINISH When the server is satisfied with the authentication, it sends along a message including the session ID encrypted with the master key. At this point, the session is officially established and both sides can add the session ID to their lists of active sessions.

When the client and the server have created a master key, then the protocol requires that both sides take the additional step of creating two new keys for the actual bulk encryption. One will be used for data sent by the client and the other will be used for data sent by the server. This asymmetry adds additional security. The actual key construction process depends on the cipher choice. In the case of RC-4, the actual key material is created by hashing together the master key with the challenge material and the connection ID number. The CLIENT-READ-KEY is the first 16 bytes of the MD5[MASTER-KEY,"0",CHALLENGE,CONNECTION-ID] while the SERVER-WRITE-KEY is the first 16 bytes of MD5[MASTER-KEY,"1",CHALLENGE,CONNECTION-ID]. A similar process is used for DES and other ciphers.

Why does Netscape use the full 128 bits of some ciphers like RC-4 even if they transmit 88 of these bits in the clear during this initialization routine? To prevent someone from creating a large dictionary for known plaintext attacks. HTTP clients often send messages beginning with GET to the HTTP server. A smart attacker could program his computer to generate all possible encrypted versions of GET that might be created by all possible keys. If there were only 40 bit keys, then it is feasible to store this successfully for fast look up. Using 128-bit keys prevents this from happening.

An attacker with a fast set of computers can still successfully attack the system, but a new set of CLIENT-WRITE-KEY and SERVER-WRITE-KEYs must be generated for each attack. Using the MD-5 hash that includes the random challenge data and the connection ID prevents the attacker from doing this in advance. This is a reasonable security problem that defends against people with large storage but doesn't defend against someone with a large amount of computing power attacking a particular message.

Using a Secure Link

Using a secure Web browser should not be any different from using an insecure browser. The protocols like SSL and S-HTTP were designed to be transparent. Still, Netscape chose to add several different visual cues to its browser so people could know if the information took a secure path to their screens. Figure 7.1 shows a sample page from the

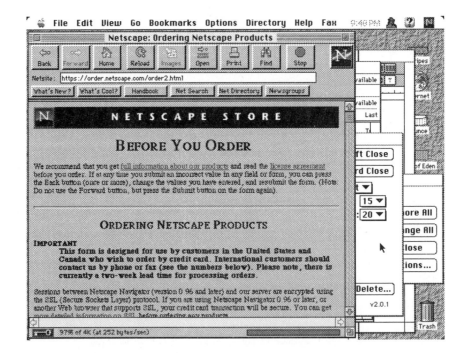

Figure 7.1. The Macintosh version of the Netscape browser showing encrypted information. The browser indicates the safety factor with a colored bar and an icon. The blue-colored bar shows up between the icon bar at the top and the window to the HTML document below. In this case it comes just above the label reading "Netscape Store." Figure 7.2 shows a closeup of the icon in the bottom left-hand corner.

Figure 7.2. A closeup of the icon in the bottom left-hand corner when a secure, HTTPS connection is in place.

Macintosh version of Netscape. If the information arrived in encrypted form, the bar at the top of the screen is blue and the box on the lower left corner contains a complete key. If there was no protection, then the bar is gray and the box contains a broken key. Figure 7.2 shows a closeup of this key icon.

There are a number of important details and questions that must be worked out in the future. Some of these include:

Transparency Netscape also enforces security by requiring separate URLs for secure servers. If you want to get a document from a secure server, you must request a URL of type HTTPS:. If your browser can't handle this, then you can't follow the link. This prevents people from filling out a form with their credit card number and shipping it off only to discover that the distant server won't accept the data. Any eavesdropper, however, would have no problem with the information. A browser that is unfamiliar with the URL type HTTPS won't bother sending this information out the door.

There are problems, though, with this approach. Its servers would still take care of nonsecure browsers. There is no reason why they cannot offer abbreviated information or other advertisement that doesn't include the dangerous forms for credit card numbers. Or perhaps these credit card number holes should be turned off. The WWW standard will flourish the best if documents appear similar to everyone.

Standard Encryption Routines The current protocols rely heavily upon RSA's public-key encryption and secret-key RC-2 and RC-4 algorithms. These standards allow for more protocols to be determined in the future and these may become available if others are willing to investigate other routines that may not be as patented.

Export Controls The HTTP protocol will probably be crippled to a point that will allow it to be exported from the United States. Although it may be possible to permit stronger services inside the United States, the Internet usually recognizes only a few standards.

The greatest danger is that criminals will develop the ability to eavesdrop on the Net and grab credit card numbers. Many cellular phone companies discounted the technical abilities of the criminals who might attack their system and now they're stuck with a system that can barely defend itself. The current set of standards is flexible enough to support longer keys should the United States government choose to accept them.

How to Set Up an SSL Storefront

Netscape invented SSL as a technology that would give them an edge in selling HTTP server software. So, one of the easiest ways to open up an SSL secure storefront is to call up Netscape and buy their software. Another solution is to roll your own SSL software. There are already some publicly distributed, third-party versions of SSL that are available for programmers to bend to their needs.

The products that Netscape offers solve several different needs and run on UNIX and Windows NT machines. The Commerce Servers come ready to offer secure links with SSL to people running Netscape's browser. The others fill similar data distribution needs. Nothing was reviewed, but here's a list of some of their basic products that was drawn from Netscape promotional material:

Netscape Commerce Server This package, which runs on both UNIX and Windows NT platforms, provides all of the tools for creating secure SSL-based links between browsers on the Net and your data. The software supports the HTTP/1.0 standard for distributing documents marked up in HTML. The forms and the actions they offer can be linked to other software using the Common Gateway Interface (CGI) with the additional help of the Netscape API (NSAPI).

Netscape Communications Server This is essentially the Commerce Server without the security offered by SSL. Offers information to the network and can check authorization but can't keep the link secure.

Netscape News Server You can build up your own network news file system using this software so your community can have local and national newsgroups.

Netscape Proxy Server This product offers a network administrator a firewall that caches frequently used pages and also initiates SSL sessions for users. Netscape claims that up to 60% of the pages requested in a recent test are re-requested soon afterward. Keeping them cached locally on the proxy server reduces Net traffic significantly and improves access time. The firewall will also initiate SSL sessions with distant machines as a proxy for the local user that might not be SSL-capable.

Netscape Merchant System This is a turnkey system that offers you the ability to get an electronic shop up and running. People can browse freely and fill an electronic shopping cart before paying and arranging for delivery of the products. The software is designed to add and subtract new products quickly. There are display templates and a new product can be added by simply filling in the template. If the template is changed, then all products using that template sport a new look.

Netscape Publishing System This is another turnkey system that offers you the ability to provide people with on-line subscriptions to publications. There are billing and accounting provisions for keeping the money flowing.

Netscape Community System You can use this to create virtual communities. I think this is essentially your own private Internet. The main difference is that the Netscape version comes with billing and metering for paying for it all.

Netscape IStore The data management of a simple commerce server with additional features for clearing credit cards and managing money.

Netscape invented SSL to sell their products and they are promising a wide range of server technology to future Net businesses.

Another solution is to roll your own SSL software. Netscape has made the standard open and others are free to adopt it. Tim Hudson offers one package that can be freely distributed.

JEPI and UPP

The Millicent program also developed a similar system for extending HTTP to negotiate a payment method. See page 226.

In the realm of computers, nothing is ever easy. Although you and I may be able to walk into a store and determine how to pay for an item, this negotiation is not automatic. Stores post credit card logos on their doors, indicating whether they accept certain brands. On the Web, a server and a client must do the same negotiation, looking for money that works. As payment systems proliferate, there are bound to be many sites that adopt only a fraction of the available systems. The only problem is that no one has created an easy way for a server to advertise with logo stickers on its door.

The UPP (Universal Payment Protocol) was developed by CommerceNet (`www.commerce.net`) and the World Wide Web Consortium (`www.w3.org`) as part of the Joint Electronic Payments Initiative (JEPI). It allows a client and a server to find a payment method acceptable to both, so money can flow and wealth can be created. At the time of this writing, the standard is circulating as an Internet draft, and source code is being tested.

The idea of stickers on a merchant's door is just a simple analogy for how the protocol works. In UPP, either the client or the server is able to ask the other what payment algorithms it knows and understands. Then each can force the other to choose. It's as if the logo stickers were available everywhere inside the store on demand.

The UPP includes a few neat programmatic solutions that may make the system more useful. The two parties can use keywords like `for` to force the other to list all payment methods that match a particular pattern. This allows the two sides to control the negotiation. This keyword was part of the Protocol Extension Protocol (PEP) being considered for the Web. It consists of a few standard ways that one machine can interrogate another to see if the other speaks a particular protocol. The UPP is just a subset of PEP.

The Protocol Pieces

The first and perhaps most complicated problem is finding a unique name for each payment protocol. In the UPP, each protocol is specified with a URL, which is unique when it is properly constructed. Presumably, any human could load this URL and find a text description of what the protocol is and how it operates. This would require major protocols to be backed by organizations committed to maintaining the domain name and keeping a Web server answering queries.

Naturally, there could be confusion if the organization moves the page often or makes copies in other sites. If the same protocol starts being used by different names, then interoperability will suffer.

The protocols can also be specified with parameters. For instance, a protocol run by the `oneword` company might look like this:

```
{http://one.word.oneword.com/PAY {params {UPP {amount
{frf}}}}}
```

This line specifies the protocol defined by the URL

```
http://one.word.oneword.com/PAY.
```

The second section specifies parameters that may restrict how it is used. In this case, the amount must be denominated in french francs (`frf`).

This line might also include a modifier that controls what pages can be bought with a particular protocol. For instance, `{for /PetesStuff/*}` means that it can only be used to purchase URLs that begin with the phrase `/PetesStuff/`.

These parameters and lines are used both in questions and answers exchanged between the two parties. Here's a list of the lines that are added to the HTTP protocol in order to exchange information about payment:

`Protocol-Query`: This is added to either the HTTP get or response. It might look something like this example from the UPP Internet draft:

```
Protocol-Query: {http://www.w3.org/UPP {for
/BobsPages/*} {upp {amount frf}}}
```

The first part of the line is the URL for the UPP metaprotocol. This payment negotiation is part of a more global system for negotiating protocols and this indicates that all of the information between the brackets will conform to the UPP approach. The `for` keyword specifies that the query is focused on all Web pages beginning with the reference `/BobsPages/`. Some payment systems may want to accept, say, MasterCard for one set of pages and Visa for another. The final parameter specifies that the payment must be in amounts denominated in french francs (`frf`). These query lines are answered with a `Protocol-Info` line.

The `Protocol-Query` line can also be used to ask whether the other side of the transaction accepts a particular protocol. If it is followed by a protocol name, then this indicates that one side wants to know what the other will do if presented with a particular protocol.

`Protocol-Info:` This line is also added to either an HTTP query or response. It includes a list of the protocols supported by a party. This list may not be inclusive—in fact, the UPP documentation suggests that each side list only its favorite methods to save bandwidth. If one side doesn't find something it likes in the list, then it can also simply generate another `Protocol-Query` message to enquire about a particular protocol.

Here's an example from the UPP documentation of a response to a `Protocol-Query`:

```
Protocol-Info: {http://www.w3.org/UPP {for
/PaymentPages/*}} {http://www.SET.org/PEPSpec {params
{upp {instrument-brand VISA}}} {for /PaymentPages/*}}
{http://www.CyberCash.com/PEPSpec {params {upp
{instrument-type ECASH}}} {for /PaymentPages/*}}
```

SET is described in Chapter 12 and CyberCash is described in Chapter 10.

This lists two types of payment, both of which can be used to pay for pages with URLs beginning with `/PaymentPages/`. The first is the SET standard and the second is CyberCash.

`Protocol-request:` This indicates that the server is insisting ("requesting") that the client use a particular protocol to pay for certain pages. It is a more serious version of `Protocol-Query`.

`Protocol:` A client makes the choice with this line.

The protocol includes several new error messages. If a client chooses a particular protocol that the server doesn't speak, then the server can generate an error and return a message with a `Protocol-Info` line including the correct protocols available.

This discussion of the UPP standard avoided some of the deeper issues about the different types of parameters available to constrain the individual protocols. These details can be found in the UPP documentation and will grow with time.

Final Assessment

Secure HTTP links are a very general way to handle information transactions. Any digital cash system is compatible because both account-based and token-based systems can ship their bits through a secure channel. The main advantage is that the same software can also be used to transmit general data and information across the link. The main disadvantage to this solution is that the U.S. government frowns upon the export of such general tools. They seem ready to approve strong cryptography like that used in CyberCash only if it is crippled and unable to secure arbitrary data.

Risk The risks depend upon the monetary transfer system used in conjunction with the secure link.

The low-quality, export-grade SSL software used by Netscape uses RC-4 with 40-bit keys. This is easily broken by anyone with a moderately powerful machine and some time. Damiel Dolgiez annouced it first after running for eight days in August of 1995. See the RISKS issues 17.27, 17.28 and 17.29 for a discussion.[1]

Several holes have been discovered and plugged in the Netscape software. The company offers a good cash reward program to encourage people to report problems and holes so they can be fixed. For instance, in 1995 Ian Goldberg and David Wagner discovered that an early version of the Netscape software did not choose its random keys very carefully. It merely used the time. This allowed them to search a small fraction of the possible keys to discover the ones that were supposedly chosen randomly[GW96]. This hole and several others have been fixed.

---

[1]Lindsay Marshall maintains a nice archive at http://catless.ncl.ac.uk/Risks.

Strengths These secure versions of HTTP can also be used to carry data, which can often be worth much more than a few dollars.

Some version of UPP must be developed and implemented. UPP is perfectly general.

Weaknesses SSL is difficult to export in its full strength. The government now allows Netscape to electronically distribute its browser with full-strength, 128-bit encryption. A user only needs to assert that he or she is not exporting the software.

Chapter 8

IBM's *i*KP

IBM's research division recently published their *i*KP protocol for securely transferring money over a network. The system is designed to work in concert with existing bank systems like credit cards or ATM networks by providing the average Net user with a secure way to transfer the information over the network. The most recent draft of the proposed protocols was written by IBM research division employees Mihir Bellare, Juan Garay, Ralf Hauser, Amir Herzberg, Hugo Krawczyk, Michael Steiner, Gene Tsudik, and Michael Waidner.

The most notable feature is that the system provides complete cryptographic protection and a solid audit trail that can be used to resolve any disputes. Other network credit systems like First Virtual's (see Chapter 6) do not use any encryption that might thwart eavesdroppers. The embedded security systems for Web browsers like S-HTTP or SSL (see Chapter 7) provide secure channels, but how the channel is used is up to the programmer. The *i*KP standard provides a good way to use the standard encryption systems to build a record of the transaction that is beyond dispute.

There are really three *i*KP protocols that represent different levels of sophistication. The lowest level, 1KP, only requires that a central authority publish a certificate guaranteeing its public key. There is no need for general public-key certificates to be issued to everyone. This means that the 1KP protocol can be adopted quickly because there is no need to establish a large-scale public-key infrastructure. The second protocol, 2KP, requires each merchant to also publish a public-key that is certified by some central authority. The third level of security, 3KP, relies upon public-key certificates issued to each potential customer as well. Obviously, requiring either every merchant or every merchant and every customer to publish a certified key pair is more complicated for everyone. But this allows the audit trail to be more secure.

The SET standard offered by MasterCard and Visa is a close descendant of the algorithms described here (see Chapter 12 for details). This chapter is kept mainly for historical interest. Also, it illustrates how the use of certificates is flexible. They may be required in many different ways.

1KP

There are three entities in the *i*KP model: C, the customer; M, the merchant; and A, the acquirer or bank. The protocol is as follows:

1. When the customer chooses an item, the merchant makes an offer containing the cost, the currency for the transaction, the date, and the merchant's ID number. The merchant also provides the public key and a certificate for the acquirer or bank that will process the transaction.

2. The customer checks the certificate for the bank. If it is okay, he adds his credit card number, the expiration date, and a PIN to the bundle of data containing the amount of the transaction, the currency, the date, and the merchant's ID number. This is all encrypted with the bank's public key endorsed by the certificate. This information is now secret and sent back to the merchant, who can't read the customer's credit card information.

   The composition of this message encrypted by the customer can take many forms. At the very least, the customer only needs to encrypt his credit card number, the expiration date, and a secure hash of the information about price and the details of the transaction. The encryption is only provided to keep this information from the merchant and give the customer some anonymity. Since the merchant already knows the details of the purchase, there is no reason to keep them secure.

3. The merchant takes the encrypted information from the customer and adds its own version of the secure hash of the transaction details. Then it forwards everything to the bank.

4. The bank decrypts the customer's information and checks to see if the secure hash provided by the customer equals the secure hash provided by the merchant. If they agree, then both the customer and the merchant agree upon the details of the trade and it can proceed. The bank charges the customer's account by the correct amount and then responds with a message that either approves or denies the transaction. The bank signs this approval or rejection as well as the secure hash of the transaction details with its own digital signature.

5. The merchant can check the signature of the bank to make sure that the transaction was approved. If it is, then the deal is done. The goods are handed over. The customer can also check this signature to make sure that everything went successfully.

The 1KP procedure provides several major forms of security for all three parties involved. For the customer, the most important feature may be the anonymity from the merchant. There is no way that a clerk or someone with access to the merchant's computer network could discover the credit card numbers. The merchant, in fact, won't even know the name of its customer unless the customer discloses it.

The merchant gains an explicit authorization of the transaction. If it saves the digital signature of the approval, then it can successfully argue with the bank if the bank refuses to pay later. In the current paper world, stores receive a verification or authorization number, but there is no way for the merchant to prove the authenticity of the number to a court or an arbitrator. If the credit card clearing company denies the verification number, then there is little the merchant can do.

All of the parties are generally protected against tampering emerging from the network. If the details of the order are changed by either the merchant or the customer, the secure hashes won't agree when the entire transaction package reaches the acquirer or bank.

2KP

The second level of the *i*KP protocol forces merchants to offer greater accountability. Each merchant needs to have a certified public-key pair that it can use to sign the transaction. The only difference between the 2KP protocol and the 1KP protocol is that the merchant adds

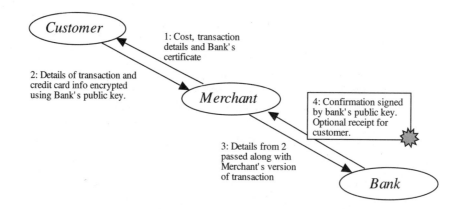

Figure 8.1. The 1KP protocol showing the movement of information between the customer, the merchant, and the bank or acquirer. The digital signatures are represented by the box around the information with the faux-foil seal.

its signature to the packet containing the customer's encrypted credit card number and the secure hashes of the transaction details. This adds the merchant's guarantee for the acquirer or bank. Now the merchant cannot deny that it made the transaction.

The merchant's certificate can also add some security for the customer. The *i*KP protocol proposal, shown in Figure 8.1, suggests that the certificate should also include the merchant's ID number, which is part of the transaction details. The merchant would provide its certificate with the initial offering data. A customer can check this certificate and know that the merchant is, in some sense, approved by the acquirer. This is a good check against widespread or high-level fraud. Merchants might need a certain amount of respectability to gain this acceptance.

The merchant can also provide a signed receipt for the customer by adding its signature to the acquirer's approval of the transaction. This digital signature would be strong proof that the transaction was made and it could either be used for tax purposes or other conflicts that might emerge.

3KP

The 3KP protocol uses the certificates of all three parties to add more security to the transaction. The major difference is that the customer now signs the encrypted version of his or her credit card number and the secure hash of the transaction details. This provides both the merchant and the acquirer or bank with undeniable proof that the customer spent the money. It also prevents anyone from forging the customer's name on a transaction by simply using the credit card number. Someone must gain access to the customer's private key before this can happen.

The *i*KP paper also suggests that the customer's certificate can include plenty of information in hashed form. It might include the hash of the address so customers could prove their addresses for shipping or billing purposes. The hash is used to protect customers' privacy. Customers could provide their certificates to everyone, but they would only reveal their addresses when they wanted to do so. Yet the details would still be guaranteed by the central certificate-granting authority.

The authors suggest that 3KP is the most desirable protocol for all parties in the system. They imagine that 1KP and 2KP, shown in Figure 8.2, will be interim solutions that could be used to start up the *i*KP system while certificates are issued to the world. This is certainly a nontrivial problem because issuing certified documents can require plenty of time and trouble.

Perhaps the most interesting aspect of the system is the structure of its partial veil of anonymity. The system provides a simple way for customers to keep their identity and credit card information out of the hands of merchants. This is a significant number of people and many

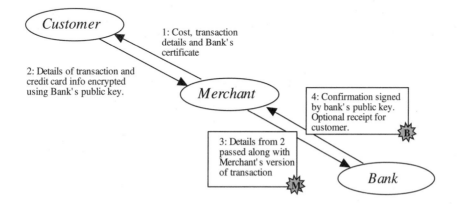

Figure 8.2. The 2KP protocol includes the signature of the merchant on the details of the transaction.

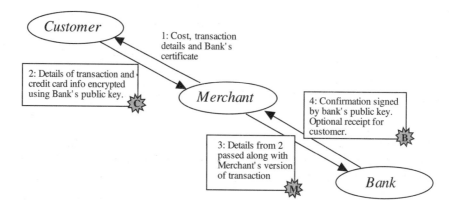

Figure 8.3. The 3KP protocol includes the signature of the customer completing the guarantees.

people may like the ability to hide their personal details from their merchants.

The *i*KP anonymity structure, though, is the direct opposite of the traditional structure produced by cash. Ordinarily, the merchant can know who is giving them the cash by looking across the counter. The banks, though, have no way of tracking the transactions in the economy. They don't know where the merchant got the cash it may be depositing.

This still leaves plenty of information in the hands of the company that processes the credit card payments. It can assemble a complete dossier of the transactions of a customer and determine much more information than any individual merchant might know. The most powerful companies are still protected in this system and they don't lose access to this information. There is still little information on how the credit card companies handle the data that flows through their computers. The raw information could be quite powerful. The credit card company would know early in the Christmas shopping season which merchants were doing better or worse than expected. This would allow them to guide their investments in the stock market with a much greater hope of making a significant profit.

Final Assessment

The *i*KP protocol is just a proposal from IBM. MasterCard and Visa, however, have produced something strikingly similar and it is certain to become a major standard for authorizing credit card transactions (see Chapter 12).

The major stumbling block will be setting up certificates for all of the users. The protocol is obviously intended to steer everyone toward 3KP. A worldwide system of certificates will be a big advance, so the push of major companies will help the cause significantly.

Risk The risk is minimized because the merchant receives confirmation. If 3KP is used, the customer will have trouble repudiating a charge because it was signed with his or her digital signature. Forgery would require someone to steal a smart card and grab the right PIN. This is not impossible, but it is harder than conventional approaches.

Strengths It provides some anonymity between the merchant and the buyer. May help push for public-key directories and certificates everywhere.

Weaknesses The anonymity model is a strange inversion of regular cash. The current transaction model does not provide much protection against insecure links. This is fixed in SET.

Chapter 9

NetCash and NetCheque

The NetCash and NetCheque systems are two payment systems designed by B. Clifford Neuman and Gennady Medvinsky at the Information Sciences Institute at the University of Southern California. NetCash is a cash system that offers a fairly strong degree of anonymity that can only be broken by the bank. NetCheque is a high-performance transfer system that is designed to clear many small payments successfully. Both of them were being tested as this book was written in 1996. Demonstration software is available for some UNIX machines, but not for the most general machines on the market.

At this writing, TEKnology-Laine, a company in Bremerton, Washington is commercializing the software. Its "mall" (`http://www.TEKChek.com`) lists several companies offering to accept payment through its system.

NetCash

The NetCash system is very similar to the classic digital cash systems described in Chapter 3. Digital coins are collections of bits with serial numbers that are guaranteed by the bank's digital signature. The designers strove to create a system that was secure against counterfeiters, reliable, anonymous, and scalable. The system itself is not secure when the payees are off-line.

There are significant differences in the level of anonymity, though, with the NetCash system. The protocols are simpler and this allows some banks to track the spending of their customers if they choose.

The designers argue that there will be many banks and currency servers available to customers so people will be able to choose one that they trust. They also argue that the banks could be contractually barred from keeping the records necessary to unravel the network of transactions and trace people's habits. Some banks might make this anonymity barrier a selling point and advertise their services based upon it.

The center for activity in the NetCash system is the currency server. This is an entity that is blessed by the government with the ability to mint digital money. In return, the currency server would maintain a direct deposit of funds with the government to guarantee any payment. It wouldn't be any different from a bank in most respects. The NetCash system proposes that the government maintain a central certificate authority that would bind up the public key for a currency server and seal it with the government's digital signature. This would allow a network of currency servers to evolve.

A digital coin produced in this system would contain these fields:

Currency Server The name and presumably IP address of the bank responsible for creating this money.

Expiration Date The date that the currency stopped being valid. This is included to allow the bank to retire serial numbers from circulation and lower the size of the database keeping track of the outstanding bills.

Serial Number The bank keeps track of the serial numbers of outstanding valid bills.

Coin Value The amount of money bound up in this coin as well as the currency type.

This data would be bound together and signed with the digital signature of the currency server or bank. The bank could either include a copy of its public-key certificate or just the ID number of the certificate. Many people might carry the complete certificates for the major currency servers on their systems.

Currency Server Transactions

These coins can be exchanged through any number of different protocols, but this basic two-step response is often adequate:

1. The customer would pack up some coins or a digital check with instructions for the currency server to exchange them for either new coins or a digital check made out to someone else. The customer would include a secret key K chosen at random and encrypt everything with the public key of the currency server.

2. The currency server would decrypt the incoming message and produce the new coins or checks as instructed. Naturally, it would check for fraud. Then it would encrypt the answer with the secret key K included in the original message.

The security of the system relies on one-way authentication. The currency server circulates its public key but each customer doesn't need to have one on file. The customer can be sure that his transaction wasn't spoofed when the return message comes encrypted with the secret key he chose at random. Plus, the customer's identity can be kept secret if he chooses because he doesn't reveal a public key or an identity bound to a certificate.

The currency server is responsible for straightening out the payments. The coins presented to it might be from another currency server across the country. The server should present the coins for payment to this currency server and get paid for them before it issues a new check or coins. The currency servers should balance up their accounts frequently and a fast national network may allow them to offer real-time clearance.

The limits of anonymity should be obvious at this point. Each currency server is responsible for generating its own coins with serial numbers in response to requests. It could simply keep track of these serial numbers and match them to names. If Bob wrote a check to the currency server on a local account, then the server could track the serial numbers of the coins issued to Bob on this check. When the coins returned, the currency server could determine their destination and watch them.

But a customer could very easily hide the information by exchanging the coins through several currency servers. He or she might withdraw coins, C_A, from server A and exchange them for coins C_B from a different server, B, across the country. This server B wouldn't know the identity of the person presenting them for payment and couldn't determine what happened even if it did track this serial number. A large chain of coin exchange could be created if the person really desired. The anonymity could only be breached if every currency server along the chain agreed to track the flow of its coins.

Payment Transfer

When coins are traded from user to user, NetCash suggests this simple protocol:

1. The two parties establish a secure channel. This might be created if the recipient has published a public key that the spender can use to initiate the transaction. Or it may be done on an anonymous basis by using Diffie-Hellman key exchange to create a pair of keys.

2. The spender bundles up the coins, a session key K_{AN}, and a session ID and encrypts them with the channel's encrypt mechanism.

3. The recipient gets the coins, checks the signature with the correct certificate for the currency server that generated the coins, and then sends the coins off to the currency server. The coins are bundled together with a new key, K_{BN}, and encrypted with the public key of the currency server.

4. The currency server checks the serial number of the coins to see if they have been spent before. If they haven't, it retires the coins and either sends the spender some new coins or deposits them in an account. These new coins are returned encrypted with key K_{BN} proving that the exchange was done with the currency server or someone who could decrypt their messages.

5. The recipient decrypts the new coins with K_{BN}. It is now fully paid. The recipient issues a receipt to the customer and may sign it with its digital signature guaranteeing the contents.

   This transaction does not require that the customer and the recipient maintain active public keys and certificates. The authenticity of the coins are maintained by the server. The coins could be used offline, but the recipient would not have any guarantee against double spending.

   The anonymity of these exchanges is just as limited. The recipient doesn't need to know the identity of the customer nor is there any way for it to find out directly. But it can find out if it conspires with the bank when it turns in the coins.

Low-Grade Anonymity and the Law

The anonymity offered by the NetCash system is a curious compromise that has several advantages. The most important one is efficiency. The banks only maintain a list of outstanding coins. A full-fledged anonymous system like the ones described in Chapter 3 needs to maintain copies of all transactions to catch double spenders in the future. These can be substantial. Disk space and tape costs continue to drop, but they are still relatively expensive. If a single anonymous transaction using the anonymous digital cash system takes 16K bytes to store, then it would cost about $.01 to store the transaction if disk space costs $.50 per megabyte. This is a perfectly acceptable cost if the transactions are larger than $10.00, but it is clear that the costs are still too large for small transactions of, say, $.50. This will change in the future as disk technology improves, but it will be several years before it is cheap enough. The NetCash system only requires that the serial number for outstanding bills be kept on-line. Each entry may be as small as 8 bytes and even could be stored as a bit in a long vector. It would be easy to keep the cost of storage infinitesimal.

Many people might be skeptical of a system that allows a bank to track the serial numbers of the bills it gives the customers. Certainly, the bank could promise not to do so and even enter into a contract not to keep the information around. But it would also hesitate to do so because of cost. Keeping track of the name of the person to whom a coin was issued would require more disk space. This might be a small amount if the bank were able to record the account number of the person requesting the coin, but it might be substantially larger if it included a certificate or the Net information of someone who came in off the Net. If each coin were stored as a bit that identified whether it was spent or unspent, then recording account information could take 8 to 100 times as much space. Clearly, the banks would consider not spending the extra cost for a feature that many customers might not want.

The limited nature of the anonymity might satisfy the needs of the law enforcement agencies, who clearly dislike any anonymous way to transfer money. The banks could keep track of coins withdrawn by certain accounts if this surveillance was requested. When the coins were returned, the bank could keep a record of the party who turned in the coins so the police could have a record. The bank might request that the police offer a warrant to activate the tracking mechanism and this could ensure that there are some safeguards. This might prove to be an ideal compromise between the widespread demands for privacy and the needs of the law enforcers.

NetCheque

The NetCheque system is a non-anonymous system that was also developed by the team at the Information Sciences Institute (ISI) at the University of Southern California. The major difference is that the NetCheque system imitates check clearance banking while the Net-Cash system imitates cash. Thus, anonymity is replaced by accountability.

Many of the other goals that led to the design of the NetCheque system are very similar to the NetCash system. The designers wanted it to scale well and offer low-cost transactions that would be appropriate to allow microbilling. The major difference comes in how authenticity and trust are generated. The NetCheque system relies upon the Kerberos system, which is described in detail in Chapter 2. Trust in this system emerges from a central server that can track all major transactions if it felt the need.

A check is created by bundling the standard information about the amount of the check, the type of currency, the name of the recipient, the name of the bank, the account number, the check number, and any other details. Call this data C. It is normally left in plaintext for all to see.

When Bob wants to sign this check, he calls up the Kerberos server for a *ticket* that will create a secure link between himself and the bank. This ticket contains a secret key $K_{Bob,bank}$ that will link Bob with the bank. It is encrypted in two different ways, once with Bob's secret password and the second time with the bank's.

Bob can decrypt this packet and get $K_{Bob,bank}$. He signs his check by computing a secure hash of C and encrypting this with $K_{Bob,bank}$. Then he appends the ticket that contains $K_{Bob,bank}$ encrypted with the bank's password. This will allow the bank to verify the signature when it receives the check.

When the bank gets the check, it knows that only Bob could have written the check because only three different entities could have extracted $K_{Bob,bank}$ from the ticket: the Kerberos server that generated the ticket (assumed to be trustworthy), Bob, and the bank. This is how security is generated using a Kerberos model.

The NetCheque system also includes plans for letting someone endorse a check with the same signature mechanism. If you receive a check from Bob made out to you, you would endorse it by generating a Kerberos signature in the same way that Bob signed the check. Then you would send it to the bank for deposit.

There is a good chance that the bank where you deposited the check is different from the bank that Bob drew the check against. Your bank would forward the check to Bob's for payment. The money would be returned through an interbank clearing system. Then it would be deposited in your account.

The NetCheque system tries to imitate the normal check clearing system in many ways. The principle advantage of the Kerberos system is that it uses private-key encryption that is generally not patented. Many good systems can be chosen without worrying about infringing upon the different patents given for public keys.

The problem with using a Kerberos model is that it requires each user to generate tickets to sign their checks. These tickets may expire frequently, which would require a more robust, on-line environment. Another major problem is that the Kerberos environment only creates secure channels between two parties. There is no way that someone can sign a check so that everyone can verify the signature. You couldn't test Bob's signature on the check because the ticket created a secure link between Bob and the bank. It would be possible to extend this and ask the check creator to include two different signature fields for both the bank and the recipient.

Sun Microsystems and HP/UX users can download binary test software for the NetCheque system from the Information Sciences Institute at USC. The authors plan to extend the test software to other platforms in the near future. Anyone who transacts a certain amount of business can get a royalty-free license. The limits range from $200,000 to $1,000,000. A similar license will probably be available when the ISI releases NetCash software.

How to Set Up a NetCash and NetCheque Storefront

Both NetCash and NetCheque were developed at the University of Southern California, which is not a software company. As such, the licensing and other options are different than many of the for-profit businesses. The developers are distributing binary files now for NetCheque that run on Sun and HP machines and they're considering releasing the source code. There is no distribution available for NetCash at this time. Several companies may offer commercial support of the system

The licensing options are designed to encourage small companies to adopt the technology. It is possible to get a royalty-free license from USC for NetCheque if your revenues from that source are less than $250,000. Details can be found with the software. For details about the license agreement contact:

Keith Johnson
Office of Patent and Copyright Administration
University of Southern California
3716 South Hope Street, #113
Los Angeles, California 90007-4344 U.S.A.
Phone: +1 (213) 743-2282 Fax: +1 (213) 744-1832
email: KJOHNSON@OPCA.USC.EDU

Pay Per View (PPV)

The NetCheque team also developed a set of software protocols that allows people running HTTP browsers like Netscape to pay for each document that they view. This protocol is built on top of HTTP by adding forms to the mix. The client must also be running the NetCheque software that will be making the payment.

When a viewer first requests a page, a CGI script at the server interrupts and sends a "preview" of the document. This may be the first paragraph, a summary, or a simple one-sentence description. The rest of the page contains a form that allows a user to authorize payment.

After the form is filled out, the NetCheque software running locally will interact with the server. When payment is complete, the document will be dispensed. This page can't be reloaded without paying for it again.

Final Assessment

The NetCheque and NetCash systems are intriguing variations on the themes in this book. NetCheque uses the Kerberos system to provide authentication. This is a good alternative to public-key cryptography when a network is always ready to provide Kerberos tickets, but it needs to be on-line nearly continuously.

Risk Both the NetCheque and the NetCash systems include a fair amount of accountability. If NetCash disappears, the cash can only be replaced by the bank if records are kept of withdrawals. The expiration date helps resolve these problems. But the holder of the cash bears the risk.

Strengths NetCheque doesn't use public-key encryption with patent constraints.

Weaknesses These systems are not backed by a major corporation with a strong consumer-minded effort. Early binaries are only available for workstations.

Chapter 10

CyberCash

The CyberCash system is another package designed to make it easy to pay for information and other goods with a Web browser. The foundations of the system are encryption and digital signatures provided by RSA Data Security software. Credit card transactions are the main vehicle for exchanging funds now but the company promises that it will offer CyberCash accounts that can be used for small-scale cash transactions. Their software runs on PCs running Microsoft Windows and it should soon run on the Macintosh and UNIX platforms. The most significant feature of the software is that it can now be exported despite the fact that it doesn't use crippled algorithms. The company was apparently able to convince the United States government that the software couldn't be used to exchange secrets.

The corporation was founded in 1994 by William Melton and Daniel Lynch. Melton also founded several different financial transfer corporations including Veri-fone, a company that makes phones for authorizing credit card transactions. Lynch gained his fame by working at SRI and running Interop, a collection of computer conferences. The team is rounded out by executives who have worked extensively with security and networking.

The corporation is also launching a micropayment scheme known as CyberCoin that is more in tune with the needs of the Net. See Chapter 11 for details.

Credit Cards

The basic credit card transactions are very similar in structure to the
*i*KP system described in Chapter 8. That package, though, is still a theoretical excursion at this writing. The CyberCash system is built out
of real code. Merchants sign up with CyberCash to clear their credit
card transactions and list the normal bank that clears the transactions.
Now, CyberCash will act as a conduit between the two and process
the encryption work. In the future, CyberCash aims to also clear regular transactions that might emerge from point-of-sale terminals or
telephone calls.

The customers set up accounts by downloading software from
CyberCash and filling out a form. The customers include the credit
card numbers that they plan to use through the system. CyberCash
will create an individualized file for each customer that includes these
credit cards and a public key that CyberCash assigns to the customer.
There are no certificates of authenticity used, essentially because there
is no certificate infrastructure in place today. The credit card numbers
are preprocessed in this way because CyberCash must check with
the issuing banks before proceeding. The preprocessing means that a
customer won't be able to capriciously decide to whip out a new credit
card to pay for something without clearing it beforehand.

The entire system, though, promises to be much more secure for
users, merchants, and credit card companies. The preprocessing and
the encryption described later add much more accountability than
provided in the current credit card system. It is not automatically
possible for a rogue merchant to steal a credit card number and run
up fake charges. Nor is it plausible that many others will be able to
traffic in fake cards. There may be some who steal the secret half of
public keys by hacking people's computers, but these won't travel
publicly. CyberCash imagines that it will be able to service many
marginal merchants who might not normally qualify for credit card
transactions because of the potential for fraud.

The steps in CyberCash credit card transactions are as follows:

1. After the merchant and the customer agree on a price, the merchant
   generates an invoice and sends it to the customer. This contains
   details about the transaction itself as well as the price.

2. The customer's software presents the customer with the preprocessed payment options. These include credit cards at this writing
and may include debit cards and bank accounts in the future. The
credit card number, the customer's identification data, and the final
agreed upon price are bound up, encrypted with the public key of
the CyberCash server, and mailed back to the merchant. The customer also signs a hash of this information with his secret half of
the public-key pair.

3. The merchant takes the customer's data and adds its own identification number and version of the final price. This is signed by the
merchant and the entire package is sent to the CyberCash server.

4. CyberCash unbundles the information and makes sure that the
customer and the merchant agree to the final price. Then it sends
the information to the bank that normally clears the credit cards for
the merchant. At this point, the credit card transaction is processed
as it would be if it began on paper.

5. CyberCash bundles up the news of the success or failure of the
transaction into two bundles, one for the merchant and the other
for the customer. Both are encrypted with the respective public key.
Both bundles are sent to the merchant, who then has the option of
forwarding the approval information to the customer.

   This packet may include other information at the merchant's
option. It might, for instance, include the credit card number of
the customer. Many companies keep the credit card numbers of
their customers on file. Although the credit card number is not
visible to the merchant in the normal transaction, CyberCash may
return the number as a benefit for the merchant. This may not be as
big a security hole in the future if everyone maintains a PC and a
public-key pair. The digital signatures are a much better guarantee.

6. The merchant may return the CyberCash-signed receipt verifying
the transaction. The merchant also delivers the goods.

The major difference between the CyberCash system and the iKP
system is the need for certificates. CyberCash is going to issue the
public-key pairs for all of the users and act, in essence, as a certificate-
granting authority for its users. There are several major effects of
this choice. First, the transactions are smaller since the customers and

merchants don't add their certificates to each packet. This is a minor consideration. Second, the entire system is more closed and proprietary. This may be good or bad for CyberCash depending upon how the market reacts to the need for an open system. There is no easy way for several competing CyberCash clearing houses to emerge in the same way that there are several competing credit card clearing agencies. There is no problem giving competing houses access to the public keys of the customer, but there may be logistical problems in giving all of the customers access to the right public key of the merchant's CyberCash clearing house.

Cash Transactions

CyberCash also promises to allow customer-to-customer cash transactions that could be very efficient. Each customer would, in essence, establish a cash account at CyberCash that could be used for payments on the Net. This account could be filled through either bank ATM transactions or checks. If you wanted, you could transfer money from your account to another's.

The cash transaction process is straightforward. Your software would send a request for transfer to CyberCash and sign it with your personal public key. CyberCash would move the money and send you a signed receipt guaranteeing the transaction.

Bit-Level Details of CyberCash

The Internet Draft describing the CyberCash protocols in detail is an excellent glimpse of how much work is necessary to build a secure way to exchange credit card numbers over the Internet. The draft, which is signed by Donald Eastlake 3rd, Brian Boesch, Steve Crocker, and Magdalena Yesil, describes all of the fundamental messages used in the version of the CyberCash system. The version of the draft dated July 8, 1995 covers CyberCash version 0.8 and can be found through anonymous FTP at `ftp.cybercash.com` in directory `pub/draft-cybercash-v08-00.txt`. Presumably newer versions will also be found here.

There are five different types of messages passed back and forth between clients and the CyberCash system: registration, credit card binding, consumer purchase details, merchant purchase details, and utility messages. All of them conform to a basic structure that consists of tags and a checksum that is not tamper-resistant. The important details are sealed inside the message by RSA signatures so there is no need for an extra cryptographically secure checksum to be computed. Here's a simple example from the Internet Draft. It shows the first message that might be sent by a new client requesting to open an account.

```
$$-CyberCash-0.8-$$
transaction: 123123213
date: 19950121100505.nnn
cyberkey: CC1001
opaque:
 iff/tPf99+Tm5P7s3d61jOWK94nq9/+1jOWK9+vr9+b+94
 n3tYzmiveJ9/+09/334ubg3rWM5Ir3ier3/7WM5Ir36+v3
 5v73ife1jOWK94n3/7T3/ffm5uD+7N339/f39/eq3ff39/
 eFiJK5tLizsoeSmpW7uLS8/7iio7Wisfv38biio7uyufv3
 tfv35uH+7N3d9/exuKX35+z3vuu4oqO7srnsvvz8/venoq
 OOv7al/7iio7WisYy+iv7s3ff3p6KjtL+2pf/wi7n43ard
 3Q==
$$-CyberCash-End-kchfiZ5WAUlpk1/v1ogwuQ==-$$
```

The start and end of the messages are indicated by the tags flanked, appropriately, by dollar signs. The last tag contains a checksum computed to identify problems in message transmission. The message is broken up into fields that are identified with tags. In this case, the transaction number is generated randomly by the client and used to identify the transaction in further communications.

The opaque section contains the important secret information encoded with DES with a session key that is then encrypted with one of CyberCash's public keys. The particular key used is identified by the cyberkey tag. RSA encryption with 768-bit keys is used for these public-key operations. The contents of the opaque section of this particular registration message look like this:

```
type: registration
swversion: 0.8win
content-language: en-us
```

```
requested-id: MyRequestedCCID
email: myemail@myemailhost.com
pubkey: aslfjflasdflasj;lfdjsl;afk
    jfjslakjf;ldskaj;flkajs;ldfjlaskf
    aslfjflasdflasj;lfdjsl;afkjfjslakjf ==
signature: alsdjflsajflksjdlkfjlsakjfl
    kdsajflksjfjslakjf;ldskaj;jfj
    slakjf;ldskaj;djlfasd===
```

This registration is announcing the e-mail address of a new person and the public key that the person would like to use. The `signature` section is a digital signature of every field in the message, including the unencrypted data such as the transaction number.

The response to this includes an official CyberCash ID that is used to identify the customer in future messages as well as other details that might be relevant. There are two other messages that can be used to update the software package if and when it falls out of date.

After users have registered and been granted a *persona*, they must *bind* their cards. This effectively preregisters their cards to save typing the numbers in repeatedly and also to allow CyberCash to block cards that might not be compatible with the system for some reason. These messages include all of the normal card details like number and expiration date. They also include one interesting technical extra: a card *salt*. This salt is an extra packet of bits that is hashed up with the card number. The central server does not store the credit card number—it just stores the hash. When a customer spends, the client software sends along the hash of the credit card number and the salt, which can be verified by the server. This makes the server files substantially less valuable if they are compromised. They don't contain millions of credit card numbers in the clear. The extra salt is added because there aren't enough credit card numbers to foil a brute-force search for a number that matches the hash in the file.

Transactions

A transaction begins when a merchant sends a message like this example from the Internet Draft to the client:

```
$$-CyberCash-0.8-$$
type: payment-request
```

```
merchant-ccid: ACME-012
merchant-order-id: 1231-3424-234242
merchant-date: 19950121100505.nnn
note;
  ACME Products
  Purchase of 4 pairs "Rocket Shoes" at $39.95 ea.
  Shipping and handling $5.00
  Total Price: 164.80
  Ship to:
        Wily Coyote
        1234 South St.
        Somewhere, VA 12345
merchant-amount: usd 164.80
accepts: visa:CC001, master:CC001,amex:CC001,
    JCPenny:VK005,macy:VK006
url-pay-to: http://www.ACME.com/CybercashPayment
url-cancel: http://www.ACME.com/CyberPaymentCancel
url-success: http://www.ACME.com/ordersuccess
url-fail: http://www.ACME.com/orderfail
merchant-signed-hash:N9MHKQoUj26kNtL2YGMiV9NgfCrux
    1AfYo2YnFsOzscLaURhcZzX/QOHwbXJr9yZzJP+LLvXyFTv
    mavLhzOTzotgcAx+jJA6W++a6mVkwxEbIyORRazBCoG9tiO
    sXdAU
$$-CyberCash-End-1SLzs/vFQOBXfU98LZNWhQ==-$$
```

The important tags are the type of credit cards accepted and the cost. The client's computer will decode this information and display it for the customer as well as a list of acceptable credit cards that are already bound to the customer's persona. The customer makes a choice from this list.

The merchant-signed-hash field cannot be used by the customer's software because the customer doesn't know the public key of the merchant. CyberCash is not extending its certificate-granting powers to this level of detail. This is a major difference between this procedure and the 3KP system in the IBM proposal. In that protocol, each of the three parties would use signatures backed by a publicly available certificate. It is unclear what the customer loses in the CyberCash approach. In some sense, the price offer is a contract and if the store backs out of it then the customer has some recourse. If the customer could verify the offer, then he could prove his case. It is not clear, however, that many customers would ever need or want to use this feature. It's nice if you're dealing with a contractor or a moving company offering a guaranteed estimate, but it is almost unnecessary for most transactions.

When the customer accepts a transaction, the client software generates this response taken from the Internet Draft:

```
$$-CyberCash-0.8-$$
type: card-payment
id: myCyberCashID
order-id: 1231-3424-234242
merchant-ccid: ACME-012
transaction: 78784567
date: 19950121100505.nnn
pr-hash:ArJfqEMfZqOBjIaoflZi2A==
pr-signed-hash: N9MHKQoUj26kNtL2YGMiV9NgfCrux
      1AfYo2YnFsOzscLaURhcZzX/QOHwbXJr9yZzJP+LL
      vXyFTvmavLhzOTzotgcAx+jJA6W++a6mVkwxEbIyO
      RRazBCoG9tiOsXdAU
cyberkey: CC1001
opaque:
 iff/tPf99+Tm5P7s3d61jOWK94nq9/+1jOWK9+vr9+b+
 94n3tYzmiveJ9/+09/334ubg3rWM5Ir3ier3/7WM5Ir3
 6+v35v73ife1jOWK94n3/7T3/ffm5uD+7N339/f39/eq
 3ff39/eFiJK5tLizsoeSmpW7uLS8/7iio7Wisfv38bii
 o7uyufv3tfv35uH+7N3d9/exuKX35+z3vuu4oqO7srns
 vvz8/venoqOOv7al/7iio7WisYy+iv7s3ff3p6KjtL+2
 pf/wi7nw3ard3Q==
$$-CyberCash-End-7Tm/djBO5pLIw3JAyy5E7A==-$$
```

The opaque section contains the amount of the transaction and a hashed up value of the bound card. The merchant can't read this information because it is signed with the private key of the customer. Only the central CyberCash computer will be able to decode it so it can be passed along to the credit card clearing company.

The pr-signed-hash is just a copy of the hashing that the merchant applied to the original price proposal. The pr-hash was computed by the customer's app and its authenticity is guaranteed by the signature of the entire message bound inside the opaque block. The CyberCash computers decrypt the pr-signed-hash with the merchant's public key and check to see that it matches the pr-hash. If it does, then both parties agree to the deal.

The merchant takes the response from the customer and binds it up in a message like this one. Notice that the opaque section is an exact duplicate. The merchant adds its information in its own merchant-opaque section.

```
$$-CyberCash-0.8-$$
merchant-ccid: ACME-69
merchant-transaction: 123123
merchant-date: 19950121100705.nnn
merchant-cyberkey: CC1001
cyberkey: CC1001
opaque:
 iff/tPf99+Tm5P7s3d61jOWK94nq9/+1jOWK9+vr9
 +b+94n3tYzmiveJ9/+09/334ubg3rWM5Ir3ier3/7
 WM5Ir36+v35v73ife1jOWK94n3/7T3/ffm5uD+7N3
 39/f39/eq3ff39/eFiJK5tLizsoeSmpW7uLS8/7ii
 o7Wisfv38biio7uyufv3tfv35uH+7N3d9/exuKX35
 +z3vuu4oqO7srnsvvz8/venoqO0v7al/7iio7WisY
 y+iv7s3ff3p6KjtL+2pf/wi7nwiff/tPf99+Tm5P7
 s3d61jOWK94nq9/+1jOWK9+vr9+b+94n3tYzmiveJ
 9/+09/334ubg3ard3Q==
merchant-opaque:
 iff/tPf99+Tm5P7s3d61jOWK94nq9/+1jOWK9+vr9
 +b+94n3tYzmiveJ9/+09/334ubg3rWM5Ir3ier3/7
 WM5Ir36+v35v73ife1jOWK94n3/7T3/ffm5uD+7N3
 39/f39/eq3ff39/eFiJK5tLizsoeSmpW7uLS8/7ii
 o7Wisfv38biio7uyufv3tfv35uH+7N3d9/exuKX35
 +z3vuu4oqO7srnsvvz8/venoqO0v7al/7iio7WisY
 y+iv7s3ff3p6KjtL+2pf/wi7nwiff/tPf99+Tm5P7
 s3d61jOWK94nq9/+1jOWK9+vr9+b+94n3tYzmiveJ
 9/+09/334ubg3rWM5Ir3ier3/7WM5Ir36+v35v73i
 fe1jOWK94n3/7T3/ffm5uD+7N339/f39/eq3ff39/
 eFiJK5tLizsoeSmpW7uLS8/7iio7Wisfv38biio7u
 yufv3tfv35uH+7N3d9/exuKX35+z3vuu4oqO7srns
 vvz8/venoqO0v7al/7iio7WisYy+iv7s3ff3p6Kjt
 L+2pf/wi7nw3ard3Q==
$$-CyberCash-End-7Tm/djBO5pLIw3JAyy5E7A==-$$
```

The merchant-opaque section includes this information encrypted with the merchant's private key. (The signatures are simulated, not real.):

```
type: auth-only
order-id: 12313424234242
merchant-amount: usd 10.00
pr-hash: 7Tm/djB05pLIw3JAyy5E7A==
pr-signed-hash:
    sfljlkjflkjseljljljwlkjrweljljlj
    wlkjrweljljljwlkjrweljljljkjrwel
    jljljwlkjrwlejrlwkjlerkjwelr=
id: myCyberCashID
transaction: 78784567
date: 19950121100505.nnn
merchant-signature: lkjladjslkjflsak
    jflkjsdljflsakjflkjsdljflsakjfl+w
    flsakjflkjsdljflsakjflkjsdljflsaj
    flksdjflksdjflsdjssf=
```

The central CyberCash computer decrypts both opaque sections, verifies their signatures and checks to see that the amounts match. If so, it sends on the information to the credit card clearing house. When the charge is authorized, the success or failure is passed along to the merchant who sends it on to customer.

The return receipt from CyberCash includes information for both the merchant and the customer. The merchant information is encrypted with the session key that the merchant app used to encrypt the merchant-opaque data. The customer's message is encrypted with the session key that the customer's app used to encrypt the credit card number that passes along in the opaque section.

The return receipt may include full information about the credit card or it might just include the card prefix and the hash code. CyberCash seems to be slowly deciding just how much anonymity the market wants. Some merchants like to keep track of credit card numbers in their computers. Giving the merchants this information may be one way for CyberCash to get new merchants into the system. The card prefix and the hash are compromises that give the merchant a unique number for each credit card but don't give them the actual number itself.

There are many other messages that may be used in other types of transactions that move through the CyberCash system. There are some messages that allow merchants to process the charges they receive by telephone, effectively allowing their computer system to act like the tiny Veri-fone boxes at checkout counters. There are also information transactions and other debugging messages. Many of these are described in detail in the Internet Draft.

The Internet Payment Framework

Donald Eastlake of CyberCash is currently circulating an Internet Draft that outlines a basic framework for linking payment throughout the Internet. The draft lays out a standard grammar for speaking about prices and suggests how the grammar might be built into many of the existing Internet standards like telnet or FTP. Ideally, these extensions to the standard forms of communication will allow digital commerce to emerge out of the standard mechanisms and not require everyone to develop new software for payment.

The draft lays out these items of basic syntax:

Prices The basic format of the price is a number followed by a set of characters that identifies the underlying currency. 12.05usd would stand for $12.05 in U.S. dollars. The standard ISO 4217 codes would be used for most major currencies. Specialized currencies or private currencies would begin with an x-. For instance, if doll hairs became a commodity in the Barbie community, then x-dh might stand for the doll hairs.[1]

Payment System Tags The draft also suggests that payment system tags be developed. These would include the bank or service providing funds transfer and a certain amount of account information. cybercash:1423241, for instance, would stand for account number 1423241 in the CyberCash system. The 1423241 value is payment system specific and it is up to the bank or transfer mechanism to decide how it is used.

---

[1]Barbie's perennial youth makes this viable. Older dolls would lose all their hair and flood the marketplace, bringing inflation. Dog and cat hairs conjure nightmares of Weimar Germany.

Price Tags The prices and the payment system are bound together in price tags. If some item was only clearable using a particular payment system, then you would place the price after the payment system tag. A price tag of `cybercash:1423241 1550.00usd` would signify that you could buy an item if $1550 were transferred through the CyberCash system into account 1423241.

Receipts If a service takes money, it might generate a receipt that contained some unique ID for the transaction and perhaps a digital signature guaranteeing receipt of the payment. These would be encoded with the service's name followed by a string of characters carrying the receipt information. `cybercash:1241jasdlj214/ 12341;jajwejrw` is one hypothetical example. The structure of these receipts is not standardized and it is up to the service to control their content.

The Internet Draft also spells out how these prices might be incorporated into the standard Internet protocols so they might be extended to absorb cash. These suggestions for the different protocols are as follows:

Web System Eastlake imagines that the costs will be embedded in the anchor of a link. The browser could display the cost and warn the user before the link is followed. This allows the HTTP server to charge before the information leaves its machine if it so chooses. One suggested tag might look like this:

```
<A COST="paymentsystem:xxxxxx 1.00usd 1.40cad"
   HREF="http://newray.com/stuff">
   This costs 1 US dollar and 1.4 Canadian ones
   </A>
```

The draft also suggests that the payment systems be built into parts of the forms with an example like this from the draft:

```
<p>Your quality of service: <select name="quality">
 <option value="bronze"> Low<p>
 <option value="silver" cost="0.10usd 0.17cad">
    Medium<p>
 <option value="gold" cost="0.20usd 0.34cad">
    High<p> </select>
```

Choosing the silver option would cost 10 cents and the presumably better gold option would cost 20 cents.

FTP Services The FTP protocol could be extended by adding some new numbers that indicate different types of messages for payment. The number 332 would be followed by a price tag like this: <COST= "cybercash:xxxxx 0.10usd">. This would tell users that they must arrange to pay 10 cents to see the document. A receipt would be carried by a 233 command.

Eastlake also provides enhanced protocols for telnet and SNMP so that entities can charge for these connections. He suggests that protocols like Finger and DNS be left free because they are essential foundations of the network. Charging for these would be like charging for air.

The current proposal is just an Internet Draft at this time and it will certainly go through many iterations before you read this text. I hope that it will spawn other explorations into extending basic Internet protocols. I'm often amazed at what level of attention to detail is necessary before the Net can be wired for money.

How to Set Up a CyberCash Storefront

CyberCash currently has agreements with several merchants and one major bank (Wells Fargo). If you want to set up Web pages, it offers a form on its Web server. You must fill it out and they will call you to discuss opening up shop.

At the time this book was completed, CyberCash merchant packages were evolving. The basic merchant software is currently drafted in PERL scripts, but they are working on converting it into compilable software. The PERL scripts can't be exported, but CyberCash hopes that they'll be able to export the binaries of the merchant software in the same way that they can export the binary versions of the client package. Eventually, CyberCash will have a turnkey version for small merchants with fairly standard needs.

Final Assessment

CyberCash is now a fully developed system for processing transactions. The list of merchants includes many small companies and sev-

eral major brand names, including JD Power. Many of the merchants
sell music CDs and different information. The client software package
is impressive, exportable, and designed to negotiate firewalls.

Risks For the consumer, the risk is minimal. In the United States,
credit card companies must cover any loss larger than $50. The
system mimics the regular banking system.

Strengths CyberCash uses the strongest crypto software and is run
by people with solid experience. The approach is designed to successfully build upon the current credit card clearing system.

Weaknesses No security weaknesses are apparent at this time. The
structure of anonymity is weak because CyberCash may disclose
certain information to the merchant if the merchant requests it. It
is unlikely that the system will evolve to offer greater anonymity
than the current credit card system.

Chapter 11

CyberCoin

The CyberCoin system allows CyberCash users to make micropayments across the network. The basic CyberCash system is a front end for both the credit card and the ATM clearing houses (see Chapter 10) and is intended to facilitate larger transactions. The overhead of credit card and ATM wire transfers, however, is too high for the penny-sized transactions that people are used to spending on information. CyberCash estimates that each credit card transaction costs about $.75 to clear; that is more than most newspapers cost today. Any payment mechanism for the Web must charge less.

The CyberCoin system is a ledger-based system. There are no data packages ("bag o' bits") acting as tokens or a coin. The money resides in a special account within the bank until it is spent. The CyberCoin central computers keep track of this money and control its dispersal, but the accounts are reconciled each evening within the bank itself. CyberCash has even arranged for a special ruling by the Federal Deposit Insurance Corporation to extend deposit insurance to these accounts. This insurance of $100,000 per user probably won't be necessary because CyberCash is currently limiting each account to $100 because of Regulation E.

The system, in essence, is a lower-cost version of the ATM and debit card networks. When a customer steps up to a Web site and offers to spend $.25, the customer's message includes an account number and authorization for transferring $.25 to the merchant. The merchant sends this to the CyberCoin central server, which collects its cut and transfers the money out of the account. All of the work is done with CyberCash's ledgers, not within the banking network.

Why did they choose this approach? CyberCash argues that being a bank is hard work. The regulations are difficult and constraining. If the money is believed to stay within the bank until it is spent, then the bank can handle the regulations and the merchants can avoid understanding anything about banking law. Other payment mechanisms like Millicent (see Chapter 19) require the merchant to issue their own scrip. While this has great flexibility, it can open the door for regulatory hassles.

The other great advantage is assurance. The banking customers inherit all of the protections they already have on their traditional accounts. Depository insurance covers them in the event of a bank failure and Regulation E forces the banks to limit the customer's exposure to losses. A lost hard disk, just like a lost credit card, may only cost the customer $50. Some banks may resist these measures because of the high cost of providing this assurance, but this safety may prove critical to widespread acceptance of the system. Many computer users have already experienced a hard disk failure and suffered from the trauma of losing potentially critical files. If their money could disappear "just like cash," many people could balk at adopting the system.

Transaction Details

The CyberCoin system avoids using public-key digital signatures for as many operations as possible. If a customer goes to a Web site and spends $.25, then the messages authorizing this transaction are sent without public-key signatures. All of the "signatures" are created using hash functions or DES with a shared secret. Each customer holds a secret value that only he and the CyberCoin central server know.

The Millicent system uses a similar hash-based signature system.

Public-key algorithms are used, but only to set up accounts and distribute these secrets. This ensures that the load on the servers is minimized. CyberCash estimates that a public-key signature takes 10,000 times longer to generate than a hash-based signature. When an account is opened for customer i, the user's machine ends up with two major secrets or keys: D_i and S_i.

D_i is used as the basis for key material and has a limited lifespan measured in days or transactions. Each new transaction is encrypted with DES using a unique key. The secret value, S_i, is hashed together with a unique transaction ID. The CyberCoin server also knows both S_i

and D_i and can take the transaction ID and redo the hashing to generate the key. This protects the security of the data inside the transaction.

Many of the fields are similar to the transaction fields described in Chapter 10. The signatures, however, are produced by using a keyed version of MD-5 instead of RSA. The key for the signatures is the secret value S_i.

1. When the merchant and the customer agree on the terms of the sale, the merchant ships the customer a hash, $h(data)$, of what he or she will get.

2. The customer replies with a message that includes the customer ID number (C_i), the amount of the transaction, and the expected hash value of the purchased data, $h(data)$. This is signed by appending the customer's secret value, S_i, to all of these fields and then hashing the result. This hash is sent to the merchant, but S_i does not go along.

3. The merchant takes this data packet and adds its own signature by appending the merchant ID number, M_j, and hashing. This goes to the CyberCash central server.

4. The CyberCash central server checks the signatures using its own knowledge of C_i and M_j. If the money is available, it signs off on the transaction by mailing the merchant an authorization and signs it by appending the merchant's secret value, M_j, and hashing it.

5. The merchant receives the signature and decides that the money is available. The data goes to the customer.

6. The customer checks out the data, hashes it, and constructs a message verifying that everything was delivered according to plan. This message includes $h(data)$ and is signed by appending the customer's secret key, C_i, and hashing.

7. The CyberCoin computer releases the money to the merchant on receipt of the message from the customer.

Final Assessment

The CyberCoin system is another good example of how private-key algorithms can be used to simplify the transaction process. Seeding each user with some secret key material can be done in advance and

this makes it possible to process transactions in real time. The CyberCoin solution for leveraging a small amount of secret material by
hashing it with a transaction ID number is also used in other systems,
including Millicent.

Strengths The CyberCash corporation has a strong group of some
of the smartest cryptographers around. They also have executives
with a thorough knowledge of the transaction processing world,
and this knowledge is essential for setting up a business. The cryptography is quite well done.

Weaknesses There are no known weaknesses at this time. There is no
anonymity.

Risks The money in your CyberCoin account is kept is a separate
escrow account controlled by CyberCash. The major risk of a bank
failure has been removed because CyberCash was able to get a
special decision from the FDIC. The only other risk is that someone
will be able to break into your computer and extract the secret
material used to prove your identity. This risk is common to all
PC-based systems without smart cards. There is no reason why
the CyberCoin system couldn't be expanded to use smart cards.

Chapter 12

SET

Visa and MasterCard[1] produced SET to be their standard for processing credit card transactions that travel over networks like the Internet. The system includes a large amount of strong cryptography to authenticate transactions and ensure that the system remains secure. A large portion of the cryptography is based on public-key systems, and SET makes heavy demands upon a certification authority for support.

The SET system itself is similar to many of the other credit card front ends like CyberCash (see Chapter 10) or IBM's *i*KP (see Chapter 8). The major difference is the level of encryption and how information is compartmentalized. Merchants, for instance, won't have access to a customer's account number.

The definitive work on the SET protocol is the *Programmer's Handbook* distributed by MasterCard and Visa, which is longer than 400 pages. This book cannot provide the same level of detail, and interested programmers or others who want to examine the deep details should turn to this document. The handbook can be found, at this writing, from the Visa home page (`www.visa.com`). Visa and MasterCard also intend to distribute sample code that programmers for various companies can use as the basis for their own implementation of SET.

---

[1]GTE, IBM, Microsoft, Netscape, SAIC, Terisa, and Verisign are also credited by the documentation as providing technical commentary and suggestions.

Overview of the Transactions

The best place to begin understanding SET is to review the credit card transaction process. The customer negotiates with a merchant to buy a product. When the price is set, the merchant calls the acquirer to request authorization for the customer. The acquirer is most likely a bank that processes transactions by calling up the issuer and requesting that $n be set aside to cover the transaction. If the credit is available, the merchant receives authorization and gives the goods to the customer.

Later, the merchant *posts* the transaction by officially requesting repayment. This may occur several days or even months afterward because the merchant may not deliver the goods immediately after receiving authorization. During this time, the $n of credit is in limbo. The customer cannot use the credit elsewhere because it is spoken for by the merchant, even though the charge has not officially been made. Hotels, for instance, often ask for a large authorization to handle extra charges like meals.

When the charge is posted, the acquirer informs the issuer of the amount which may be smaller than the initial authorization. The credit is consumed, the charge is entered onto the customer's bill and the issuer gives the acquirer the funds. Eventually, the acquirer gives the merchant the money after an amount of time that differs from contract to contract.

The SET project aims to support each of these operations over the Internet through a mixture of digital signatures and encryption. The customers, merchants, acquirers, and issuers will each sign off on their stages of the transactions, building up a solid audit trail that can solve all arguments about who gets paid when.

Certificates and SET

The wide variety of people and companies in the SET universe sign their transactions with digital signatures. Such a widespread use of digital signatures requires a solid infrastructure for maintaining certificates guaranteeing public keys. These certificates form a chain of responsibility that vouches for the public part of every key pair so people know whether to trust it or not. A certificate is like a letter of credit because it states that someone is willing to stand behind this signature.

The SET standard relies on a particularly strong chain of what are called *certificate authorities* (CAs), that is, an organization that offers to back up a person's signature and vouch for its authenticity. A customer or cardholder using the SET system will have his or her own public-key pair and the public part of it will be packaged in a certificate that includes the digital signature of the issuer. This is generated by the *cardholder certificate authority* (CCA), which works in cooperation with the issuer. Any merchant can examine the certificate and see that the issuer is going to stand behind the charges made by it because the public key was signed by the CCA that works for the issuer.

But how does anyone know that the CCA's signature is really good or worth trusting? Well, it comes with its own certificate that is signed by a still higher authority. Can you trust this signature of a higher authority? The chain of certificate authorities can go on and on, but it must stop eventually. At the top is the *root certificate authority* or Root CA. This Root CA may guarantee the signatures of many different groups. Beneath the Root CA is the *Brand CA*, which is set up by each brand (e.g., Visa, MasterCard, Discover, or Amex). The SET standard also imagines that there may be an optional *Geopolitical CA* that would guarantee local signatures. So either the U.S. government or some other state would provide some backup for the authenticity of a signature.

If a customer begins to sign off on a charge, the merchant must check at least four digital signatures and their certificates. First, the customer's signature is backed up by the signature of the CCA. This signature is backed up by a certificate issued by the Brand CA, which, in turn, is backed up by the Root CA. A Geopolitical CA may also exist in the chain or it may provide separate assurance about the CCA.

Checking out all of these signatures need not be done with each transaction. The merchant can be certain that the CCA's certificate is good because it is unlikely to go bad from customer to customer. Many customers will have their cards issued by the same bank and backed up by the same CCA, so there is no need to confirm all signatures in the chain.

There are also similar organizations backing up the merchants and the acquirers. The merchants have their own set of digital signature pairs that are backed up by the *merchant certificate authority* (MCA). A customer might want to check out the signature of a merchant on a receipt, and the MCA's job is to stand behind these signatures. There is also the *acquirer payment gateway certificate authority* (PCA), which will back up the signatures of the acquirers. These signatures will be verified by the merchant to make sure that the credit is correctly issued.

Both the PCA and the MCA issue certificates that are backed up by Brand CAs. If an acquirer supports multiple brands, then it may have several certificates issued by several Brand CAs. They may either validate the same or different keys.

Revoking Certificates

Certificates, in essence, are like the plastic cards available today. If a CCA issues a certificate, then it is willing to stand behind the card. But cards get lost or stolen and people abuse their credit limits, forcing the credit card issuers to withdraw cards. The certificate authorities also need ways to withdraw their support of a certificate.

The solution is a list of *revoked certificates*. This is much like the old, thick multipage pamphlets that were distributed to stores before electronic clearance of credit card payments became common. These lists contained the numbers of the bad card accounts that would be refused by the issuer. Each certificate authority maintains a list of revoked certificates and distributes it.

Revoking certificates is a messy procedure and it is best to minimize the amount of times it needs to be done. The easiest solution is to give each certificate an expiration date after which it is automatically revoked. This minimizes the size of the revoked list.

The SET protocol includes a technique, known as the *thumbprint*, which is used as a surrogate for the list of revoked certificates. It is just the hash of the entire list. Someone who wants to check a certificate must return to the certificate authority to get a list of the revoked certificates to make sure that it hasn't gone bad. Someone who wants to do an up-to-the-minute check of a certificate must make sure he or she has an up-to-the-minute list of revoked certificates.

The thumbprint allows a merchant to maintain a list of revoked cardholder certificates. When a new customer offers a card, the merchant can check its own local list to see if the certificate is there. If it isn't, then the merchant can ask the CCA for the thumbprint of the latest list of revoked certificates. If the thumbprint matches the hash of the merchant's local list, the merchant can be sure that no new accounts have been added to the bad certificate list.

The Contents of Certificates

The certificates act as a match between a cardholder and the digital signature. In many ways, they are just like the plastic cards issued to people today. These cards contain the expiration date, the account number, the person's name, and maybe even a photograph. The SET certificates could contain all of this information, but they don't.

In fact, no personal information is to be gotten from a SET certificate. The name is not included and the account number is blinded from view. So the merchant may receive a signature and make sure it was generated by the private key matching the certificate, but the merchant can't extract the name of the customer or the account number. This shielding helps prevent fraud by dishonest merchants or their clerks.

The blinding algorithm uses a *keyed hash algorithm* that acts like a public-key signature. The cardholder and the CCA agree on a shared secret by exchanging random values (a.k.a. *nonces*). This acts as a key to the hash of the actual credit card number when it is appended to the credit card data before the hash function is computed. The result is a unique value that acts like a pseudonym for the customer. It uniquely identifies customers, but it won't reveal their actual identities or their account numbers.

The actual details for computing a keyed hash are important to people implementing the procedure. They are left out of this book, but programmers should turn to both the programmer's reference and the sample code distributed by Visa.

The certificates for merchants and the acquirer clearing houses also contain extra information. Their name and identity are left in the clear because there is little value in keeping their position pseudonymous. In fact, their whole authority derives from their stability and reputation. The certificates also can contain data about transaction limitations.

The SET protocol imagines that certificates will not be used at the beginning because of the large overhead involved in distributing keys and certificates to all cardholders. So merchants will be able to present their charges to the acquirer without certificates or signatures from the cardholders to back up the transactions. Eventually, as certificates become widely distributed the acquirers will require the merchants to provide this information.

The certificates for the acquirer could contain a description of what the acquirer requires from the merchant. When cardholder certificates become required, the acquirer would attach a flag or a note to their certificates and distribute it widely. The merchant would be responsible for watching for changes in the certificates.

The certificates, in essence, can be used to promulgate binding transaction requirements. When one party changes its transaction limits, it would revoke its old certificate and issue a new one.

There are many possible ways that this could be used. Cardholder's certificates, for instance, might include a maximum (or minimum) transaction size. This might be as large as the entire credit limit or as small as a few pennies. The cardholder could use this to enforce some policy. A parent, for instance, might not want his or her child spending more than $20 on a credit card given to the child. A business might set a limit on petty cash spending. The current SET protocol includes no provision for these examples, but there is no reason why it couldn't be extended to encompass them.

The Transaction Data Flow

The SET protocol involves three parties: the cardholder, the merchant, and the acquirer. The flow of data, at the highest level, is pretty simple. The cardholder asks to purchase something, the merchant asks the acquirer for enough credit to cover the transaction, and the acquirer responds. If there is enough credit, the merchant hands over the goods and then asks the acquirer to finalize the payment.

For a better understanding of the process, turn to Chapter 8, which describes IBM's iKP. It is an early effort that is quite similar to the SET protocol.

Although this may take only two sentences to describe at a high level, it takes at least 40 pages to describe in the SET programmer's handbook. The data structures required to handle all of the miscellaneous data can be quite involved. The protocol must be able to anticipate many contingencies and adapt to allow them. Also, the protocol provides a way for transactions to be processed without certificates to back up the digital signatures. This means that almost two separate protocols are in place.

This next description of a typical transaction is a mid-level description. While it will discuss each message passed between the parties, it won't go into enough detail for a programmer to build the system. If you are interested in that level of detail, you must turn to the SET *Programmer's Handbook.*

PInitReq—**The Initialization Request** This is an optional message that the cardholder's machine may generate to start the transaction. Its main job is to introduce the cardholder, select the card brand (MasterCard, Visa, etc.), and synchronize the certificates.

The cardholder's machine will make a list of the certificates it holds and produce a thumbprint (i.e., hash value) of them. This is sent to the merchant, who will determine whether the cardholder has access to the latest version of these certificates. The merchant is assumed to be more in touch with both the acquirer and the certificate authorities.

This message also includes a random value, Chall_C, that stops replay attacks.

PInitRes—**The Merchant's Response** The merchant decodes the message and starts up a record for an upcoming transaction. The most important job is for the merchant to check through the list of certificates to make sure that the cardholder's machine has the latest ones. This message contains updated certificates for the different CAs, the acquirer, and the merchant, if they're necessary.

The response also includes a copy of Chall_C. When the entire message is signed by the merchant, the random value prevents this message from being reused by any eavesdropper.

PReq—**The Payment Request** When ready to pay, the cardholder sends this message containing the data about the card and the amount. The details of the order are transmitted "out of band," which is to say that the SET protocol really doesn't care how the merchant and the cardholder come to terms on what will be sent and how much it will cost.

This message is broken into two parts. The order information (OI) is for the merchant and the payment information (PI) is for the acquirer. The merchant doesn't touch the PI and may not be able to read much of it. The customer's account number is scrambled in the certificate.

The OI's main job is to carry a hash value of the order data to the merchant. This hash of the details of the transaction prevents any party from disagreeing with the purpose of the transaction. When the merchant receives the OI, its machine takes it apart and compares the hash value against the merchant's version of the order data. They should agree. The merchant will send this version of the hash on to the acquirer when payment is requested, because the PI also contains the same hash value. This way the acquirer can be sure that all three parties agree on the hash value of the order data.

The OI also contains several more random values, which are used as salts to prevent replay attacks. If the transaction began with a PInetReq, then the same value of the random challenge value is included. Otherwise, a new one is generated. Also, the hash value of the order data is "salted," which means that an additional random value is appended to the data. This random value also travels in the OI.

The PI contains information for the acquirer, including the customer's description of the transaction. This includes the merchant's ID number, the payment amount, the scrambled version of the customer's account number (PAN), and a hash of the order data. There is also a slot for the customer to include a random key for establishing a secure link directly between the customer and the acquirer.

The OI and PI data are mixed together with a "dual signature." In this case, this means that the PI is encrypted with the public key of the acquirer. Before this is done, the OI and the PI are hashed together in a fairly complicated procedure to ensure that neither can be changed without affecting the final signature. The result is signed by the cardholder.

If the cardholder has no certificate, then the result is simply hashed together and the PI information is encrypted with the public key of the acquirer. No extra signature is attached.

PRes—**The Merchant's Response** The merchant acknowledges the cardholder's request with this message. Before sending it, the merchant must verify some of the information in PReq. That is, the hash of the order data must correspond to the merchant's idea of what is being ordered. Also, the merchant may check to see that the challenge values produced during the optional PInit phase are copied over correctly. This value, Chall_C, is copied over again and again in this transaction to prevent replay attacks.

The merchant can also check to make sure whether the correct signature is in place. Eventually, the acquirer will require all customers to have certificates and refuse to process transactions without certificate-based signatures. This requirement is noted in the acquirer's certificate, which the merchant already has on hand. A quick check is all the merchant needs to make sure that the acquirer will accept the transaction. This is one advantage of distributing information through the certificates.

At this point, the SET protocol leaves the merchant several options. The PRes message is issued only when the merchant is willing to sign off on the transaction. This usually will be after the merchant receives authorization from the acquirer but not necessarily. The merchant may choose to announce that the transaction is complete before authorization to save time. If the amount is small enough and the loss is small, the risk often is worth taking.

The merchant also can delay sending the PRes message until after capture is over; that is, until after the merchant and the acquirer have completed the transaction and the acquirer is sending the money directly to the merchant. This adds an additional delay, but the merchant may choose to do this.

The PRes includes all of the available information. At the very least it includes the transaction ID, Chall_C, and a code indicating the status of the transaction. If either the authorization or the capture is finished, then the result codes are added to the end. This may include a separate message from the acquirer back to the cardholder.

The entire message is signed by the merchant.

InqReq—**A Status Request** The cardholder may request information on the status of the transaction any time after sending the PReq message. This message is quite short and it only contains a new challenge number and a copy of the transaction ID. The random challenge numbers ensure that the merchant will be able to distinguish between multiple InqReq messages.[2]

This message also may be sent after the merchant has approved the transaction. The cardholder may want to find out additional in-

---

[2]The SET protocol is designed to be *idempotent*. This is a mathematical term that asserts that it doesn't really matter how many copies of a message arrive. A customer may send ten copies of PReq without knowing how many will get through. The customer won't be charged ten times. The merchant will use the identification numbers and the challenge numbers to sort it out. The InqReq message, however, is different. The customer may generate many of these at different stages of waiting. Each should receive its own response. That is why each gets its own challenge number.

formation about the authentication and capture of the data. These might not have been present in the merchant's first approval message if the merchant chose to send approval before everything was processed.

If the cardholder has a certificate, then he or she will sign this message.

InqRes—**The Merchant Responds** The merchant responds by sending the current version of the PRes in the same format, which includes the latest value of the challenge number, the transaction ID, and a code indicating the status. If there are either authentication or capture responses from the acquirer, then they are included in this message.

The response code encapsulates all of the various responses from the merchant. These include the finality of the transaction and any potential errors.

This is signed by the merchant.

AuthReq—**The Merchant Requests Authorization** When the merchant requests authorization for a payment, this message carries the data. It normally is sent by the merchant before responding to the customer but it may be sent afterward if the merchant chooses to absorb the risk.

This message has two jobs: to synchronize certificates with the acquirer and to pass along the transaction data. The merchant has a copy of both the customer's and the acquirer's certificate. This message includes a thumbprint of both of these certificates to ensure that they're current. A merchant who doesn't have these values must pause and exchange PCertReq messages to get all of the right certificates.

If all of these are available, then the merchant must send along the PI information from the PReq message. This is the customer's card data and the customer's version of the transaction. The merchant includes its hash of the order data so the acquirer can confirm later that both are in agreement concerning the terms of the transaction.

The merchant may also include additional data about the customer's address that may be used to verify the cardholder. Merchants often refuse to ship to anything other than the billing address on the card. If the merchant is suspicious about the customer, an additional flag can be sent to alert the acquirer to take special care to check for the signs of credit card fraud.

The final information depends on the details of the transaction. If the merchant wants only to authorize a card for payment, then the message includes the authorized amount. This may be larger than the initial charge. If the merchant wants to both authorize *and* capture the money from the transaction, this can be accomplished in a single transaction by setting the appropriate flags.

If the merchant chooses to separate the authorization and capture phases, then the merchant later must send a CapReq message requesting capture.

AuthRes—The Authorization Response The acquirer checks out the request for a transaction and sends this response back if everything is in order and the money is available. Otherwise, it sends an error message.

The acquirer checks that the copy of the PI from the cardholder's PReq has a valid signature, if it is required. Then it makes sure that both the cardholder and the merchant agree on the hash value of the order data.

The customer's account number is bound up in a scrambled field (PAN) that must be decoded. After it is in the clear, the account is checked and the appropriate authorization and capture is done. This account number may be returned to the merchant in the AuthRes message if the merchant is set to receive it. Many merchants keep spending records on their customers. This data traditionally was provided to them in the past, before encryption. If the merchant and the acquirer agree to it, then the merchant gets this information and the transaction is not anonymous.

If the merchant's versions of the certificates were wrong, then the acquirer would include new copies in this message as well as new versions of the thumbprints. The merchant would use this data to update its database after checking that the chain of certificates is valid.

The details of the authorization and capture codes can be found in the SET Programmer's Handbook.

The rest of the message is filled with the proper response codes to the authentication and capture requests. These are sent on to the cardholder when the merchant receives the AuthRes and generates the PRes message.

CapReq—**A Separate Capture Request** When the merchant chooses to separate authorization from capture, the merchant must follow up with this message at a later date. This message can seek to close out multiple transactions with the same message to save time.

The CapReq message is a fairly complicated structure that also includes fields for synchronizing certificates and passing PAN tokens back and forth. The details are found in the SET *Programmer's Handbook*. The most important detail here is that multiple transactions can be captured together.

The key piece of data is a token returned with the authorization. This identifies the transaction and allows the acquirer to correlate the two. If the amount being captured is less than the authorization, then this is also noted.

CapRes—**The Capture Response** When the acquirer processes all of the capture requests and determines that they are in order, it sends this message and begins the transfer of money. This includes all of the capture codes that may be sent through to the cardholder if the cardholder executes a InqReq.

AuthRevReq—**Reducing the Authorized Amount** When a merchant wants to reduce the size authorized for a particular transaction, it issues this message. The message contains the transaction ID, a new random challenge number, and the new authorization limits. Everything is signed by the merchant.

As before, the copies of the certificates are synchronized by including a list of the certificates and a thumbprint that is a hash of the certificates. Also, all of the previous data included in the AuthReq and the corresponding AuthRes are copied over. These include the authorization codes and tokens.

The AuthRevReq can also be issued after capture. It might be used when a cardholder returns some merchandise for credit—if it is returned soon afterward. When the authorization is zeroed out, then most of the extra data is not included.

AuthRevRes—**The Acquirer Approves** When the authorization is reduced, the acquirer responds with a signed message including the correct certificates, the new authentication codes, and the transaction details. This includes the random challenge number included in AuthRevReq to prevent replay attacks.

CapRevReq—**Capture Reversal** This message is syntactically almost the same as the CreditReq. Both of them return money from the merchant to the acquirer to cancel a previous transaction. They are almost the same because both must include the same details about the previous capture. It includes these details, new transaction tags, and a signature.

This message contains the same thumbprint mechanism for synchronizing certificates as the other messages between the merchant and the acquirer.

CapRevRes—**Capture Reversal Response** If the acquirer approves the credit, then this message includes the appropriate tags and random numbers. Everything is signed by the acquirer.

CredRevReq—**Credit Reversal** If something goes wrong with CapRevReq or CreditReq, then this message can set it straight. The usual details about the transaction and the approval codes are present.

CredRevRes—**An Answer to Credit Reversal** This is the response of the acquirer to a mistake made in the credit process.

PCertReq—**A Request for More Certificates** When the merchant determines that it lacks the proper copies of the certificates, it sends this message requesting the certificates. The message includes a tag requesting the certificate by name. These certificates are in the X.509 standard.

Separate certificates distributed by the acquirer's gateway also can be used to set up a secure, private-key channel. These may be replaced more often than the signature certificates.

PCertRes—**The Certificates** The certificates arrive bound up in this message. They also contain a new thumbprint to ensure synchronization.

Final Assessment

The SET standard is one of the most highly evolved standards available to the public. The documentation available from www.visa.com is some of the most complete, and interested readers should turn to it for a deep discussion of the details. This chapter provided a high-level look at the various messages that float back and forth.

It is possible to summarize the entire process on an even higher level: SET involves three parties, the cardholder, the merchant, and the acquirer. Eventually, all three will hold certificates issued by separate certificate authorities. These certificates are backed up by a chain of signatures that ends with the Root CA. Eventually, all messages between parties will be signed using these certificates.

Each party keeps a list of certificates that are necessary to verify signatures. A cardholder, for instance, might hold the certificates of the last several merchants, the merchant's CA, the Brand CA, and the Root CA. When two parties begin to exchange messages, they also include a list of certificates they hold and a "thumbprint," which is really a hash of the certificates. This allows them to make sure they hold the same certificates without wasting bandwidth. Some messages include extra fields for passing new copies of the certificates.

The cardholder encrypts the account number and a hash of the payment information in the PI. The merchant takes this, adds its own version of the hash of the payment information, and then passes it on. The merchant can't see the cardholder's data and the cardholder is essentially pseudonymous. The acquirer compares both parties' version of the transaction and processes it if both agree.

Many details about authorization and capture are left out of this description. For the most part, this covers the process in enough detail. Programmers and people with a deep knowledge of the credit card clearing process should turn to the *Programmer's Handbook*.

The SET standard is not universally accepted at this writing, but the code is not finished. The brand names behind it, however, guarantee that it will be a heavy favorite.

Strengths It is a solid system built with the highest level of available encryption. Hash functions are used liberally to ensure that messages can't be changed in any way. Each party can verify the accuracy of the messages.

Weaknesses Certificates are a good idea, but no one has much experience distributing them to a large population. The standard can process payments when the customer doesn't have a certificate, but clearly the standard is tuned to requiring them. Only time will tell whether this is practical.

Risks There are no known holes in this system. But protecting certificates will be a big challenge. Many home computers are quite susceptible to viruses, and there is no reason why a virus can't be written that will search out certificates. Copying keystrokes is easy, and a clever virus might be able to snatch any PIN code used to encrypt the certificate. Clearly, smart cards are a good idea even if they're not 100% tamperproof.

Chapter 13

CheckFree

The CheckFree corporation of Columbus, Ohio is one company that offers an incremental solution for moving money. Its clearing house is well-integrated with the major credit cards and the Federal Reserve Bank's electronic transfer network. CheckFree markets its services to consumers who use CheckFree software to pay monthly bills, to corporations who need access to automated processing, and the companies like health clubs that need bills processed each month. The company took many of the major electronic transfer systems available to large businesses and crafted software solutions aimed at people who hadn't used them before.

An average consumer can use the CheckFree software for DOS, Windows, or MacOS machines to pay monthly bills. The subscription costs $9.95 for the first 20 payments and $3.50 for each subsequent batch of 10 payments. This approach is not far from the cost of paying bills the old-fashioned way with checks, if you add in the cost of stamps.

Transactions occur between bank accounts. You provide a voided check with your bank information when you open your CheckFree account. This is provided to the Federal Reserve Bank's wire transfer system. All the money you spend will come out of this account as if you had written a check.

When you wish to write a check to a merchant, you type the merchant's name and address. CheckFree's computers then determine the best way to pay the merchant. In some cases, the recipient will be hard-wired into the electronic payment system. Mortgage companies are a good example. In this case, CheckFree moves the money directly in a pure electronic transaction. If this option is not available, CheckFree will send the merchant a paper check through the mail. This may be a check written on CheckFree's corporate accounts that might aggregate several payments at once. Or it could be a CheckFree laser copy drawn upon your personal account.

The user schedules the payment dates with the CheckFree software. Although the transfers are electronic, the time limits are not much of an improvement over paper. A transaction must be entered four business days before its effective date. A stop payment order must be issued five days in advance. The company suggests that you schedule your payments well in advance as a convenience. They won't process the payment until the correct day. The four-day limit is largely because CheckFree must print out a paper version of the check if the merchant doesn't accept electronic transfers. In the future when most people have accounts that are electronically linked, there is no technical reason why this lag time couldn't be shortened.

CheckFree's Wallet

The CheckFree company announced plans to team up with the Spyglass Mosaic group to release a money system for the Web. The system, known as the CheckFree Wallet, will reportedly be an extension of the company's current links to the banking and credit card industry. Here is a sample from the press release:

> Finally, there's an easy-to-use Internet transaction product! No vouchers, no "Internet bucks," no coupons. And best of all, no transaction fees or service charges! Using CheckFree Wallet will be just like buying a product over the phone or in a store. All you do is type in a password to open your CheckFree Wallet, check the information, and click "pay."

> Because your shipping and credit card information is already stored (under heavy encryption for security) in the CheckFree Wallet, you won't have to fill out lengthy order forms every time you make a purchase. Just point and click on your payment type!

It is clear that the system will operate similar to the *i*KP system or the CyberCash system. Adding the address and shipping information is a simple idea, but one that will be bound to both reduce fraud and make life more convenient.

The Wallet became available in the later half of 1995. No further information is available at this writing.

How to Set Up a CheckFree Storefront

The CheckFree system is largely aimed at allowing consumers to settle their bills. The easiest way to set up a CheckFree account is simply to register your bank account with them. Then, the CheckFree company can forward any payments to you directly.

If you run a business that regularly bills customers, you might want to seriously consider investigating the services that CheckFree offers. They produce a turnkey system that lets a health club send out monthly bills to customer's credit cards. This isn't the Web, but it still might be useful.

No information is available on how to sell information with the CheckFree Wallet at this time.

Final Assessment

It is difficult to judge the success of the CheckFree Wallet before it is introduced, but the limited press releases indicate that they won't be taking a substantially different course than the other manufacturers. The regular CheckFree system is a good but far-from-perfect complement to regular checks. There are so many 3- or 4-day deadlines that seem out of place in an electronic realm.

Risks For the consumer, the risk is minimal. In the United States, credit card companies must cover any loss larger than $50.

Strengths CheckFree is easily integrated with the standard banking community. It already offers nice turnkey systems for billing credit cards.

Weaknesses It is impossible to assess how CheckFree is planning on solving the standard problems of encryption and security at this time. As the book was going to press, CheckFree and CyberCash announced plans to work together to develop software.

Chapter 14

Open Market

Most of this book is devoted to answering the question of how a bundle of bits can be made to encapsulate promises. Building a nice digital store is another important part of creating a digital world where people can buy and sell goods. If the architecture of a digital storefront is not well designed and secure, the business may fail because of potentially avoidable losses. There must be simple and effective ways for people to trade money for information, and both the store and the customer should feel that they haven't been ripped off.

The Open Market Web-based system was developed by Open Market Inc. of Cambridge, Massachusetts, to provide a secure handoff of goods. The system was created to include many different levels of authentication of customers. Some low-level deals may be transacted on password alone. More valuable deals may use more complicated cryptographic algorithms if the circumstances demand. The system can expand to include all of these options.

The Open Market Web servers are impressive and complete. It is easy to access them and easy to experiment before jumping in. The software recognizes many different forms of cash including "Demo Dollars" that you can spend on demonstration items like colors. Lexis-Nexis is one of their major customers and they sell information from their Small Business database. You can search by keyword and even look at a short, two- or three-paragraph synopsis before buying. All of this is accomplished through standard HTML with forms.

There are ten steps to a standard Open Market transaction according to internal documentation. They are:

1. The client starts a transaction by sending a GET request to the HTTP server. The items on this page include *payment URLs*, which encapsulate plenty of information into a URL.

2. When the client chooses an item from the choices, the payment URL is sent as a request to the HTTP server.

3. The HTTP server sends the URL to the *payment switch* which is responsible for making the transaction. This switch seizes control of the transaction so it can control the authorization.

4. The payment switch requests the buyer's name and password. Open Market suggests that you use your e-mail address as an identifier.

5. The payment switch gets the identity and the password. It also discovers additional information about the client including the IP address from which the request is coming, the software running on the client, and the security level of the channel. The payment switch can use this information to decide how much it can trust the channel. If the request is small and the IP address is a known hangout for the individual, then the switch could let it go without checking further.

6. The payment switch might ask for more authentication as an option. Open Market obviously imagines that the user might have some extra authentication software. This might be a piece of software that would hash together a password and a challenge string. Open Market would forward a challenge string across the network, the user would supply the password, and the local software would hash them together before sending the result across the network. This would never reveal the password to eavesdroppers.

   Open Market also imagines more robust forms of authentication including hardware smart cards that would control access even more by forcing the user to hold a physical device.

7. If authentication is necessary, the user and his computer responds. Open Market suggests that the computer system can also check addresses, accounts, "velocity checks," and other authentication, based upon the parameters of the transaction. It obviously imag-

ines a future that includes the credit card company's systems for checking for strange patterns.[1]

8. If the payment switch approves then it forwards an access URL. This includes a pointer to the data, the buyer's IP address, an expiration time, and the digital signature of the entire URL as signed by the payment switch.

9. When the user presents this URL to the HTTP server, the server checks the signature to make sure that it was created by the payment switch. Then it forwards only the data to the IP address embedded in the URL. This further prevents fraud and sending copies of the data to multiple people.

10. The client finally ends up with the goods.

There are many clever details in this system. The system is an excellent way to vend information to people on a one-time basis. They will have trouble passing the URL on to their friends or reusing the URLs. Naturally, there is always the problem of people copying the raw information itself to disk. This can be fixed in the future by using restricted browsers that don't give the average user the ability to save HTTP pages to disk.

There is also a framework for a flexible authentication strategy. Although it is not immediately obvious how extensive it will become, it is clear that the system includes the ability to check the IP addresses and other details about a potential client. This may end up giving the company some substantial leverage to counteract fraud.

First Virtual vs. Open Market

The Open Market system is presented here as a strong contrast to First Virtual's exchange mechanism. (See Chapter 6). Both are mere shells for exchanging funds that use more conventional credit and debit card

---

[1]One trigger is apparently using the automated gas pumps to fill up your car. I was recently called by a credit card company after I used a reserve card one weekend for several errands. The first stop was a gas station with automatic payment. This triggered them to call me the next day to check up on my purchases. Apparently card thieves check out the cards at the pumps to see if the card has been reported missing yet. This saves them from facing a clerk whose telephone authentication device is announcing that the card is stolen.

companies to process the actual money. Both are well integrated with the on-line world and the Web system. The fundamental difference is the level of trust. First Virtual allows people to try before they buy. Open Market designed its system for real-time transfer so people can be charged before the information is shipped.

The difference is important for users. The users may believe, quite correctly, that they have a right to browse through information before they purchase it. Bookstores allow this. First Virtual encourages this behavior by designing their system to require users to e-mail a confirmation. The Open Market system could be reworked to include this option. The Lexis-Nexis software already gives the user a three-paragraph summary as a free teaser to the entire document. There would be no problem adopting this mode of doing business.

It would be difficult to adopt the First Virtual system for faster payment. FV relies exclusively on electronic mail for its transactions. This can be slow and cumbersome. It is common for electronic mail to take several hours even when a Net connection is stable and letting the user use his or her Web browser. In this case, a user would churn through some information and then confront an e-mail queue filled with messages asking to confirm First Virtual transactions. Will they pay? The bards always passed the hat *before* giving the ending to the story because they knew that was when people were most ready to pay. First Virtual can generate a hangover effect. After the infobinge is done, the bills are waiting for you to confirm that you spent them. First Virtual says that it will actively investigate and shut down the accounts of those who abuse the system and refuse to pay too often. FV is circumspect about how often is bad, but this threat alone may prove to be enough.

Both of the systems rely heavily on network security for their own security. IP addresses and mail can be faked. But both are relying upon the fact that it will be easier to steal the information in other ways. Standard copyright infringement is easy to do. Why bother with faking IP addresses and mail?

How to Set Up an Open Market Storefront

Open Market makes its money by selling Web software and support to people and companies. They manufacture both classic Web server software that runs on most UNIX platforms as well as the more robust

Integrated Commerce Environment that offers the tools you need to set up shop.

Here's a list of the basic products offered by Open Market. I have only tested them by interacting with their Web server, not by installing the software on my machine. The products are:

Secure WebServer This is a server with support for SSL, PCT, and S-HTTP. It speaks both FastCGI and HTTP.

OM-Transact, OM-Axcess, OM-SecureLink Executive, and Active-Commerce DB These packages combine with the servers to offer a storefront. The software can handle transactions, billing, and some customer service requests like determining an outstanding balance. The Open Market demonstration software offers a good example of how to purchase information from Lexis-Nexis, as shown in Figure 14.1 and Figure 14.2.

WebReporter This analyzes the log files and produces complicated reports.

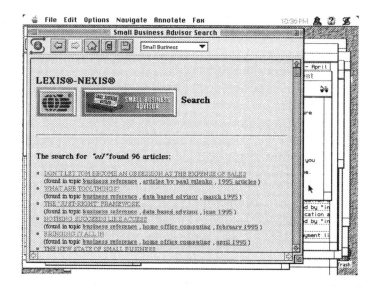

Figure 14.1. A page from Open Market's server that sells information from a Lexis-Nexis database. The page shows the result of a search. Clicking on a document will generate a short summary and a price. This is shown in Figure 14.2.

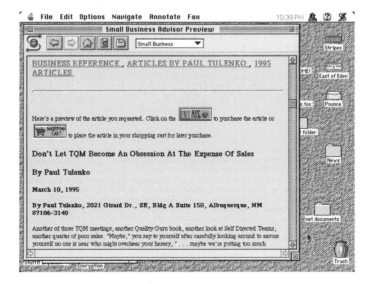

Figure 14.2. A document for purchase from Open Market's server selling information from a database maintained by Lexis. Clicking on the payment button initiates payment.

The highly proprietary nature of the Open Market system means that the best way to get on the Web is to purchase their software.

Final Assessment

The Open Market system is a fairly extensive solution for adding a turnkey storefront to your Web machine.

Risk The store owner bears the risk for items until they're cleared by the credit card companies.

Strengths Open Market has extensive storefront software.

Weaknesses The company is still expanding security options. Adding SSL would allow Open Market software to work with the popular Netscape browser.

Chapter 15

CAFE

Although Europe may be a continent that spawned 1,000 wars, the current climate of unity and cohesion is spawning 1,000 bureaucrats. Relatively quiet committee meetings, not invasion, are the preferred way to unite a continent filled with many different currencies controlled by many different central banks. In the realm of digital cash, one of the most prominent experimental projects joins companies and government agencies from seven major European countries. The consortium, known by the acronym CAFE for Conditional Access For Europe, is creating electronic wallets and smart cards that people can use to transfer cash electronically. The system is currently undergoing a trial that was due to conclude by the end of 1995 with what the project directors hoped would be a mandate to deploy the system throughout Europe.

The partners in the project are a mix of academic and high-tech industry. The universities that entered into the development contract include the Centrum vor Wiskunde en Informatica (CWI in the Netherlands), the Catholic University of Leuven (Belgium), and Aarhus University in Denmark. The research divisions from the telephone companies of France and the Netherlands are contributing as well as the German Institute for Social Research and the Institute for Information. The companies involved include Siemens (Germany), DigiCash (the Netherlands), Gemplus (France), CardWare (UK), Ingenico (France), and Delab (Norway).

The basis of the CAFE experiment is a mixture of smart cards and wallets. It is a hardware solution for people who walk to stores and want to carry digital money with them. The smart cards are the size of normal credit cards and the wallets are no bigger. The cards can be inserted into ATM machines or payment devices at merchants and the wallets can communicate with these same machines through infrared radiation devices. The system will also provide people the means to pay via the telephone or other network.

The system mimics real cash as much as possible. Cash is kept directly on either a card or a wallet. Users can transfer money between the two as they wish in much the same way that they might move paper cash between a drawer and a wallet. The cash itself is meant to be anonymous to preserve the privacy of the user. The transactions in the current test environment are not anonymous, but the final version includes the option of making each transaction unconditionally anonymous. The CAFE team notes that some European governments are requiring that electronic toll collection systems for automobiles be designed in a way to prevent tracking of individuals. They also believe that anonymity will be a positive feature that will attract people to the system. The system, though, does include a way for a user to trace back transactions to check for mistakes or errors.

The system is intended to unify European commerce by successfully handling all of the many different currencies. The wallets can hold value encoded in a variety of different currencies and the user may exchange the currencies by negotiating a rate. If these cross-currency transactions can be accomplished easily, the ease will provide a large economic incentive for development of this system. Paper money is very expensive to handle because of the security risks and it is even more expensive when the money must be transported to another country for exchange. Local banks can always recycle the local currency they receive by parceling it out to someone withdrawing money. Foreign currency needs to be transported. French francs exchanged for German marks in Berlin can't be recycled in Berlin. They must, in all probability, be shipped back to France. This huge cost could be saved through electronic transactions.

Cryptographic Foundations

The CAFE project relies upon public-key encryption for its security. This is a significant departure in many respects because many similar smart card systems in Europe simply rely upon secret-key encryption. These secret keys, however, were soon compromised through eavesdropping and reverse engineering. One of the most famous system failures involved the Pay TV system in the UK, which succumbed to technical attack within three years of being launched.

A public-key encryption system can be more secure because only the public key is distributed throughout the world. The secret half of the pair can be locked away in one place. If someone grabs one smart card and manages to gain complete access to the contents of its memory, he or she will not gain the ability to encrypt messages like the central office. The would-be thief will only find the public key for the central office and this is not useful for spoofing.

Final Assessment

The CAFE project is currently undergoing trial tests of electronic smart card products developed by DigiCash. The future of the product depends, in a large part, on the political reaction to the system. This will determine how willing banks will be to join with the forces of the research project and make it a reality.

Not much new information is available at the time of this writing so it seems likely that the project is ending its life. This chapter provides a good introduction to how a smart card system might work.

Chapter 16

DigiCash

The DigiCash company was created by David Chaum to build the software to use his cryptographic inventions. Many of the algorithms described in Chapter 3 emerged from papers and patents written by David Chaum and it is good that he is actually building implementations that rest upon the theory.

The DigiCash system is now one of the more successful systems because it has made the transition from laboratory to marketplace. Two banks, the Mark Twain Bank in St. Louis, Missouri, and EUNet in Finland, use the DigiCash software to support real accounts. The very imposing Deutschebank in Germany and Advance Bank in Australia have also announced plans to use the system. The Mark Twain Bank already lists about 35 stores that accept payment over the network.

The structure of the DigiCash system includes both account-based money and token-based money. Each person maintains a central bank account with DigiCash that is filled with their larger denominations. Each person also gets a DigiCash wallet that can be filled with token-based digital coins subtracted from an account. These coins are bundles of bits created with the basic digital cash algorithm using a blind signature.

Figure 16.1 shows a wallet that was just filled with $10.00. The bank automatically dispenses the coins in sizes that grow exponentially. This system is probably more efficient than the decimal-based system we use today, but it does increase the number of times that someone must break a bill. If a merchant must break a coin, it must interrupt the transaction to go to the bank for the right change.

```
================================================================
|  ≡≡≡≡≡≡≡≡≡≡≡≡≡≡≡≡≡  Ecash Status  ≡≡≡≡≡≡≡≡≡≡≡≡≡≡≡≡≡  |
================================================================
| ┌─Account information─────────────────────────────────────┐ |
| │   ☁      Bank balance: $90.00                           │ |
| │  ☁☁      Bank address: bank@bank.digicash.com           │ |
| │           Account ID: pcw@access.digex.com              │ |
| │            Username: Peter Wayner                        │ |
| │             In cash: $10.00                              │ |
| │  Guaranteed payments: 8                                  │ |
| └─────────────────────────────────────────────────────────┘ |
|                                                              |
|  ┌──────────────┐                        ┌─────────────┐    |
|  │  Hide coins  │                        │     OK      │    |
|  └──────────────┘                        └─────────────┘    |
================================================================
```

#	Value	Amount	Expiration
8	$0.01	$0.08	Aug 15 12:19:49 1995
8	$0.02	$0.16	Aug 15 12:19:49 1995
8	$0.04	$0.32	Aug 15 12:19:49 1995
8	$0.08	$0.64	Aug 15 12:19:49 1995
9	$0.16	$1.44	Aug 15 12:19:49 1995
9	$0.32	$2.88	Aug 15 12:19:49 1995
7	$0.64	$4.48	Aug 15 12:19:49 1995

Figure 16.1. A glimpse at the ecash wallet after $10.00 was withdrawn from the central bank account. Note that many smaller coins are included in the package to lower the number of times that the bank must break a coin to allow change.

The current system only provides anonymity for the buyer. When the digital coins are withdrawn from the bank, they're created with blinded signatures and this prevents the bank from matching the serial numbers of the coins with a user. The merchants, however, receive no anonymity because they must turn the coins in immediately upon receipt. The incoming money is credited to their DigiCash account. DigiCash argues that this form of cash is worthless to the lawless because records are kept of one side of the transaction. A drug dealer who accepts cash would still have to deposit them in his account.

In theory, people could subvert the system by exchanging disks with all of the cash stored upon them. At the most extreme they would trade laptops loaded with digital cash. This would make it possible to exchange the digital coins without processing them through the DigiCash computers. It is clear that anyone who attempts this is risking losing the money because there are no cryptographic protections against double payment in this system. DigiCash simply keeps a record of the serial numbers. The laptops and files would have the same identity and digital signature.

A Sample Transaction

The transactions occur between the merchant's machine and a Digi-Cash wallet running on the customer's computer. Both need to have full IP addresses and Internet access.

The transaction described here is a donation of $1.00 to the Electronic Privacy Information Center through the Web page show in Figure 16.2. Figure 16.3 shows the TCP/IP connections begun by Digi-Cash's electronic wallet. The process starts when the Netscape browser sends an HTTP request to the merchant's server. In this case it is the server at DigiCash accepting donations for the Electronic Privacy Information Center. The request triggers a script that runs a program that manages the transaction. This program dials up the ecash wallet running on your TCP/IP server and asks for some cash.

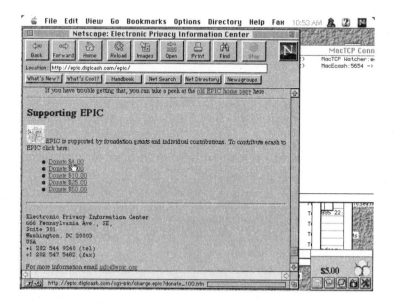

Figure 16.2. A simple storefront designed to let you donate ecash to the Electronic Privacy Information Center.

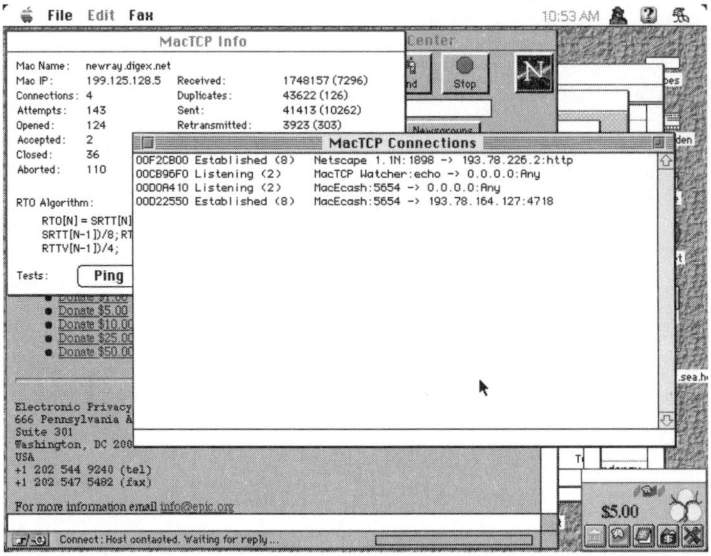

Figure 16.3. A glimpse of the TCP/IP connections begun by DigiCash's electronic wallet.

If the wallet successfully starts a connection like the one shown in Figure 16.2, then the wallet asks for confirmation from the user. This is shown in Figure 16.4.

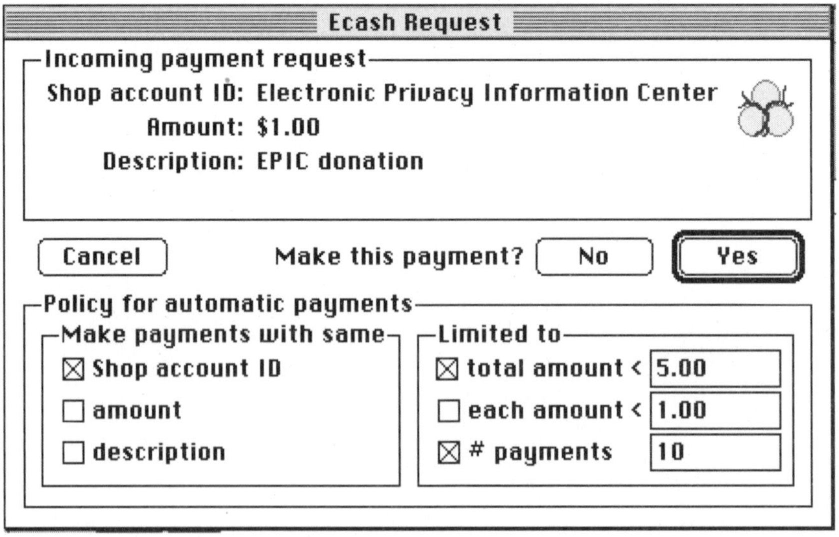

Figure 16.4. The wallet asks for confirmation before proceeding.

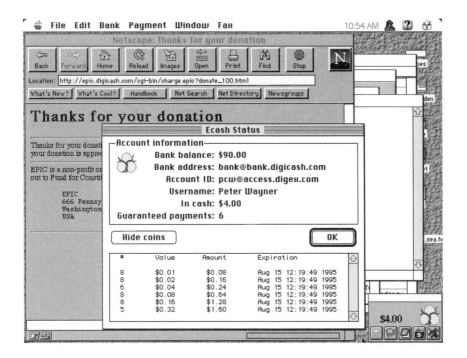

Figure 16.5. The wallet contains $4.00 in coins after $5.00 and $1.00 were donated to EPIC.

When the transaction is finished, the number of coins has changed. Figure 16.5 shows the coins in the wallet after $5.00 and $1.00 were donated to EPIC.

How to Set Up a DigiCash Storefront

There are two major ways to set up a DigiCash storefront. Both require that you have an HTTP server up and running. In one case, you process the monetary transactions on your machine using some DigiCash software. In another case, you simply hand over the task to DigiCash's computers. Both are acceptable solutions.

Using DigiCash's Server

Many people may choose to let DigiCash's computer server process all of the cash transactions. This saves you the trouble of setting up the DigiCash processing software, which only runs on a UNIX system at this time. To use their Remote Store software, you only need to have a machine running an HTTP server. Your machine holds a directory that can only be accessed by digicash.com and then you refer all requests to digicash.com. Everything else is the same. Figure 16.2 shows a simple storefront operated for the benefit of the Electronic Privacy Information Center. At this point in time, only toy dollars can be donated to them.

The steps are:

1. Place the information in HTML form in a directory and close off access to all but digicash.com. For instance, if you run an NCSA HTTP server, DigiCash suggests doing this by adding this to the file .htaccess:

```
<Limit GET POST>
order deny,allow
deny from all
allow from digicash.com
</Limit>
```

2. Set the prices using a file called either price_conf or price.cnf. The first line of this file must be your ecash account name and the second must hold the account to receive payment. The rest list the goods and their price. The first entry in the line is the name of the file and the second is the price in cyberbucks. DigiCash offers this as a sample:

```
myshop@myserver
myemail@my.host.name
goods.xyz 6.66 Nice Goods
other.gif 0.50 Nice picture
.gif 0.99
#all other pictures are $0.99
```

3. Produce an HTML page that will be shown to users when they're having trouble paying. This happens when they try to buy something without a wallet running on their machines or when a firewall gets in the way. This is why DigiCash suggests that you include a form for them to fill out with the proper address and port numbers of their machines. This allows people to negotiate firewalls. An image of DigiCash's sample page is shown in Figure 16.6.

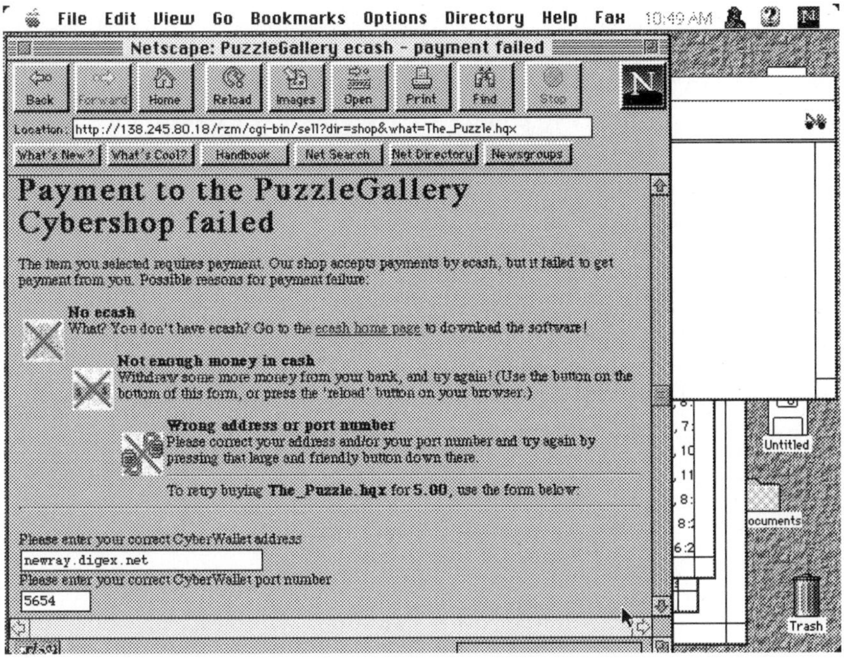

Figure 16.6. The HTML page displayed to a purchaser who fails to complete a trade. This often happens when DigiCash can't access the purchaser's wallet.

4. Produce your page and place pointers to DigiCash's Remote Shop Server. For example:

```
<a href="http://www.digicash.com/cgi-bin/shop-
    gate2?http://pete.machine.com/full/path/Se-
    cret.html">Buy this for $3.00! </a>
```

This tells the DigiCash server that someone is trying to buy the file `Secret.html` for $3.00. It should retrieve the file from `pete.-machine.com` in directory `full/path`, charge the user $3.00, and deposit that cash in the account specified in the `price.cnf` file described above. Note that the DigiCash machine will use the `price.cnf` file to determine the price. The text in the link above, "Buy this for $3.00!" is what is shown to the user.

Running Your Own Ecash Server

If you're using a UNIX machine to run your HTTP server, you can consider installing the ecash transfer software directly on your machine. This will allow you much more flexibility in the transaction. You write the scripts and can use the ecash as an atomic command to transfer money.

The ecash software, which comes without source code, runs on most major UNIX platforms. The key command is one called ecash, which comes with four major options: -v sets verbose debugging mode, -R means collect payment from an address, -b sets the home directory of the account receiving the money, and -p starts a payment transferring money to someone.

Here's an example of a shell script charging someone $5.00 for something:

```
if ecash -v -R 5.00
  ''A charge for secrets" "\$REMOTE_HOST:6000"
    >>/tmp/goodlog 2>>/tmp/badlog
then
  echo Thank you!
else
  echo Too bad...
```

The remote host's port is set to 6000 here. The default is 5654. This may need to be changed if a firewall is in the way. A payment transaction might look like this:

```
ecash -v -p 4.00 @ "Here's what I owe you."
    "\$REMOTE_HOST:6100" >>/tmp/paylog &
```

ecash will try to transfer $4.00 to wallet software running on the remote host and listening to port 6100.

DigiCash offers many sample scripts for shell, PERL, or CGI interpreters. You can easily build up a storefront using them.

Final Assessment

DigiCash is one of the most ambitious and technically robust digital cash efforts being made on the network. It is also one of the few token-based solutions. Most are merely extensions of the credit card system. As is discussed elsewhere in the book, there are advantages to token-like cash.

Risks If you lose your cash, it's gone. If it's still in the account, then it is the bank's responsibility.

Strengths Token-like cash can be used in many network applications similiar to agents. The system offers limited anonymity to buyers and sellers. No one can trace where people spend their ecash, although it is possible for the banks to watch for accounts showing a large number of transactions.

Weaknesses Even partial anonymity seems to make some nervous.

Chapter 17

Citibank's Transaction Cards

Citibank is one of the largest banks in the world so it should not be surprising that it is experimenting with different forms of electronic transaction systems. The bank is already one of the largest providers of credit cards so it already has a connection with the burgeoning world of Internet-mediated credit card transactions. Anyone who may use systems like First Virtual (see Chapter 6) or CyberCash (see Chapter 10) may already be using the Citibank system if he or she uses a Citibank credit card.

But the bank is also experimenting with a smart card carrying digital cash. Its system, which was demonstrated to me as a prototype, uses data packets bearing the digital signature of the bank. The packets contain information about the bank that stands behind the packet and the amount of value. The system is quite similar to the digital cashier's checks described on page 53.

The smart card has two jobs: maintain a secure file system that catalogs the cash on hand and apply a secure digital signature to back up each transaction. The cards are intended to be tamper resistant and the demonstration included a nonworking prototype that will fit into a PCMCIA card.[1] Other smart cards may also be used in the future, but they must be able to produce digital signatures.

The current version of the system can support multiple currencies and even credit lines. Each can be exchanged and two smart cards can buy and sell foreign currencies between themselves.

---

[1] The work that normally would be done by the card was done by a laptop in the demonstration.

The prototypes include a clean front end that runs on Windows-based systems. These interact with the smart card and provide a simple user interface for manipulating the money. The software can link two smart cards over a local area network or the Internet.

Transactions

The transactions in the system are straightforward. Each note consists of the name of the bank, a serial number, the amount, and a certificate used to guarantee the note. This package of bits is signed with an RSA signature produced by the key pairs in the certificate. The initial note is produced by a special sealed module kept secure by the bank, presumably in a vault. Only this module has the private key pair used to create the signature and it is actually a mint.

When money is transferred from one smart card to another, the spending smart card wraps a new layer of bits at the end of the note. This data includes the amount being transferred, the smart card's identification number, the time, and the smart card's certificate. The smart card then signs the entire package, effectively guaranteeing that it obtained the note legitimately and it is now offering it legitimately.

The notes can travel through several smart cards before returning to the bank. Through each step, each smart card in the chain adds its own signature, building a chain of custody for the note and the value it contains. This chain can be used to reconstruct the flow of money through the economy to either stop money laundering or trace fraud.

The notes can also be split in parts. If your smart card contains a $10.00 note and you want to buy a newspaper for $0.50, then the smart card will create a new note worth $0.50. This note will contain the old $10.00 note at its core and the outside wrap of data will specify that only $0.50 of its value is being transferred to this new note. The smart card may then split off other fractions from the same $10.00, but it must make sure that all of them add up to $10.00.

Each note can be split into parts by each smart card that holds it in the chain. So each note can spawn a wide variety of notes with fractional values. Citibank has a program that will collect these descendants when they are turned back to the bank and make sure that they all add up to the value of the original bill. The program will also graph the tree-like structure in graphical form if necessary.

   The smart card receiving the money must validate it to make sure
it is correct. By the time a note arrives at a particular card, it might
have passed through ten other smart cards. Each card added its own
signature and a certificate used to validate the signature. The receiver
checks each signature in the chain to make sure it is valid and matches
the certificate. This is a fairly secure chain of custody. In the Citibank
system, the accepting smart card will trust a bill with a valid chain of
custody without checking with the central server.

Transaction Details

When two cards are used to buy and sell, the Citibank software follows
this set of steps:

Authentication The two "trusted agents" authenticate each other by
   exchanging digital signatures backed by certificates. That is,

   (a) The first produces a random number, r_1, signs it, and sends it
       to the second.

   (b) The second checks the signature, signs r_1, and returns it. Then
       it generates a second random number, r_2, signs it, and sends
       it on.

   (c) The first checks the signature on r_1 and r_2. Then it signs r_2 and
       returns it.

   (d) Now both cards have established that they both know the
       secret keys to the public-key pair backed up by certificates.

Secure Channel The two random numbers can be combined to make
   a key that will be used to encrypt all further communication by the
   two computers.

Exchange of Data If the transaction is being used to sell data or software over the network, then the seller bundles up data by encrypting it and sending it to the purchaser's computer.

Cash Is Tendered The purchaser's smart card produces a collection
   of notes that add up to the correct amount. These are sent to the
   seller's smart card.

Cash Verification The seller's card examines the digital signatures in notes it received. If they check out, then the seller's card sends a receipt, R_1, acknowledging that the notes arrived safely.

Purchaser Accepts the Transaction When the purchaser's card receives the acknowledgment, it marks the notes as spent. The purchaser's card acknowledges the receipt (R_1) with another receipt (R_2) releasing the cash.

If the first receipt (R_1) never arrived at the purchaser's card, then the card would assume that something went wrong and it would continue to believe that the notes were all its own. They would appear as valid on the list of notes contained inside the card and it could spend them again later.

Seller Accepts the Money When this final receipt (R_2) arrives, the seller's card knows that the notes are now its alone. It has sole possession, and it knows that the transaction is completed. The notes can now be spent again.

If this final receipt (R_2) does not arrive, the seller's card cannot assume that it owns the notes. The original receipt (R_1) may have gotten lost in the network. The smart card freezes the note in its memory for later reconciliation.

Seller Releases the Data The seller has now received the money, so it releases the decryption key for the data. The purchaser can now decrypt the data and use it.

Any disputes about the transaction can be resolved in the future. If the seller, for instance, accepts the money without sending the final decryption key, then the purchaser can provide the original encrypted data as evidence in any investigation. It would presumably be signed by the seller. If any of the receipts fail to arrive, then the smart card will lock up the notes and the bank will be able to investigate later to make sure that no counterfeiting occurred.

Multiple Currencies and Credit

The Citibank system can handle notes in any of the major currencies. If the bank wants to issue currency, then it must build a special generator for that particular currency. This would be controlled by the laws of the nation that backs that currency.

The Citibank cards also have a novel feature that allows them to trade notes of credit. That is, the note would represent $1000 of credit extended by someone else, not $1000 of cash backed by some government. The distinction is important because it allows this smart card system to also offer many of the features of a credit card. A bank would issue a note worth credit instead of creating a limit on a credit card.

The credit is traded like any other note. If you want to buy an item worth $42.00 with a credit note, then the fraction of $42.00 would be split off. The digital signatures can act as a fairly good guarantee that the credit is good.

The recipient of the credit note must process it another step. It must offer the credit to the issuer and ask for real cash in return. The current version of the Citibank system does not allow credit to make multiple hops from card to card. This is because bank regulators might view this as the creation of a new currency. When the credit is presented, the issuer must return the correct amount in digital cash or face legal action.

The company issuing the credit could start charging interest as soon as it exchanges the credit note for real currency. Even though the credit note may flow through the network like real cash, it doesn't become activated until a recipient turns it in. That is when the credit is truly extended.

This distinction is, in some ways, deceptive. The recipient who accepted the note of credit did it with the understanding that it would be backed up by the full faith of the issuer. If the recipient got a note of "real" currency, then it would be accepting something backed up by the full faith of the central government. In the first case, the recipient got the right to ask some bank or credit issuer to pay up. In the second case, the recipient merely got something that could be used to settle a tax bill. Forcing the recipient to exchange credit notes immediately for real currency is, in effect, just a way of giving government-backed currency a senior status in the realm.

This feature, however, is a clever way to unify a currency-based system with a credit-based system. Credit cards can be a very lucrative source of income for a bank like Citibank, and it is understandable that it wants to preserve that income. This feature allows the cards to replace credit cards without removing the credit lines from the system.

Decentralized, Off-Line Transactions

The system itself is quite decentralized. Many of the digital transaction systems in this book require all bills to be validated by an on-line check before proceeding. That is, the bank must make a quick decision and tell the merchant whether it will stand behind a note with a particular serial number. This requires a significant investment in network resources to process the transactions at peak times like the Christmas holidays.

The cost of any central approval network can be astonishing. The most important problem is that the central approver does not scale. There must be one list and one list only. Many Web-based systems can easily be expanded to handle double or triple the traffic by adding more computers. But approving transactions is different. This central computer must keep track of which bills have been spent and which are still outstanding. What if the same bill is sent for approval to two different machines simultaneously? Both would be relying upon a list of valid bills that may only be a few minutes old. But both would approve the transaction. Later, when the lists were reconciled, the problem would appear.

This cost cannot be underestimated. Although many credit card transactions are approved through the phone network, many are not actively investigated. If the amount is small, then the system may not bother to add up all of the recent transactions to see if the limit was reached. Several fast, small transactions in a row could easily breach a credit limit in this case.

The Citibank system does not require any central server to certify each bill. Two smart cards can transfer cash between themselves without calling up the central service. The receiving card examines the digital signatures on the note and accepts them. The system relies on the integrity of the smart cards to protect against double spending. Double spending is technically possible—but only if one is able to break into the smart card and duplicate what it does.

The design of the system also includes several layers of protection. The smart cards lack the ability to mint money. They can only spend notes that were produced by the central money creator. Every transaction must be guaranteed by a digital signature. If double spending occurs, the bank can determine which card is double spending. This may not identify the cheating person immediately, but it can produce a good trail of where the notes were spent again and again. The police would be able to interview the clerks and other people involved in the transactions and perhaps find some information that would identify the crooks.

The decentralized nature also means that it is impossible for the bank to shut down a rogue smart card. If someone found a way to work around the tamper-resistant packaging of a smart card and turn it to do his or her bidding, then the bank could not shut down that person. The bank would quickly be able to identify the serial number of the smart card because it would receive the multiple duplicate versions of the bill from other customers. But it couldn't stop the smart card from appearing legitimate to every other smart card that came along. There is no central verification of charges.

The solution to this problem is to periodically change certificates. Legitimate cards would be able to download new certificates and public-key pairs from an ATM or the Internet. The illegitimate card owner could not present this rogue card successfully without identifying himself or herself. This would substantially limit the effect of cloning or removing one card.

The system also requires that the money "age." That is, each note comes with an expiration date. After that, the notes must be exchanged for new notes from the bank. This forces the notes to flow through the bank every n days and allows the bank to identify any fraud or double spending at that time. This process is quick and can be accomplished through an ATM or the Internet. In fact, the Citibank software automatically refreshes all cash in a smart card whenever the card interacts with the bank.

This limit means that Citibank hasn't removed the role of the central computer, it has merely relaxed its role. Instead of responding on a minute-by-minute basis, it must only enter into the picture every n days (currently about seven days). This allows the central computer to be smaller and more manageable but at the risk that more double spending will occur.

The lack of a central server also makes the system more usable. The central system need not be involved in every transaction, so transactions can take place in many different locations. A small business at a street fair could accept Citibank's smart cards without installing a link to the network to approve the transaction. A father who wants to give $20 to a child would not need to use the central system.

Anonymity and Citibank's System

Citibank's system offers a certain amount of anonymity to the customers. The smart cards do not bind the spender's name into the transaction. If you go to the store to purchase something, the latest version of the note is guaranteed by the digital signature, but this signature doesn't include your name. It contains only the identification number of the smart card.

At the very least, this keeps your name from the store's computers. The store may be able to gather some data on the spending habits of its customers by examining the IDs of the smart cards, but it won't be able to gather the names.

But there will be a tight connection between a smart card and a person. While the cards may often be lost, stolen, or given to a friend, each person will be closely identified with the smart card. The Citibank system requires fairly powerful smart cards, and these will not likely be manufactured at a low enough cost to make them fairly disposable. If the bank recorded the ID number and the name as it issued smart cards, it would have a complete record of the spending of a person.

Final Assessment

The Citibank system is only a prototype, but it offers some good insight on how to develop a smart card system that balances the risks of double spending with the need for decentralized access. The system is currently backed by several patents. Citibank hopes to roll out the system gradually in the future.

Risks For the consumer, there may be minimal risk. Citibank could offer to replace lost or stolen cash because it could identify the notes that flowed through a particular card. If they don't appear until long after the expiration date, then the bank could replace them as a service. If the card was reported stolen, the thief might be identified through investigation. But the bank does not have to offer this service, and it would require a customer to surrender his or her anonymity to use it.

Strengths The system requires a smaller centralized server because each transaction need not be cleared. The system uses centrally created digital notes that can be minted only by a special computer card, which presumably will be well guarded. This forces a rogue card to use double spending to create wealth, which leaves a strong trail of where the money was spent that could be used to identify the crook.

Weaknesses The system relies upon the strength of the smart card to help maintain the security and stop double spending. The strength of these cards is untested at this time. People who spend time developing ways to break them would presumably not make this information public.

But Citibank relies less on the strength of the smart card than other vendors. Each note or bill can be created only by a central machine, which presumably is in a safe vault. Anyone who breaks into a particular smart card will gain only the ability to double spend the money that is in the card. To the crook, there is little difference between double, triple, and quadruple spending a $100 bill instead of merely counterfeiting several new ones. But to the bank, there is a big difference. All of the bills eventually will return to the bank with a trail that may allow investigators to close in.

Chapter 18

Smart Cards

At least two major companies (NatWest and Visa) are actively exploring distributing "smart cards" with embedded chips that can act as cash. Anyone with a card can insert it into a terminal and transfer money between the card and another entity, which may either be another card or a merchant's computer system.

These major smart card systems will place the value "on the card." That is, the card will be considered the respository for the money. If it is lost or stolen, the money may be gone, although the central companies may have the ability to replace it much like traveler's checks.

The main difference between the smart card systems described in this chapter and the other systems is the amount of central control. The smart cards act like branch offices of a business. They have the ability to transfer money in and out without getting permission from the central office. For instance, two people can meet on the street and move money between their Mondex smart cards without discussing the matter with a central computer. Systems like DigiCash must get central approval before any money moves.

The most obvious advantage in the lack of central control is cost. The network infrastructure required to process all of the payments between parent and child, neighbor and neighbor, or customer and merchant is extremely high. This price must be paid by someone, and it will be, in all likelihood, amortized over the cost of the cards. People will pay it in fees or interest.

Of course, the lack of central control means that the system must be designed to defend against "rogue" cards. That is, cards that are reprogrammed to act like they have a million dollars in them. Each card must have the integrity to resist this.

No one is quite sure how strong these cards can be. While the cards may employ a variety of different antitampering solutions, the types of attacks can often be surprising. Paul Kocher, for instance, discovered that RSA keys could be extracted by timing the process of signing a value [Koc96]. This attack surprised many people (including me) because it was easy and simple to compute. It may be impossible to prove that there are no other such attacks out there.

Mondex

The Mondex system is a project of the NatWest Bank in England that grew into a separate company. It was effectively sold to MasterCard International, which announced plans to purchase 51% of the company on November 18, 1996. MasterCard was clearly influenced by the fact that many major banks throughout the world had already announced their intention to utilize the Mondex system. These banks include Wells Fargo, Westpac, and Commonwealth Bank.

The Mondex system is built around the smart card, which is a tamperproof card the size of an ordinary credit card. It contains a small chip with enough memory to store a program and some data. This program will interact with outside computers and either accept or dispense money while keeping an accurate audit trail.

Mondex also uses a more useful, albeit larger, device known as a *wallet*. This is just a smart card with an LCD display, a keyboard, and a port for connecting with another smart card. The wallet also can hold money, and its main job is to transfer funds on and off the smart card connected to it. You might use the wallet to give $10 to a child or pay a friend. Mondex expects that the wallets will be reasonably priced and perhaps integrated into even more powerful devices like a cellular phone. These wallets are manufactured by companies like Oki, Keycorp, and GIS.

The Mondex card has been tested extensively in Swindon, England, a small town where all of the residents and merchants have machines. The pay phones even have the ability to accept a Mondex card and transfer money to another card inserted in the phone at the other end of the call. This test began in 1995 and continues today. Other tests are underway at two English universities, Exeter and York, as well as in New Zealand and San Francisco.

Mondex is guarded about the design of its cash system. While the basic elements can be gathered from simple white papers distributed by the company ("Mondex: Security by Design"), the company provides detailed specifics only to manufacturers. Therefore, it is possible to provide only a general assessment of the strength of the system.

At the simplest level, the Mondex card may simply keep a counter inside of the card. If money is added, the counter increases. If money is transferred out, then the counter decreases. This type of system could be weak if someone determines a way to access the counter or clone the card. Once this happens, there is no way to distinguish between legitimate cash and illegitimate cash.

The cards, however, are designed to make it difficult to access the counter. The early versions use a tamperproof smart card, and the company maintains laboratories that aim to keep improving the resistance of these cards.

The cards also are programmed to ensure that money is not created by mistake. Each transaction between two cards uses several steps designed to eliminate false transfers:

1. Both cards exchange identity numbers and prove they are valid by signing random numbers provided by the other. They also exchange certificates. The Mondex system is algorithm independent so it can switch between different signature schemes if a problem is found in one.

2. The "merchant" card asks for the money and signs this request (Message A).

3. The "customer" card acknowledges the request (Message A) and confirms that the money is available by sending Message B. It sets the money aside and adds this transaction to a list of pending transactions. If communications were cut off at this point, the money would be frozen until the central bank could step in to clean up the transfer.

4. The "merchant" gets the acknowledgment (Message B) and sends its own acknowledgment (Message C). This effectively finalizes the details of the transaction.

5. When Message C arrives, the customer's card finally deducts the money. It is now gone and the details of the transaction are moved from the list of pending transactions to the list of completed transactions. A new Message D confirming the end of the transaction is sent.

6. On receipt of Message D, the merchant adds the money to its ledger. Also, the transaction is changed from pending to final.

If any problem or error is detected in the transaction, a new entry would appear in the exception log. This is used to stop fraud and debug the system. If it becomes full, the card must be returned to the bank for clearance. The transaction log only stores the last ten transactions.

Migration

Mondex anticipates that it will be necessary to upgrade its security over time. For that reason, it includes two protocols for transferring money in each card. These protocols have different keys, algorithms, and perhaps even software. The presence of two different protocols allows new cards to be issued to replace old ones without introducing a large amount of disruption.

For instance, the first batch of cards to leave Mondex may support protocols A and B, but start off using protocol A. Eventually, protocol A will grow old or insecure. Mondex can switch to protocol B unannounced. Suddenly, all new cards may support protocols B and C. When an old card and a new card meet, they'll be able to exchange money using protocol B. Eventually, the old cards must be turned in to the bank and replaced with new ones, but this does not have to happen immediately.

This method of producing a "currency exchange" is a common way to catch cheaters. The United States military, for instance, would issue scrip to its soldiers fighting in foreign lands. At random intervals, the military would issue new scrip and force soldiers to redeem their old scrip in a currency exchange. Anyone caught with a large amount of currency would be immediately suspect as someone dealing illicitly.

These currency exchanges were always a logistical nightmare. The military tried to make them as unannounced as possible to prevent people from converting their soon-to-be-invalid old currency into hard assets like gems or gold. But unannounced plans had to be accomplished on a widespread basis, so a large force of people was needed to execute the exchange simultaneously. The size of the effort lowered the level of secrecy.

The Mondex method of updating cards offers some serious advantages. Cards do not become invalid immediately, and people can update their cards over time. It will be much more orderly and regimented. Of course, if someone is able to penetrate the tamper resistance of a card, shifting from one protocol to another won't make much difference. A person who has access to the certificates and secret keys used in protocol A would be able to get at the certificates and secret keys used in protocol B.

Mondex clearly anticipates updating both the algorithms and the keys as technology permits. Key lengths will certainly grow over time as new smart cards with enhanced computational ability become available. Algorithms may be enhanced as new approaches become understood.

Levels of Cards

Although all "cards" in the Mondex system can talk to each other and exchange money, not all cards are created equal. In fact, the most complicated may not even be smart cards at all but full-fledged computer systems.

The primary level will be smart cards that can maintain a balance. Mondex will limit the amount of currency each card can hold and also the number of transactions in its lifetime. A certain number of transactions will be recorded internally. These levels will be set as low as is still practical to reduce fraud and lower the amount of money laundering. These cards correspond with the bank only when a customer goes to an ATM to withdraw more funds.

The next level up is the wallet. This is just a smart card with an input/output device for checking value and transferring it to other smart cards. It may have different limits, but probably not if it is widely distributed.

The merchant terminals are effectively smarter cards. These keep longer records of transactions and correspond more frequently with the central bank. A merchant may sweep its receipts into a bank account once a day to start receiving interest. These terminals also may have more sophisticated fraud detection schemes. They may be programmed, for instance, to lock out certain cards. Smart cards could also do this, but it may not be practical to embed a long list in such a small amount of memory. Merchant terminals could be built with more memory or even a hard disk drive to facilitate this approach.

The bank would maintain its own set of "cards," which service accounts and transfer money between accounts and cards. These would be hooked up to ATM machines and merchant networks. At the highest level is a set of cards with the ability to "mint" money. These will be controlled, in all probability, by the central banks and kept locked away.

Each of these levels has a different set of limitations. The most general cards used by the population may have low cash limits. The central cards will have higher limits. Some cards may not talk to other cards. The central bank card, for instance, may only distribute cash to the local banks, not to individual cards. The stratification of the levels can change over time as new protocols are rolled out.

Anonymity

Early reports suggested that the Mondex card was anonymous. This is, in reality, far from true. Each card keeps a record of the latest transactions and you can even read this out yourself with a special version of the wallet. This transaction-level detail might prove valuable to travelers on expense accounts and budget freaks addicted to programs like Quicken. But the only anonymity that will exist will come if someone's name is not matched with a card.

Visa Cash

Visa has also developed its own cash-like system that runs on smart cards. Its system also uses a small, cheap card with an embedded microprocessor that keeps track of the money available.

The most visible use of the Visa Cash card was at the 1996 Olympic Games held in Atlanta. Visa outfitted many major chains around the city with card readers and also dispensed cards throughout the city. The reaction, however, was mixed because people found that they could spend the money only in these locations. Perhaps the reaction will be better if the money is more universally accepted.

Visa intends to test the card in New York City in 1997 as well as in selected other places throughout the world. It claims, for instance, that it will distribute 2 million Visa Cash cards in Spain.

Final Assessment

Smart cards offer a nice decentralized mechanism for trading cash. People can easily exchange money without linking up with a central computer system, and this can reduce the costs significantly. But such decentralization also offers dangers, because people may find a way to either clone or manipulate the smart cards.

Smart cards can also be used as part of any of the other systems described in this book. DigiCash, for instance, doesn't need to exist on someone's hard disk. It could live on a smart card. So could many of them. Smart cards might simply be used for identification. They would hold the person's keys in a more secure setting.

Other cash card systems can be found in Chapters 17 and 15.

Risks Smart card companies typically distribute much of the risk to the cardholder. If the card is lost, the money is gone, too. It may be possible for companies to protect the smart cards with PINs and then offer potential reimbursements like traveler's checks. But this may not be possible if smart cards have the ability to trade money between themselves. This would effectively act as a "laundry" of cash from a card that is already reported lost.

Obviously the issuer holds much of the risk of someone discovering how to clone a card. Chapter 25 contains a long discussion of how several Japanese companies fell prey to criminals that were smarter than the cards.

Strengths Smart cards are distributed. They don't need central permission to do their job. This can significantly lower the cost of central administration.

Weaknesses Smart cards are distributed. If someone finds a way to clone them, then there is a universe of cards out there waiting to interact. It may be functionally impossible to shut down a card even if you know that it is in the hands of a crook.

Chapter 19

Millicent

Millicent is another attempt to lower processing costs to an acceptable level to facilitate Net commerce. The system was developed by Mark Mansasse at Digital's System Research Center and it is still being explored actively by the group of scientists there. The project generated a standard method for making digital "scrip"[1] as well as a set of extensions to HTTP that would allow someone to pay for a Web page when he or she requests a URL. Both parts of the system are interchangeable, and you can use the Millicent scrip outside of the HTTP framework or you can use the HTTP framework with another digital cash system.

The Millicent system is a fairly complete realm that lives separate from the normal monetary world. There are customers, brokers, and vendors. A *customer* begins by establishing an account with a *broker*, who will somehow get paid by the customer for everything the customer buys. This may be either a credit or debit relationship that would probably be assumed by a bank. The vendors also establish relationships with the brokers. Whenever a customer wants to start spending, he or she must contact the broker and withdraw scrip that is good only at a particular vendor. Now, whenever the customer wants a Web page from a vendor, that customer sends the scrip along and the vendor verifies it.

---

[1]The term *scrip* is used here because it is also used in the Millicent documentation. For most intents and purposes, it is intended to be just like a digital "coin," that is, cheap to process. But it is usually only valid at specific vendors so it does not have general currency throughout an economy.

The Millicent team believes that this vendor-specific scrip can lower costs for vendors because only the brokers will have to worry about maintaining accounts and settling payment between customers. The vendors only need to worry about checking the scrip coming through their doors to make sure it is valid. At the end of each time unit, they return it to the broker who handles settling the accounts.

Millicent Scrip

See Chapters 21 and 20 to read about two other systems, MicroMint and PayWord, that use hash functions to replace digital signatures.

The Millicent scrip lowers processing costs by using cryptographically secure hash functions instead of public-key signatures. These are faster to compute and more easily exported. The Millicent system adds a layer of secrets that is shared between the user and the vendor or broker to establish identity. Someone who knows the secret value can generate a signature. Any cryptographically secure hash function can be used in this context. If h is the hash function, x is the message, and s is the secret value, then $h(sx)$ is the signature where sx is created by concatenating s in front of x. The major difference between this form of signature and the public-key version is that both sides must share the same value of s. There is no way to publish one half of the key so anyone can verify a signature.

Secrets

The secrets, which are merely random strings of bits, are established when an account is opened. Each customer gets a secret, which for customer i will be called CS_i. This value is known by both the customer and the vendor.

This network of secrets is quite similar to the Kerberos system of security invented at MIT and used extensively by DEC, among others.

The customer secrets could simply be stored in a large database, but this can be an expensive solution that requires plenty of disk space and memory. Millicent scrip uses a smarter solution. Each customer gets an identification number, CI_i, that identifies him or her. A direct and fairly easy to compute function converts this number, CI_i, into CS_i.

The heart of the function is the *master customer secret*, MCS, which is also a pile of random bits. The function extracts a portion of the MCS based on some part of the CI_i. For instance, the MCS, might consist of 256 bits that can be treated as 16 parts, $MCS_0, \ldots, MCS_{15}$.

The last four bits of the CI_i are extracted and used to pick one of these 16 parts. Call this mapping process g. Then the customer secret is produced by hashing these bits together with the customer ID, CI_i. That is, $CS_i = h(MCS_{g(CI_i)}CI_i)$.

The master customer secret is known only to the vendor producing the scrip. When a customer purchases some scrip, the vendor uses the MCS to produce CS_i and send it to the customer through a secure channel.

When a customer uses the secret to sign something, the vendor can verify this by using the CI_i and the MCS to produce the CS_i. There is no need to access a database or even go outside of the processor cache. The MCS should be kept at a reasonable size to ensure fast response.

A *master scrip secret*, MSS, also is used by the vendor to sign the scrip. A function similar to g is used to extract part of the MSS to create the vendor's signature of the script. For the purposes of simplicity, the letter g will be used again and the MSS will be considered to be the same size as the MCS. But there is no reason why any arbitrary function or set of bits could not be used here as well.

Producing Scrip

A Millicent scrip consists of the following pieces of data:

Vendor This is the company that produced the scrip and will accept it. It could be a name, a number, a domain name, an IP address, or some combination of these things.

Value This is how much the scrip is worth. It could be one frequent flyer mile, one ice cream sandwich, one song file from an Internet jukebox, and so forth.

ID# This is the serial number of the scrip. It is used to prevent double spending. The vendor keeps a list of all spent items and uses this to watch for someone passing the same scrip twice. This serial number is also used to derive the hashing signature of the scrip because it is used to extract part of the MSS.

Customer ID Scrip is produced for one customer only. This is the customer's identification number, CI_i, used to construct the CS_i.

Expiration Date The vendor must maintain a list of spent scrip, which will grow with time. If the scrip expires, then the vendor can replace this database from time to time and keep it manageable.

Extra Data There is an extra field for more data that might be used to add exclusions or extra features to the scrip.

Certificate The Millicent documentation uses the word *certificate* in a different way than most. The word is usually used to refer to a person's public key that has been endorsed with the digital signature of some central, trusted authority. Here, the word merely means the vendor's signature guaranteeing the scrip. This is computed by hashing together the other fields in the scrip with the value $MSS_{g(ID\#)}$.

The vendor can easily check the certificate when it arrives by computing $MSS_{g(ID\#)}$ and hashing it up with the rest of the scrip. As long as MSS remains secure, only the vendor will be able to check the veracity of the scrip. Digital cash schemes that use public-key systems can publish the public key of the bank and any vendor can check the veracity of its bills.

The parts of the scrip can be bundled up into a fairly compact package, which may range between 36 and 52 bytes. Actual implementations will standardize the size.

The Broker's Role

The broker must act as an interface between the regular banking world and the Millicent system. If a customer wants scrip, the broker must determine if the customer's account or credit history can support the request and then arrange to deliver it. This relationship will surely evolve to be somewhat similar to the credit card system. A broker may solicit customers in the same way and then determine who to use as partners.

The scrip can be minted by anyone who knows the MSS and MCS. This may be the vendor or, probably, the broker. The Millicent documentation imagines that the vendor will contract with the broker to produce scrip by giving the broker a range of serial numbers and a copy of the MSS and the MCS. The broker will then generate customer-specific scrip by inserting the right CI_i into the scrip and computing the hash function.

A broker that doesn't generate much scrip for a small company may act merely as a warehouse. The vendor could generate a small number of notes and then send them off. There would be no reason for the broker to know the MSS and MCS. This might also be a good approach if the broker and the vendor have a less than trusting relationship. A vendor might be issuing particularly valuable scrip and not want to risk the potential for disclosure of the MSS and MCS.

Of course, the broker will also serve as a senior member of the community. Banks often take a strong local interest in the economy because they've invested heavily in many local loans.[2] A functioning local government and a low level of corruption are in their best interest. This makes it worth their trouble to invest in a long-term infrastructure and do what is necessary to make the economy work.

It is entirely possible that major backbone providers of the Internet will become aligned with the brokers. It is, after all, in the broker's best interest that the requests for information make it safely between the customer and the vendor. The broker may offer large-scale discounts or preferred routing for their vendors to generate demand.

Vendor Specialization

The most important difference between Millicent and most other digital cash systems is that each piece of scrip is only good for one combination of customer and vendor. Customers that go elsewhere must purchase a different batch of scrip to use there. One of the major roles for the broker in the realm is to make sure that the customers can easily acquire scrip for specific vendors. The Millicent system is intended mainly for micropayments on the Internet. The broker acts as a clearing house between this Internet world and the rest of the banking system.

The main advantage of vendor-specific scrip is that it scales neatly. Imagine, if you will, a one-world digital currency issued by some all-controlling world bank called, maybe, *Credit DeutscheCitiNippon*. Each

---

[2]Some in my home town, Baltimore, for instance, are concerned because many of the strong local banks were purchased by multistate conglomerates with headquarters far away. The bank's senior executives will no longer have first-hand experience with the city and its problems.

digital note would have a serial number and this serial number would need to be checked against a corresponding master list to determine whether it is still valid. This list must be centralized, and multiple copies of the list would open a window for double spending and fraud.

Vendor-specific scrip is the simplest way to scale. There are still millions of companies around the world that haven't been purchased by Coca-Cola, Disney, or one of the Japanese conglomerates. Splitting up the load for maintaining the list of unspent currency is easily done at this level.

Vendor-level scrip also allows each vendor to create coupons that can serve many purposes. A vendor might issue a particular type of scrip like frequent flyer miles. This decreases its central bookkeeping responsibilities and may allow customers to easily pool their resources.

But, for all of these advantages, it is not clear whether the highly specialized nature of the scrip will be feasible on the network. A person may visit hundreds of Web sites in a single session. Buying, storing, and processing 100 different types of scrip is certain to be a burden. There is no easy way to compress them.

Coalitions between vendors issuing general currency for their members are also not possible. One central server must keep track of the notes to prevent double spending. While the small value of the scrip might be low enough to make it possible to sacrifice some potential losses to slow synchronization, there is a limit to this. Multiple vendors also mean multiple parties will know the MSS and MCS, making it possible to forge scrip.

But if each user has, on average, 50 units of 50-byte scrip from each of 200 major Web sites, then that only works out to be a database of about 500K. This is a relatively manageable number for desktop machines in today's world. In fact, it would probably cost no more than $0.10 of disk space at the time this book was written. The cost will only go down.

Anonymity and Refreshing

The anonymity of the transactions is more subtle in the Millicent system and it is related to the problem of refreshing old currency. Most digital cash systems with serial numbers will want to force currency to become obsolete in order to restrict the size of the database watching for spent currency and also to add some regulation to the environment. Each consumer must have a way to trade in old currency for new.

Some level of anonymity can be achieved if the customer trades old currency for new regardless of the expiration date. Ordinarily, the broker has the opportunity to keep track of the serial numbers of the notes handed out to a customer. If there were some relationship with the vendor, then it might be possible to trace transactions. One of the Millicent papers[3] [Man95] suggests that it would be possible for someone to return scrip to the vendor and get new scrip with new serial numbers to prevent the broker from tracing the transaction.

It is not clear if this protocol would have much real effect. If the broker sells a customer scrip from Corporation X, then that scrip is going to be good only at Corporation X. Changing the serial numbers would only prevent the broker from recovering exactly what the customer purchases. Of course, if the relationship between the broker and the vendor is good enough so the broker knows the matching between bill serial numbers and items bought, then it is likely that the vendor may also be selling the names behind the transactions.

Of course, the general level of anonymity in the Millicent system is fairly low. Each piece of scrip is minted for a unique customer ID. It can only be spent by someone who knows the associated secret, CS_i.

But another layer of anonymity could be grafted onto the system. A broker that is given a range of serial numbers as well as copies of the MCS and MSS could create a unique customer ID for a person who wants to buy the scrip anonymously. If the customer trusts the broker to keep this new identity a secret, then it may be possible to generate scrip that carries no information to the vendor.

The lines of trust in such a scenario are still intact. The broker generates only n units of scrip for a customer who pays n units from his or her account. When the vendor receives the n units, it can receive payment in real money from the broker. The customer ID will only help establish the corresponding customer secret.

I know of no way to use a blinding factor with the types of digital signatures proposed here. They use a cryptographically secure hash function that is fast to compute but also very noncommutative. The commutative property of multiplication is the basis for Chaum's blinded digital signature.

For information about the blinded digital signature, see page 33.

---

[3]http://www.research.digital.com/S RC/millicent/papers/mcentny.htm.

Refreshing Cash

Let B be the scrip that includes all of the information about the value, the serial number, and the company that will redeem it. A vendor that wants to refresh a piece of scrip could send customer i a new version to replace it, $\bar{B}$. The cash could be delivered through any standard means of encryption. For instance, the current secret known to the customer can be used if the vendor sends the customer a random value N and the value $\bar{B} \oplus h(CS_iN)$. The hash function would convert the value N, shipped unencrypted, into a secret key.

The $\oplus$ stands for exclusive OR.

Another solution is to maintain a set of public-key pairs for the vendors or the customers. The customer may ship a value, R, to the vendor encrypted with the vendor's public key and expect to receive $\bar{B} \oplus R$.

Integrating Millicent with HTTP

The Millicent team at Digital is also exploring adding new fields to the HTTP protocol to make it easier for browsers to pay for the information they consume. The standard protocol includes a few fields where the browser indicates the data it wants. The distant server responds with either the data or some explanation of why it can't proceed. The new proposals enhance HTTP by offering a place for the money or scrip to be added to the request and ways for the server to respond if it isn't properly paid. The extensions are tailored to the needs of the Millicent system, but they could be used with many other token-like systems.

The core of the proposal is a set of new fields that might be found in an HTTP request:

`Payment-Protocol:` This is the name of the payment scheme; the officially designated version is `Millicent-1.0`. Others may follow. If the client and server are opening up a connection, this field may contain multiple protocols separated by commas. This indicates that the sender of the message is willing to exchange money in any of these. This is known as an `inquiry` request. Later, when payment is offered in a `purchase` request, only one should specify the final choice.

`Payment-Cash:` This field holds the actual bags of bits that act as cash. They should be in the format specified by the `Payment-`

`Protocol:`. If multiple notes are placed in the field, then they should be split by commas.

`Payment-Authorization:` Some protocols require a customer or merchant to sign the process using some form of digital signature. The Millicent system requires a customer to use the customer secret to authorize a transaction. This information should be supplied here.

`Payment-Bid:` This field is used by the customer to propose the price for an upcoming transaction. The price in the `Millicent-1.0` version of the protocol is specified by a real number and the ISO 4217 currency code. These are usually straightforward. `3.1415usd` means 3 dollars, 14 cents, and 15 hundredths of a cent.

The protocol also includes the possibility for negotiation. The price offered by the customer does not need to be accepted by the vendor. If the customer is paying a listed price that is believed to be guaranteed, then the entry can include the word `guarantee` after the price separated by a semicolon. The entry "`Payment-Bid:` `0.001gbp;guarantee`" means that the customer expects to pay one thousandth of a British pound.

A customer that just wants to inquire about the price should submit a blank `Payment-Bid` entry.

`Payment-Offer:` When the vendor needs to respond with its price, it uses this field to carry the information. This might be a higher price in response to `Payment-Bid:` or it could merely be a price quote made in response to a blank request.

Each entry in this field should contain three subparts separated by slashes. The `Millicent-1.0` protocol suggests the entries should contain the price, the vendor name, the expiration date, the URL of the information, and a vendor signature certifying the guarantee.

`Payment-Receipt:` This field contains a receipt for the cash or scrip tendered. It may include a public-key-based signature in some versions of the protocol. Also, if change is returned, then it is accompanied by a `Payment-Cash:` field.

`Payment-Error:` If the server doesn't like the client's request or its form of payment, it issues an error. This field carries the description. Here's a list of the new codes that are to be added to the current set of error codes:

402 Insufficient Payment Not enough money enclosed. The correct price is held in the Payment-Offer: field that must accompany it. Note, this "error" is generated if someone is merely requesting a price.

420 Bad Payment The cash or scrip is not in the correct format or it is expired or already spent. The offending notes should be found in the Payment-Cash: entry.

421 Unknown Payment Protocol The client is proposing to pay with some scheme that is not understood. Only Millicent-1.0 is recognized at this time. The allowed protocols must accompany this response in the Payment-Protocol: field.

422 Payment Rejected A generic response when things go wrong.

Adding Millicent to HTTP

Any browser using HTTP to request documents can add these fields to its request with a minimal amount of effort. The greatest chore will be building a database to maintain the different vendors' scrip and keep it straight. This may also be the biggest roadblock to the incorporation of Millicent into the world.

The Universal Payment Protocol also has a scheme for negotiating for a payment method. See page 118.

The details of the format for the information in many of the fields in the HTTP protocol are only specified by the payment protocol. So if a Digicash-1.0 protocol emerged, it might use a completely different format for the price guarantees returned in the Payment-Offer: field.

The most important detail is the name of the vendor. These must be unique because the names are used again and again in determining where scrip can be spent. The Millicent version uses either an IP address (4 bytes) or a domain name (i.e., www2.dot.com) followed by the port number. A colon separates the two.

The digital signatures are computed using MD-5 (RFC 1321), but the details of the formatting and the structure of the messages are too complicated for this book. For answers to these questions and others surrounding this standard, turn to http://www.research.digital.com/SRC/millicent/.

Legal Details

The vendor-specific nature of the Millicent system may have technical advantages, but it has legal ones as well. Creating a generally circulating currency like DigiCash requires heavy regulation by the government(s). They often view this as their prerogative as the sovereign. But coupons and other vendor-specific systems like scrip are completely different. If something can only be redeemed at one vendor or for one particular product, then it falls outside of the regulation of many laws aimed at duplicate currencies.

Final Assessment

Millicent is one of the most ambitious projects in the digital cash world because it attempts to produce vendor-specific scrip for each customer. This increases the amount of scrip that must be stored by the customer, but it simplifies the process of accepting and verifying the scrip. The process also offers a third role of the broker for the bank or credit-card-like organization that provides much of the central billing and bookkeeping for the vendor.

Risks The greatest risk in this system is that someone will find a way to aggregate many tiny payments and still make off with a significant sum. This system is engineered to make small payments feasible and that means cutting overhead to reduce transaction time and computation. Ideally, the value of these items will be small enough to make it too expensive for someone to try and steal them.

Computers are highly automated and programmable. The greatest danger may be unseen. Little amounts can add up, especially if accounts are reconciled long after the transaction.

Strengths The strength of the system is the low-cost digital signatures constructed using hash values. This reduces the cost of running a server that authenticates the scrip and also removes the need to license public-key patents.

The vendor-specific nature also enforces a distributed network. This reduces the possibility of a catastrophic failure. The Disney Web site may go down but not the Time-Warner or the Fox site.[4]

Weaknesses The vendor-specific requirement of the Millicent scrip is also a weakness. It requires each customer to maintain separate

---

[4]At this writing, these three companies are still separate entities. They may buy or merge with each other by the time you've read this.

piles of cash for each vendor. This can add up in the fragmented world of the Web. It is entirely conceivable that a Web page owner may write the text to a Web page but license the photographs from different sites. That means you may need ten or more different types of scrip just to view one Web page—one type to pay the initial site and nine to pay for the pictures.

There are no obvious weaknesses in the hash function signature system, but it does force each customer to maintain a separate secret that must be sent via a secure channel.

Chapter 20

MicroMint

Many of the algorithms in this book use public-key encryption to generate signatures that provide guarantees. This is a powerful approach, but it has its drawbacks. Public-key encryption is more computationally expensive than simpler cryptographic solutions like hash functions. Smart cards are very low-power devices and many can't handle the extensive calculations needed to do RSA. The algorithms are also covered by many overlapping patents held by people who want to be paid for using the algorithms. Finally, the U.S. government frowns on exporting software using general security algorithms like RSA and requires a great deal of assurance that the software will not be used to protect anything except financial information.

MicroMint[1] is a public-key-free approach developed by Ron Rivest and Adi Shamir who were the R and the S in the troika that developed RSA. This system uses cryptographically secure hash functions like MD-5 (see page 36) to replace public-key encryption. This is not difficult to do because hash functions offer some of the same features as public-key encryption.

In both cases, if you know $f(x)$, then it is practically impossible for just anyone to determine either x or find a y such that $f(x) = f(y)$. The major difference is that public-key signature algorithms make it easy to do if you own the private half of the key pair. Cryptographically secure hash functions are difficult for everybody to reverse.

---

[1]MicroMint is also the name of a hardware manufacturer that builds neat, inexpensive embedded controllers (see www.micromint.com). There is no relationship between the company and this algorithm.

The MicroMint algorithm uses this feature of cryptographically secure hash functions to duplicate the factors of the public-key encryption system. Unfortunately, to do this it must go to extreme lengths to duplicate the features of public-key encryption system. The MicroMint system requires a large super computer to "mint" each coin or token, and this super computer must be significantly larger than the machines available to the average person. Rivest and Shamir chose to include the word *mint* in the name of the algorithm because it invokes the image of the government's mint, which also performs large capital-intensive operations. Stamping out metal coins is not easy to do unless you're able to invest in heavy-duty presses. The low value of the coins is a pretty effective barrier to counterfeiting.

A coin in the MicroMint world consists of n values, $x_1, x_2, \ldots, x_k$ such that $f(x_1) = f(x_2) = f(x_3) = \cdots = f(x_k)$. This is often called a *k-way collision*. The function f is some cryptographically secure hash function.[2] Anyone can test the validity of the coin by computing the hash function for each value of x_i. If they match, then the coin must be valid. The definition of a cryptographically secure hash function means that it should be practically impossible to counterfeit the coins—if the hash function acts correctly.

Minting Coins

If it is hard for the average person to counterfeit the coins, how can the government or the monetary authority produce them? After all, there is no trapdoor in a cryptographically secure hash function. The solution, which may be too high priced to be considered practical, is to choose a huge number of random values, $\{y_1, \ldots, y_m\}$, and compute $\{f(y_1), \ldots, f(y_n)\}$. If the number of values, m, is large enough, then the odds are actually fairly good that some subsets of k values will hash to the same value.

This is often called the *birthday paradox* because its effect is often described in terms of birthdays. For instance, if you have a group of m people in a room, what are the odds that two of them ($k = 2$) have the same birthday? If $m = 2$, then only one pair is possible and the

---

[2]You could use public-key encryption here as well, but that would spoil the speed effect. The algorithm succeeds because someone can test whether $f(x_1) = f(x_2) = f(x_3) = \cdots = f(x_k)$ much faster than checking a digital signature.

odds are 1 out of 366. If there are $m = 3$ people, then three pairs are possible. The number of potential pairs is $m(m - 1)/2$, which clearly grows much faster than m.

This result produces two effects. First, it is still hard to simply mint a coin. A simple match requires about $2^{k/2}$ hashes if n is the number of bits returned by the hash function f. If n is larger than about 100, then it becomes quite impractical to mint a single coin. But the second effect is just as important. Generating a new coin becomes easier and easier. When you generate value y_m, there are $m - 1$ chances $f(y_m)$ will match a previous value.

These effects are even stronger when $k > 2$. The first k-way collision should appear after approximately $2^{n(k-1)/k}$ values of y are examined. So finding one coin becomes harder. But now the number of potential subsets of k values of y increases like m^k so the collisions will come faster.

Details of Minting

Finding k-way collisions can be a difficult task that could require an enormous super computer. The greatest problem would be building the memory to store these values as they are generated. Rivest and Shamir have come up with a number of suggestions to make life easier for anyone minting a large number of coins. Here are some of them:

Expiration Date Coins will last only a short time, say, a month. After that time, they will be replaced. How do you know whether a coin is valid for a particular month? At the beginning of each month, the mint announces some criteria for the values of x_i. For instance, the first five bits of each value of x_i might have to be 01100. But the solution could also be more complex. It could be any arbitrary Boolean function.

Rivest and Shamir suggest that this can even be taken to the extreme. The mint could produce 30 different Boolean predicates and only use values of y_i that satisfy all 30 of them. Each day, a new predicate would be revealed to the public. The merchants could add it to the list of ways that they test each incoming coin. None of the month's coins would be affected by this, because the mint took all 30 predicates into consideration when it made the coins for the month.

But these predicates prevent any forger from slowly but surely building up a large database of numbers and their hash values. Only a small fraction will meet the current criteria. The mint, on the other hand, will work only with values of y_i that meet this criteria when they are minting the coins for the next month. Forgers will have to begin anew each time a new predicate is announced.

Rivest and Shamir also point out that the hidden predicates can be constructed in such a way that they can't be discovered by examining a large number of coins. They cite the work of Avrim Blum, Merrick Furst, Michael Kearns, and Richard Lipton, who describe how to construct these unlearnable functions in [BFK93].

Bad Coins The mint might decide to keep only values of y_i where the first t bits of $f(y_i)$ match some set value. The rest are simply ignored. This trades memory for computation. The mint will cut the size of storage it needs to look for collisions by a factor of 2^t but at the cost of increasing computation by another factor of 2^t.

This bad coin feature also allows the detection of counterfeits. The mint does not need to make this criteria public because it is using it merely to trade computation for storage. If coins start appearing with hash values of $f(x_i)$ that don't fit this criteria, then someone has compromised the system.

Multiple Denominations The same technique for creating publicly known predicates can also be used to create multiple denominations for the coins. There could be a collection of predicates, p_i, and any coin that satisfied p_i would be worth i units of money.

This might be defined at a lower level to make minting easier. That is, a coin would consist of k values, $x_1 \ldots x_k$. The value of the coin might be defined to be the highest value of i such that there was a j such that $p_i(x_j)$ was true. This means that the mint would not need to create a different batch of y_i for each denomination. It could simply mix them together in one batch and take whichever coins emerged. The number of coins with some value of x that satisfies p_i would be roughly proportional to the number of values of y that satisfied p_i. The number of coins of each denomination would follow from this observation.

The problem with this approach is that it may be easier to "counterfeit" coins by increasing their value. Imagine you had a batch of coins worth, say, a penny. You could simply try values of y that satisfy p_{25} until you found one that fit into the collision in one of the existing coins. Then, you could increase the value of the coin.

One defense against this is to give the coin the value of the smallest predicate satisfied by any x. This curtails the production of high-value coins and probably isn't worth the tradeoff.

User-Specific Coins There might be circumstances when you would like to mint a special set of tokens that could only be used by a small group of people. These coins or tokens would be much more resistant to theft because they could only be used by members of this group. For instance, you might want to mint coins that could only be used by IBM employees to view a Web page. The HTTP server could make sure that the request was coming from within IBM by doing a reverse DNS lookup on the IP address.

One simple solution is to come up with yet another set of predicates for each coin. For instance, a hash function, h, could return some bits that indicate the group. When $h(x_1, \ldots, x_k)$ is computed, it would indicate who is allowed to spend the coin. The major problem with this is that it may be difficult to balance the demand of the different groups. If there are 2^a different groups, then the mint must produce about $2^a M$ coins, where M is the largest monthly demand of any of the groups. The random nature of a hash function like h makes it impossible to control which coins emerge.

Of course, if h is merely applied to the values of x individually, then some scheme like the one for multiple denominations could be more specific in how it produced coins. That is, if there are predicates $p_1 \ldots p_n$, then a coin could be used by group i if p_i was the first predicate that would be satisfied by any member of x in the coin's collision.

More Complicated Predicates Rivest and Shamir propose generalizing the concept of a "collision" to make it easier to create more complicated coin identification schemes. A coin will be valid if

$$x_i - x_{i-1} = d_i \bmod 2^n$$

for $i = 2$ through $i = k$. If $d_i = 0$ for all i, then this scheme would reduce to the normal version of a collision described throughout the beginning of this chapter.

The values of d_i become a way of identifying who can spend the coin. A mint might use a different vector of values each month or it might assign a vector to each potential group of customers.

Minting coins that satisfy this definition of collision could be easier. The values $\{f(y_1) \ldots f(y_m)\}$ are computed as before. These are probably stored in memory or on a disk. Instead, for k values of y that hashed to the same value, the mint would choose one arbitrary value to be x_1. Then it would add d_1 to $f(x_1)$ and look for the value of y that generated it. If it were found, then the step would be repeated using d_2 and repeated again until k values of x were identified. Otherwise, the process would begin again.

The principle value of this scheme is that it is not necessary to compute coins for different users in different batches. Any value of y might be used in a coin for any user. It all depends on the values of d. You could easily mint 10 million coins for one user and 10 for another using the same batch of y.

This size of n can be adjusted in this scheme to change the accuracy.

Overlapping Predicates The job of the mint could be reduced by arranging the predicates so that they accept coins from the previous few months, which for the sake of example will be 12. That is, p_i is a predicate that returns true if a value of x is valid for month i. Call the batch of values of y constructed in month i to be Y_i. So p_i is true for all members of Y_i.

The workload can be made lighter if the predicate p_i is also true for the members of the previous 12 batches, $Y_{i_1} \ldots Y_{i-11}$. If this could be accomplished, then all of the previous 11 batches could be used in month i to help find collisions.

A Practical Example

Rivest and Shamir have developed a practical example for the parameters of the system that they feel might be used to implement it. Here are their numbers:

- Each coin is worth one penny ($0.01).

- The bank, broker, or mint charges a 10% commission by giving a merchant $0.009 when a coin is returned.

- Coins are built from four-way collisions ($k = 4$) with parts x_1, x_2, x_3, and x_4.

- Each month, the mint would create 2^{30} pennies.

- To do this, the mint would create 2^{31} bins for sorting the values of $f(y_i)$. Each bin would have space to hold four values of y that had the same last 31 bits. The top $n - 31$ bits would be fixed to some constant to restrict the size of this database. This would require about 128 gigabytes of storage.

- The mint would fill the bin by looking for values of y that produce hash values with the right $n - 31$ bits at the beginning. This would require $m = 4 \times 2^{n-31} \times 2^{31} = 2^{n+2}$.

- On average, half of the bins would be filled if the hash function is purely random and a Poisson distribution holds. That means that 2^{30} coins would be produced.

- To hash 2^{n+2} coins each month, field-programmable gate arrays could be configured to encrypt DES. The hash function, $f(x)$, could be set to the result of encrypting some fixed random value with the key set to be x. This is a well-understood problem in silicon design ([Way92]). Rivest and Shamir estimate that 256 chips would cost $400 a piece, giving the machine a cost of $100,000.

- This machine could hash 2^{33} values in a second and there are 2^{21} seconds in a month. So a good value of n would be $n = 52$.

- If all of the coins were used each month and returned by a merchant, then the profits from the commission of $0.001 per coin would be approximately $1 million. The cost of the machine would be $150,000.

Anonymity

The mint must keep track of each coin when it returns to make sure that it isn't spent twice. This may be accomplished by simply keeping a list of the values of $f(x_1)$ that return. The bank could watch who receives these values and who returns them to determine who is spending how much where. So no anonymity would be offered to users.

Final Assessment

The MicroMint proposal is merely an academic paper, but it illustrates a novel way of thinking about how computational resources act to prevent counterfeiting. Normally, the strength of a public-key system is used to stop counterfeits, but here a clever insight into the birthday paradox allows a bank to achieve economies of scale that small counterfeiters will never achieve.

Rivest says that he and Shamir have no intention of pursuing patents on the invention, and it is not clear whether it will ever become practical. The use of hash functions, however, makes it much easier to achieve the computational requirements with a small smart card. It also lowers the needs of the bank or mint that must test each incoming coin or token to see if it is valid.

Risks Barring a loophole in the hash function, the major attack would be a machine that is larger than the mint's. This might be able to evade some of the predicates and do enough computation each day to generate some value. But this could easily be combatted by watching for vendors passing counterfeit coins.

Strengths No public-key encryption means less export headaches and lower computational overhead.

Weaknesses Secret computation predicates can help defend against counterfeiters, but they can't eliminate the threat. Nothing can stop a serious attack from someone willing to build a machine that is several orders of magnitude bigger than the standard machine. But if the value of the coins is kept low, this will discourage such counterfeiting.

Chapter 21

PayWord

Hash functions can be a valuable substitute for digital signatures. Chapter 20 describes one unique payment system designed by Ron Rivest and Adi Shamir that uses hash functions to produce coins on a very large scale. In the same paper ([RS96]), they also described a system they called *PayWord*,[1] which used a chain of hash functions as small-value tokens. Rivest and Shamir noted that this system was also developed independently by Ross Anderson, Harry Manifavas, and Chris Sutherland at Cambridge University ([AMS95]) as well as Torben P. Pedersen at Aarhus University ([Ped95]).[2]

This system is very straightforward and uses the principle that a cryptographically secure hash function is practically impossible to invert. That is, if you are given $f(x)$ it is difficult to compute x, but if you are later given x then it is easy to verify that the x value matches. You could easily use a public-key digital signature function as f, but this is computationally impractical. Hash functions execute between 100 to 10,000 times faster than public-key operations, depending upon the key length.

The basis for the PayWord scheme is the *chain of hash values*. That is, the numbers $x_1, x_2, \ldots, x_n$ form a chain if $x_i = f(x_{i+1})$. A chain is

---

[1]This book uses the name *PayWord* to describe the system because the author first learned of the scheme from the paper by Rivest and Shamir. No other attempt was made at discovering the "correct" name through forensic citation.

[2]Similar systems are also used in password control. See Leslie Lamport [Lam81] or Neil Haller [Hal94].

generated in reverse order by starting with some random number as x_n and working backward, computing the hash functions. If you wanted to create n coins recognized by some bank, broker, store, or Web site, you would create a chain with $n + 1$ elements and give x_1 to the ultimate recipient. You would spend the first coin by tendering x_2 and the recipient would check it to see if $x_1 = f(x_2)$.

These coins are easy to create and relatively small. Some hash functions like the SHA return 160 bits. Only a few bytes of identification need to be added to allow the recipient to determine who is spending some cash. Also, the recipient only needs to maintain the last coin spent and a counter for the remaining coins. The database may be no more than 25–40 bytes per account.

Minting Details

The PayWord system can be implemented in a number of different ways to satisfy the various needs of users. Here are some different suggestions:

Public Signatures A user who registers a chain of hash functions with the bank, Web site, or other recipient by sending the first value, x_1, must somehow validate his or her identity. This may be accomplished by a public-key signature and certificate. When someone opens an account, he or she may be issued a certificate that contains a public-key pair to be used when authorizing new spending.

A public-key signature is not necessary if the transactions are conducted in person. A user might bring a smart card into a bank or store, give the clerk some cash, and then the smart card would be allowed to register a chain of values.

Credit versus Debit This scheme can be used to support either credit or debit. When a chain of hash functions is registered, the recipient may consider this as either extending credit or debiting from an account as necessary.

Verified Addresses Rivest and Shamir suggest that the PayWord tokens ($\{x_i\}$) be bound to a particular address. That is, each value in a chain could only be used to purchase information that is sent to a particular location. There is no particular reason why this is necessary. Imagine that someone intercepted the coin x_i en route to being spent. There is no publicly known way that the eavesdropper could reconstruct coin x_{i+1} or any of the other unspent coins.

Anonymity Someone must provide payment when the chain of coins is created. If this payment is provided in a secure way, then there is no reason why the coins can't be largely anonymous. Whoever possesses the chain of values ($\{x_i\}$), possesses the coins. Even someone in the bank can't steal them.

But, aside from anonymously offering something of value in person to the bank or recipient, there is no other way to provide anonymity with this system. Other systems allow someone to withdraw cash from an account in such a way that the bank doesn't know the serial numbers of the notes or coins. This is not possible with this approach. The bank must know the value of the last coin spent, and it must also keep a count of how many coins are left in the chain. Although the bank may choose not to tie a customer's name to a chain of coins, the information is readily available.

Theft Resistance If the PayWord coins are not anonymous, then the recipient can provide replacements in the case of theft or loss. The central account ledger determines which coins are valid and when they can be retrieved. If someone can provide proper documentation and swear that the coins were lost or stolen, then the account can be closed out and the user can provide a replacement chain of hash values.

Final Assessment

The PayWord system is an ideal example of how hash functions can be used to create digital coins. The approach may be a good solution for low-end smart cards used to pay tolls, purchase phone calls, or buy items from vending machines. The system, however, requires that each coin be cleared through a central list to prevent double spending.

Ron Rivest says that he has no intention of patenting this process so it is likely to fall into the public domain.

Risks The PayWord system is highly resistant to security breaches. Someone who intercepts a coin between the spender and the recipient can't practically generate another coin from the chain.

Strengths The PayWord system works like all other systems with
central accounts and central control. Using a chain of hash values,
($\{x_i\}$), is implicitly stronger than simply producing serial numbers. Imagine, for instance, that someone simply sent in the values
$1, 2, 3, \ldots$ as he or she spent coins. An eavesdropper could easily
construct the next coin in the sequence. Also, the recipient could
easily close out an account and claim that a user has spent all of the
coins. If a chain of hash values is used, then the recipient can prove
that someone spent coin x_i simply by knowing the value of x_i.

Weaknesses The coin system's major weakness is that each coin must
be worth the same amount. If you want to spend five coins, there is
no need to send x_1, x_2, x_3, x_4, and x_5. It is enough to send x_5. But the
recipient must compute the hash function five times to validate x_5.
There is no easy way to make change but no reason why different
chains can't be created with different values.

Chapter 22

Magic Money

One of the best ways to experiment with a digital cash system is to play with Magic Money, a very nice text-based implementation of the basic blinded signature described in Chapter 3. The software was written by Pr0duct Cypher and distributed freely throughout the cypherpunk community. You can get a copy of the software through anonymous FTP. Copies can be found in both the cypherpunks archive (`ftp.csua.berkeley.edu`) or in Italy (`ftp.dsi.unimi.it` in directory `/pub/security/crypt/code`).

The Magic Money system uses the basic PGP routines to provide encryption and exponentiation. The software uses RSA for the digital signatures and uses the blinded algorithms patented by David Chaum to provide anonymity. Generally, experimental use of patented ideas is permissible. Commercial or personal use, however, is not.

There are two application programs for the software: the client and the server. The server acts like a bank: it validates coins, exchanges old coins for new ones, and maintains a list of spent coins to prevent double spending. The client program validates coins, maintains a wallet filled with coins, and turns in coins to the bank server when they are received. The system is essentially on-line because the coins must be turned in immediately. They do not encode the identity of the user to catch double spenders like the more ambitious approach described in Chapter 3.

The software comes with C code for UNIX systems. The server can and probably should be hooked up with its own account so that incoming mail can be fed directly into it. This allows it to process coin exchanges autonomously. The client software is best run as an application.

Setting Up a Magic Money Server

Creating your own server is pretty simple. After the code is compiled, you simply execute the server with parameter i that indicates initialization. The software prompts you for the name of your bank, the name of the coins, the denominations of the currency, and the size of the PGP key that will be used to protect it.

The process of creating the key pairs is simple. First, the system finds two large primes, p and q, that produce a modulus, n, that will be used for all of the encryption. Here n was set to be 1024 bits long. This is a good beginning. The program chooses a different value of e_i and d_i for each denomination of the coin where i is the value of the coin. The values of e_i are distributed with n as the public key. When a customer presents a coin to the bank for signing, the bank will choose the right value of d_i for the denomination. The signature can only be verified with the right e_i.

The server software also has the provision for changing the pairs of e and d. This is a way to expire coins and it is necessary because the software must keep a list of all spent coins. This list can grow quickly with use, so expiration is the only way to clear out the system. If you were to set up a serious Magic Money system, then you might notify people that their coins would expire every three months and they must be refreshed. Many of the commercial systems like CAFE or DigiCash have a built-in refreshment mechanism. Ideally, you might arrange to honor the old coins, but do so at a long delay. The lists of old, expired coin serial numbers would be stored on slow, cheap tape.

The other job of the server is to mint new coins. Magic Money coins are very simple. They have two numbers: the serial number, S, and the value of e_i that is used to verify its authenticity. The serial number has a standard format: 16 random bytes that identify the coin and 18 fixed bytes that are the same on all coins. The rest of the serial number is padded with FF until the serial number is the size of n.

The coins are distributed as a pair, e_i and S^{d_i}. Anyone can verify a coin by computing S^{e_i} and checking to see that the serial number is in the right format. The bank server can generate new coins by simply constructing random serial numbers and then signing them with the value of d_i that corresponds to the value.

A client can only create a new coin by turning in a new coin. When it has a coin to turn in, the client requests a new coin from the bank by generating an S and blinding it with a blinding factor. After the bank server returns the new signed coin, the client unblinds it and stores it. The coin can be shipped to another client who would then repeat the process.

It is important to note that the Magic Money coins are not structured like standard Chaumian blinded coins. The Magic Money coins don't use a hash function as an intermediate step to mix up the serial number and other information. That is, the banks compute $f(S)^{d_i}$ where f is a cryptographically secure checksum like MD-5. This is an important step because RSA encryption preserves multiplicative associativity. That is, $RSA(ab) = RSA(a)RSA(b)$. That means if you want to convert S^d into some more valuable bill, T^d, then you only need to find R such that $SR = T$. If you get the bank to sign R, then you can produce $R^d S^d$ to get T^{d_i}. One solution to prevent this is to use a hash function. Magic Money avoids the problem by fixing a large part of the serial number. Finding the right factors like T seems intractable.

Here's a sample script from setting up a Magic Money server:

```
Server setup will create a PGP key for
your server, ask you for a list of coin values,
and create an e-d pair for each coin.

Enter a name for your server
(this will be the PGP key userid)
Stripe's Bank

Enter number of bits for the key: 1024

Enter a name for your digital coins.
stripes

Enter values for your digital coins.
Each value can be between 1 and
2^32 stripes(s). Press return after
each one, enter 0 to end.
```

```
1
2
4
8
16
32
64
128
256
512
1024
2048
0
```

```
Generating key pair
ppPppPppppPppppppppppPpppPppppppppppppppppPpppppP
ppppppppppppppppPpppPpppppppppppppppPppppppppppppP
ppppPppPppppppppppppPppppppPppppppppPppPPPPqqqqQq
QqqqqqQqqqQqqqqQqqqqqqQqqqqqqQqqqqqqqqqQqqQqq
qqQqqqqqqqqqqqqqqqqqqqQqqqQqqQqqqqqqqQqqqqqqqQq
qqqqqqqqqqqqqqqQqqQqqqQqqqqqqqqqQqqqqqqqqqqqqq
qqQqQqqqqqqqqqqqqqqQqqqqqqQqqqqqqqqqqqQqqqqqqqQqqq
qqQqQqqqqqQqQqqqqqqqqqqqqqqqqqqqqqqqQqqqqqqQq
qqqqqqqqQqqqqqqQqQqqqQQQQffffffff
Key generation completed
```

```
Creating value list
1 2 4 8 16 32 64 128 256 512 1024 2048
```

```
Generating e and d lists
Finding e and d for value 1
Finding e and d for value 2
Finding e and d for value 4
Finding e and d for value 8
Finding e and d for value 16
Finding e and d for value 32
Finding e and d for value 64
Finding e and d for value 128
Finding e and d for value 256
Finding e and d for value 512
```

```
Finding e and d for value 1024
Finding e and d for value 2048

Initializing hash file

Your server is initialized. An ASCII-armored
copy of your public key has been placed in file
(bank.asc).
```

The seemingly random collection of p's and q's are exactly that. The software prints them out during key generation to show that work is still being done. A file, rand.dat, is used as a source of randomness.

The Magic Money Client

The client software is just a wallet that maintains coins for the user. It has four different functions:

Process Coins If someone sends you a file filled with coins, then the client checks the signatures and creates new replacement coins. The old and new coins are shipped off to the server encrypted with the server's public key. In the interim, the blinding information is stored in file proto.dat.

Accept New Coins After the server exchanges the old coins for the new coins, it ships them back to the client encrypted with the client's public key. The client decrypts the package, unblinds the coins, checks the signature, and stores them away. When they are accepted, they're stored in the file allcoins.dat.

Bundle Coins for Payment If you want to pay someone something, then you ask your client to unpack certain coins from the wallet file and pack them up for shipping. Ideally, you'll have the right denominations. If you don't, you'll need to send off for change. The results are stored in the file coins.dat which you would probably include as an attachment to your electronic mail.

Retire Old Coins If the bank notifies you that it will be retiring coins, then you must send in the old coins for new ones. You can only do this when the bank sends along the new versions of e_i that it will start using.

A Sample Transaction

A good way to understand the flow of the bits and the money they
represent is to follow a simple transaction. This must begin by creating
coins. When the system first begins, there are no coins in the system.
Only the server can mint coins and it is clear that this is a nice position
to be in. This is accomplished by feeding a list of denominations into
the server:

```
access5% s m 256 256 512 1024 128
Minting coin of value 256
Minting coin of value 256
Minting coin of value 512
Minting coin of value 1024
Minting coin of value 128
```

When it is done, the coins are stored in the file coins.dat. This
is the standard file format for exchanging coins. This file makes its
way across the Net to whoever is receiving payment. In this case,
the bank/server is paying off someone with the money that it mints.
This is equivalent to the U.S. government paying its bills. When the
client receives the file, it needs to check out the quality of the bits and
make sure that they haven't been double spent. After the signatures
are verified, the client creates a new set of coins with the same value,
blinds them, and encrypts them with the bank's public key. Here's a
transcription:

```
access5% c coins.dat
Input is coins for deposit
Coin of value 256 stripes(s)
Coin of value 256 stripes(s)
Coin of value 512 stripes(s)
Coin of value 1024 stripes(s)
Coin of value 128 stripes(s)
Total value to deposit 2176 stripes(s)

Denominations: 1 2 4 8 16 32 64 128 256 512 1024 2048

2176 stripes(s) remaining
Enter value of coin to create: 2048
```

```
128 stripes(s) remaining
Enter value of coin to create: 54
That coin denomination does not exist.
128 stripes(s) remaining
Enter value of coin to create: 64
64 stripes(s) remaining
Enter value of coin to create: 64
Creating new coin of value 2048 stripes(s)
Creating new coin of value 64 stripes(s)
Creating new coin of value 64 stripes(s)
Send the file output.asc to the server to deposit
coins.
```

I got 2176 stripes (the currency name) and asked for one new 2048-stripe coin and two 64-stripe coins. The result comes in file output.asc and is mailed off to the bank server where the coins will be signed. The Magic Money server will work as a mailing program that automatically processes and checks the coins, retires their serial numbers, and blindly signs the new coins before returning them in encrypted form. When the result returns in the mail, you feed it into your client. Here's a transcription:

```
access5% c out-10.asc
Input is message from the server - good signature
Coin of value 2048 stripes(s)
Coin of value 64 stripes(s)
Coin of value 64 stripes(s)
```

Now the wallet, allcoins.dat, is 2176 stripes richer. If I wanted to pay money to someone, I would withdraw the coins from the wallet into a file with the same format as coins.dat. The process continues.

Final Assessment

The Magic Money system is an excellent experimental system for understanding how digital coins work. It is secure enough to act as the foundation for a system for exchanging coupons or other items. The biggest limitation is the software, which is built for hackers with UNIX boxes. PC and Macintosh versions exist, but they are not designed for general consumption.

Risk If a `coins.dat` file or an `allcoins.dat` disappears, then whoever owned it has lost it. It's gone. Internet electronic mail is pretty secure, but letters do get lost. If you send the `coins.dat` file to someone, you should definitely encrypt it. Otherwise, someone could snag the coins from the ether.

Strengths It's a nice implementation that integrates well with PGP.

Weaknesses Magic Money is just an experimental system.

Chapter 23

NetBill

The NetBill project at Carnegie-Mellon University in Pittsburgh, Pennsylvania recently announced another collection of protocols for exchanging money over the Internet. The system relies upon a central accounting computer to keep track of the accounts. In many ways it is a mirror image of the debit or credit card system. This may be one reason why Visa is working with the main designers, Marvin Sirbu and Doug Tygar, to develop an experimental system for selling information. Some of the experience may find its way into the development of the Visa system.

The basic exchange protocol involves a central server that maintains account balances and any number of clients who might be interested in buying information. The clients and the central server exchange encrypted and digitally signed purchase orders before exchanging cash between the servers. The protocol also prevents clients from using any information they receive before paying the bill. The system is most similar to the *i*KP protocol described in Chapter 8.

A Simple Exchange

A simple transaction in the NetBill environment involves three parties: the customer, the merchant, and the central cash server. The NetBill literature refers to the software used by the customer as the *checkbook* and the software used by the central server as the *till*. The merchant receives communiqués from the till telling it what the customer wants to buy or sell. The steps of a simple transaction are as follows:

1. A customer selects a piece of information to purchase. The checkbook sends a request for a price quote to the till, which forwards the request to the merchant. This process of requesting a price quote is included because a merchant may choose to offer different prices to different people. Some organizations, for instance, might own a site license to all issues of a particular electronic journal. This might be what a subscription becomes.

2. The merchant returns a price quote signed with the merchant's digital signature. The till acts as a middleman again. When the customer or the customer's software decides to pay the price, it sends a message announcing this and signs this request with a digital signature.

3. The till gets the request to buy the information and requests it from the merchant. The merchant encrypts it with a random key before transmitting it to the till, which computes a secure checksum of the encrypted information before transmitting it to the customer.

4. When the customer receives the entire block of encrypted information, he or she computes a checksum of the data and sends this checksum back to the till in a packet that includes a timeout stamp, a description of the purchase, and the final accepted price. This block is known as the *electronic purchase order* and it signifies the customer's final commitment to purchase the information.

5. The till receives the customer's checksum and verifies that all of the data arrived at the customer unscathed. Now it can safely transfer the money between the accounts. It checks the accounts and notifies the merchant that the transfer is complete.

6. The merchant transmits an invoice that contains the price and the secret key for decrypting the data. This invoice is signed by the merchant.

7. The till transfers the money and forwards the key to the customer.

8. The customer decrypts the data.

The most noticeable part of this protocol is the process of encrypting the data. The merchant and the till are protecting themselves against a malicious customer who might receive the data and then cheat by saying, "Gosh, it never arrived. I don't think I want it anymore." Forcing customers to give the checksum of the data before giving them the key prevents them from cheating in this way.

This is a more robust way to exchange data than the First Virtual system (Chapter 6) or the Open Market system (Chapter 14). The needs for such a robust system are hard to assess at this time. As I discussed in Chapter 12, the solution lies in the domain of marketing, not mathematics. The need for such a system depends to a large amount on how honest people are.

Encryption Details

NetBill uses two popular key management systems, RSA and Kerberos. The public keys built out of the RSA system are used for the final signature approving the transaction. This cannot be repudiated. The private half of these public keys is provided when the account is opened, and is usually stored in encrypted form on the workstation. When the final step of a signature is required, the user provides a PIN number, which is used to decrypt the half of the key pair necessary to generate the signature.

All other communication is handled using private-key encryption algorithms built on top of the Kerberos key management system. This requires the central server and the customer to keep shared secrets that only each other knows. This encryption can be much faster and this is why it is used.

Using two different systems for encryption and authentication is becoming more popular. Although it would be possible to use the public-key system to distribute the keys, this adds an additional potential for compromise. If the public-key system is used only for signatures, then it may be more secure. Also, there is no need to distribute new public keys as frequently.

Setting Up a NetBill Storefront

The NetBill project is only a university project at this time, albeit a project from Carnegie-Mellon with ties to Visa and the Mellon Bank.

At this time, the NetBill team is producing software that will integrate with a Web server to make it possible to sell information on the network. The process uses a new MIME type for HTTP called *x-netbill*. When a browser receives a document with type x-netbill, it turns around and gives it to the local Money Tool running on the client machine.

This "Money Tool" requests to speak to the merchant's *product server*. This software is being written by the NetBill team and you need to install it to become a merchant. This software will determine prices for the documents and arrange for payment to take place. It announces the prices and sends transactions to the central bank for payment.

This generic tool will make it relatively easy for a merchant to open up a store. The only necessary step is configuring a price table. Everything else will be handled internally.

At this writing, NetBill is quoting transaction prices of 5% of the value and $0.02 for transactions under $2.00, and 3.5% and $0.02 for transactions above that amount.

The software is currently in alpha testing and it is not clear when it will be available to the general public for full-scale use.

Final Assessment

NetBill is a research project that offers a few interesting ideas. The most important is the ability to escrow information until payment is delivered. This is very different from the First Virtual system, which ships out the data and hopes people will be honest.

At this writing (November 1996), the NetBill project is beginning an alpha launch of software that only runs on Sun's Solaris OS. The system also only trades in *bibliobucks*. In the future, the project intends to use real accounts drawn on the Mellon bank.

Risk The encryption system substantially reduces the risks to the merchant. Customers can't decrypt information until they've paid.

Strengths NetBill offers a more secure way to distribute information on the network.

Weaknesses Extra encryption may not be worth the trouble if First Virtual is right about the strengths of social controls.

Chapter 24

EDI

Money is not the only thing on earth. Electronic commerce needs more than just money, it needs something for people to buy. The term of art, EDI, which stands for Electronic Data Interchange, refers to the process of doing business electronically. The process was originally begun by large corporations who wanted to streamline transactions with their suppliers. The process mushroomed and now the world is blessed with a pair of major standards to choose between. The ANSI X12 standard is embraced by the U.S. government and its Department of Defense, while the EDIFACT standard is supported by the United Nations. The field is by no means closed because many businesses continue to use their proprietary standards or smaller standards to communicate with suppliers.

The process of digitalization is simple in theory. The standards define simple electronic formats for every major business document like the invoice, the purchase order, or the request for a quotation. If both ends of the transaction use this standard, then they can send orders and invoices electronically without worrying about the flow of paper. The accounting systems will be able to track the transactions automatically and everything will be cleaner.

In practice, the process of coming up with a standard is quite complicated. Most invoices and purchase orders are simple, but many can involve strange and nonstandard discount arrangements. It is common, for instance, to grant volume discounts that might kick in after someone purchases a certain number of items. Expressing all possible discount arrangements in a computer-legible form can be complex.

Most EDI transactions are not intended to handle money flows. Businesses continue to use banks to transfer money through electronic payment and checks. This places the topic largely outside of the scope of this book. Readers who are interested can turn to one of the many books that concentrate on the topic. Some are [Ley93, Emm90, Bau91].

The rest of this chapter covers some of the basic EDI transactions as an inspiration. Most of this book is concerned with creating digital money—an item that comes in atomic quantities that are meant to mimic some physical substance. But there is no reason why people need to trade $100 for an item. They could write a contract that guaranteed $50 and 10% of the gross. Standard electronic contracts with well-defined terms could also serve a monetary function. The only problem is standardizing them enough to make trading simple and convenient.

X12 Standard

The ANSI X12 standard covers many standard ways that businesses interact. Each type of contract or business communication has its own substandard that is usually refered to by its number. These substandards are often called *transaction sets* because they define a particular type of transaction. The most important ones are:

810 Invoice

820 Payment Order/Remittance Advice

824 Application Advice

836 Contract Award

838 Trading Partner Profile—Vendor Registration

838 Trading Partner Profile—Confirmation of Vendor Registration

840 Request for Quotation

843 Response to Request for Quotation

850 Purchase Order

855 Purchase Order Acknowledgment

864 Text Message

997 Functional Acknowledgment

The X12 standards were taken by the U.S. government, studied, and turned into Federal Implementation Guidelines. These cover the details for how each of the different messages or transactions are formatted. The National Institute of Standards and Technology is responsible for creating these guidelines and promulgating them to companies that may need them to carry on business with the federal government and its Department of Defense.

Each of the transaction sets is divided into *segments* and each segment represents a specific part of the action. For instance, an invoice contains one segment specifying the names of the parties and their addresses. Another segment describes the items in the order. Each of these segments is broken up into a set of *data elements* and *codes*. The particular data elements are defined within each segment.

Invoice (810)

Here is a short description of the major segments in an X12 invoice as well as some of the data elements that make up each segment.

Transaction Set Header This contains the code that identifies the transaction as an invoice (810) as well as a unique ID number for this particular invoice.

Beginning Segment This specifies all of the particular data about the invoice and why it is being created. That includes the invoice number, the invoice date, the purchase order number that started the invoice, and the date of this purchase order. There is also a data element for identifying the type of invoice and a set of codes for filling this element. It may be a credit or debit invoice, or a credit or debit memo. Finally, there is a field to indicate that additional modifications are being made.

Currency Segment This defines the currency used as a basis for the transaction. This segment might include information on the exchange rate agreed upon for cross-currency transactions or the currency exchange market that will provide a market rate for the transaction. There are additional fields for indicating which party authorized payment in which currency.

Name Segments The names of each party and their addresses are filled out here. There is great flexibility in how this can be achieved. The simplest method is a text name and address field, but codes are also possible. For instance, the Dun and Bradstreet company issues DUNS numbers to companies. This is good enough to specify a name and address because another database maintains the link. There are also entries for DODAAC, CAGE, and MAPAC numbers. There are also specific codes for countries, states, and local political entities.

There are at least six different parties that can be part of a transaction including the payee (PE), the Party to Receive Goods (PO), the Party to Receive Remittance (RI), the Service Performance Site (SV), a Metering location which might measure the goods provided (MQ), and a shipping location (ST). Each of these parties can be specified by using the codes, names, and addresses.

Reference Numbers This is an additional segment for additional numbers without which the world might stop revolving. Seriously, these could include the Old Account Number, the Old Meter Number, the Sequence Number, the Government Bill of Lading number, the Customer Reference Number, and the Final Sequence Number, among others.

Administration Contact Segment This tells whose head will roll if things don't work out.

Terms of Sale Segment This details when the payment must be made and what discounts are available. There are data elements for the number of days in the net due date, the day this commences, and the dates that discounts kick into play.

F.O.B. Instruction Segment This specifies who pays for the shipment and who covers the risk of loss.

Baseline Data Segment This specifies the basic format of each line of the invoice. One example might be Case, Color, Drawing No., UPC No., ISBN No., Model No., SKU. Each line of the invoice would include seven entries for each of these areas. There are also standard entries for the quantity used, the unit price, the basis price, identification numbers, and qualifiers.

Tax Segments There are specific segments for federal, state, and local taxes as well as FICA taxes.

Terms of Sales This specifies when discounts can apply and when they begin.

Carrier Detail The carrier who will deliver the goods and the route that might be taken.

Total Monetary Amount Segment This measures the total value of the invoice, that is, how much needs to be paid. In typical EDI style, this is not one number. There is the total amount, the amount subject to discount, the discount percentage, and the final discounted amount.

Here is an example of an invoice drawn from the Federal Guidelines. The actual data that would be transmitted are printed in this font and the comments provided by the author of the Federal Guidelines are *in this font*. It is clear that the typography of the EDI standard was not defined by someone aiming for readability. It seems to hark back to the punchcard era when FORTRAN was coded with many fixed idiosyncrasies. Data storage and transmittal costs are not that great any more, so it would not cost much to increase the data.

ST*810*0001 N/L   *An 810 invoice with a transaction set control number of 0001.*

BIG*940330*12345*940102*DAAJ9994C0001***DI*00*F N/L   *Indicates an original (00), final (F), debit invoice (DI) number 12345, dated March 30, 1994, against contract number DAAJ9994C0001, dated January 2, 1994.*

CUR*PR*US N/L   *Indicates that the payment will be made in U.S. dollars.*

N1*PE**1*246801234 N/L   *Indicates that the party submitting the invoice (PE) is known by its DUNS number (1) 246801234.*

REF*BL*123321 N/L   *Indicates that the cited items were shipped under a Government Bill of Lading (BL) number 123321.*

REF*SI*ABC999 N/L   *Indicates that the applicable shipment number (SI) is ABC999.*

PER*AF*SUE SMITH*TE*1234567890 N/L   *Indicates the party who can be contacted regarding questions on the invoice (AF) is Sue Smith at telephone number (TE) 123-456-7890.*

N1*PO**1*086429876 N/L   *Indicates that the federal government invoice receiving office (PO) is known by its DUNS number (1) 086429876.*

ITD*21**2**10**30 N/L   *Indicates that the invoice is subject to the Fast Pay provisions (21) of the Prompt Payment Act. Also indicates that a discount of 2%–10 days, net 30 days, applies to all line items in the invoice.*

DTM*011*940330 N/L   *Indicates that all line items were shipped (011) on March 30, 1994.*

FOB*PE N/L   *Indicates that transportation charges were prepaid and added to the invoice (PE).*

AT**********123Z00999ABCXYZ001 N/L *Indicates the appropriation data (long-line accounting data) applicable to all line items in the invoice.*

IT101*0001*10*EA*20**FS*6240009991234 *F1*94-1*MG*A3344 N/L *Indicates that line item number 1 (0001) is for 10 each (EA) items at a unit price of $20.00 (20) and the item can be identified by its National Stock Number (FS) of 6240009991234, from catalog number (F1) 94-1 and its manufacturer's part number (MG) A3344.*

PID*F****WIDGET OF GREAT SIGNIFICANCE, WITH RED STRIPE N/L *Provides a clear text description (f) of the item.*

REF*K5*9876 N/L   *Indicates that CLIN 0001 was performed under task order (K5) number 9876.*

CAD*A****1 N/L   *Indicates that the items were shipped by air (A). The number 1 satisfies an ASC X12 syntax requirement.*

SAC*C*I250 **20 N/L   *Indicates that a transportation (I250) charge (C) of $20.00 (20) was paid to ship the item by air.*

N1*ST**33*55555 N/L   *Indicates that the items were shipped to (ST) an address identified by its CAGE code (33) of 55555.*

IT101*0002*1*LO*100**SV*PROGRAMMING N/L   *Indicates that line item number 2 (0002) is for 1 lot (LO) of a service that can be described as (SV) programming, at a lot price of $100.00 (100).*

TDS*330*200*326*4 N/L   *Indicates that the total invoice amount (including all charges) is $330.00 (330); the amount subject to the terms discount is $200.00 (200); the discounted amount due is $326.00 (326); and the discount amount is $4.00 (4). Note: Look at the SAC segment following the TXI segment to pick up another charge that was added at the end because it did not apply to any specific line item.*

TXI*LS*****8 N/L   *Indicates that the invoice is exempt (8) from paying state and local sales taxes (LS).*

SAC*C*G970**10 N/L   *Indicates that a small order (G970) charge (C) of $10.00 was added to the invoice.*

CTT*2*11 N/L   *There are 2 line items (2) in this invoice and the sum of the quantities invoiced is 11 (10 +1).*

SE*24*0001 N/L   *There are 24 segments included in this transmission bearing a control number of 0001.*

Chapter 25

Security

If eternal vigilance is the price of liberty, it is also the price of installing widespread, efficient digital transaction systems. Computer security and cryptography seem like daunting subjects that are hard for everyone to understand, but they are also very fragile creations. Criminals have a strong incentive to probe and poke at digital transaction systems until they bleed cash. Security breaches can emerge in the most surprising places. Any company that chooses to create a digital transaction system should have a strong commitment to keeping a close watch on security. New holes can emerge from strange places and the only real solution is for companies to keep a close watch on their products.

There are two important policy goals. First, each system should include a wide range of auditing checks that make it possible to flag counterfeiting as soon as possible. Central servers need not be used constantly, but the systems must have some way of checking the veracity of the currency in circulation.[1]

The second most important policy is for the systems to be easily replaceable. Encryption algorithms are notoriously fragile. Many algorithms that were once thought strong are now easily broken. The best algorithms on the market today—DES, IDEA, and RSA—may have

---

[1] Some of the most philosophical members of the U.S. Treasury Department are fond of saying that a small amount of counterfeiting is no major problem. The government just wants to produce a stable currency and it doesn't matter who does the work of printing it. The counterfeiters just save the government some time. Clearly, private companies can not take such liberties with their balance sheets.

endured years of assault by some mathematicians, but that doesn't guarantee that they'll be secure tomorrow.

By its nature, cryptography rests on uncertain foundations. If humans understand one branch of mathematics backward and forward, then humans can compute functions and their inverses. Cryptography, however, needs functions that we understand only in one direction. They must be easy to compute but hard to uncompute. Unfortunately, very few problems are provably hard to uncompute.[2] So we end up settling for ones that seem to be hard. No one knows how to invert them, so we use them for a cryptographic solution.

The rest of this chapter will survey some of the ways that digital cash systems can fail. This survey is not complete, but it should build a good foundation for understanding what can go wrong. A good source for deeper exploration is Ross Anderson's essay "Why Crypto Systems Fail" [And93].

Hardware Problems

All cryptographic systems and their descendants, digital cash systems, require that some files be kept secret, accessible by only a trusted few. Even the system with no cryptography, First Virtual, must keep its central log of transactions secure to prevent people from deleting their transactions. Any system that uses public-key cryptography must keep the private half of the key secure.

Guaranteeing perfect security throughout the system is probably impossible. Home PCs have very little security. The electromagnets in a computer monitor generate a fairly strong signal when they paint an image on the screen. This signal can be picked up from a relatively short distance. Similar taps can easily be placed inside a computer to watch for relevant data. Writing a hidden program that records key sequences is surprisingly easy.[3]

---

[2]The best guaranteed lower bounds on a problem that are proven involve sorting. Given n objects, sorting them will take time approximately proportional to $n \log n$. But even this bound is not so strong. If the numbers to be sorted are of a bounded size, then the computation time is linear.

[3]My version of the Iomega Zip drive for the Macintosh installed a backup program that would record all key clicks in a file. This was a safety mechanism to help me recover from a computer crash but the software is so transparent that it could easily be used for nefarious purposes.

Although these attacks are not likely to be used on home personal computers that might control only a few thousands of dollars, they could easily be used on central servers for the bank. Any institution must consider physical access to its central machines to be essential. The vaults that once protected paper cash can be reconfigured to protect cybermoney.

Many home computer systems are also prone to holes in the operating system. These may emerge from an original design flaw or they might be inserted by a virus. In either case, they are increasingly dangerous because of the world's growing connectivity. A few years ago, most personal computers were islands. If some rogue part of the operating system wanted to ship out secret data to a distant host, there was no way to do it. Now, Internet connections are increasingly common. Any virus could easily phone home and send personal data out the pipe, and may never be noticed.

Smart Cards

The lack of security of desktop machines makes smart cards attractive. These cards do not have to be physically tamper resistant to be useful. One possible solution is for people to carry their personal keys locked away on a smart card. When some data needed a digital signature, the data would be handed off to the smart card, which would do the computations and return it. Smart cards capable of doing RSA computations are more expensive because they can handle more complicated computations, but they may be worth the cost to avoid copying the private key into the general computer with its insecure OS.

The smart card could be designed to have a very simple architecture, proven to be free from holes. It would not run new software, so viruses and other Trojan horses could not insert holes. The smart cards could even be protected by a PIN to prevent casual thieves from accessing the data inside them. This PIN, however, would be collected by the host computer, which might be insecure. A determined attacker could still get at the data inside the card.

Even though smart cards could be accessed if the PIN is uncovered by some snooping software, the presence of such cards can still be an important deterrent to crime. The greatest danger of these digital transaction systems is that a hole could be exploited remotely and programmatically. If someone were to discover a flaw, he or she could program his or her own computer to relentlessly exploit it from a safe haven. Someone may be able to recover a PIN number remotely, but the smart card must be physically recovered to use the data inside.

Unfortunately, attacks are still possible. Any virus or hole that could open up a way to eavesdrop on the person's PIN code may also be able to open up a tunnel though the operating system that would pass all transactions in and out of the smart card. The best solution may be for people to keep their smart cards in their pockets unless they are using the cards at the time.

"Tamper-Resistant" Smart Cards

Some smart cards are said to be tamper resistant. This means that someone who wants to recover the data inside the cards may find it practically impossible. These cards usually provide this additional layer of security through physical devices. The chips are encased in tough plastics, and these plastics have embedded abrasives like sapphire granules that make it difficult for someone to grind off the outer layers without affecting the internal ones.

There is no well-defined and understood theory behind producing these tamper-resistant packages, and it is not clear whether any well-understood theory would be any stronger. Humans are remarkably ingenious when confronted with a barrier. Some, like space travel at the speed of light, may seem pretty strong, but any practical digital cash system can't rely on these stronger barriers. The cash and the data must be accessible to those with the proper authorization so no absolute barriers can be used.

Many of the current techniques are quite strong, but it is unclear how they will resist time and ambition. I don't think anyone in the cellular phone business in the United States expected the cloning problem to become as severe as it is today. In some cities, the half-life of a phone may be only three months before someone clones it and forces the legitimate user to get the phone rechipped. These losses are much easier for the phone companies to absorb because they often have unused capability. The "stolen" phone calls just absorb this unused bandwidth.

Money, however, is a different concept. Criminals have been remarkably clever in exploiting smart cards in the past. Some early smart phone cards were cracked by people who would solder tiny wires to contacts before inserting the card into the telephone. This allowed them to watch the signal levels and learn how to spoof a fully loaded card.

The most dramatic story to date comes from the Japanese pachinko parlors. In May 1996, two companies that make cash cards for pachinko machines reported that they sustained losses of 55 billion yen (about $588 million at the time) because of counterfeit cards [WSJ96a]. Pachinko is a popular form of Japanese pinball that involves a mixture of mainly luck and some skill. You begin with a number of tiny balls and fire them into a complicated arrangements of pins. If some land in the correct slot, you can win more balls.[4]

The parlors attracted fraud because the balls could be turned in for prizes. The more balls you have at the end of the game, the bigger your prize. Japan bans gambling, so these prizes are all you can technically win, but many pachinko parlors support shops nearby that repurchase the prizes for cash. So, by reselling the gift, the balls could be exchanged for money. Some pachinko parlors even generated phony prizes made up of pretty paper that had value only at the redemption center [Ish96].

The cards were worth between 10,000 and 1,000 yen and they would lose value as more balls were purchased. Many pachinko parlors noted an increase in business after the cards came into use, because people found it much easier to buy balls. The early card readers on the machines did not check the serial numbers of the cards, so it was possible to make exact clones of cards. Later, new card readers were installed to check for counterfeits and clones, but it was too expensive to put them on all machines.

The problem, however, also had a political side [WSJ96b]. The *Wall Street Journal* reported that the cards were invented, in part, because of the possibility that money was being laundered through the pachinko parlors. Many are run by ethnic Koreans living in Japan, and some theorized that the money was heading to support the North Korean nuclear weapons program. The card readers were supposed to bring accountability and the ability to audit the system. Before, the steel balls were anonymous and fungible—the two key requirements for money laundering. The article suggests, but does not prove, that the money ended up in Korea. There is no solid evidence, however, and the only

---

[4]The funniest part about the original story in the *Wall Street Journal* is that it reported that there were 18,244 pachinko parlors in Japan. How could a system lose $588 million yet know the number of parlors to five significant digits?

thing that is certain is that the money has disappeared from the card manufacturers.

In any case, it is clear that even small amounts of currency can quickly build into a large loss. Some reports suggest that a criminal would be able to remove only 2000 yen (about $20) from a card before returning to an illicit magnetic reader to recharge the card. Yet, over time, $588 million disappeared through little drips like this.

Advanced Attacks on Smart Cards

As this book is going to press, some clever attacks on smart cards are being described publicly for the first time.[5] These are serious techniques that make it possible to recover the secret key information held inside a smart card with a relatively small amount of work. While there are some correspondingly simple defenses against the attacks, they illustrate why it is difficult to assume that any smart card will be tamperproof.

The attacks were noted by Dan Boneh, Richard DeMillo, and Richard Lipton of Bellcore. They showed that the secret half of an RSA key could be recovered from a smart card if the smart card could be forced to make several simple errors in processing. This is somewhat ironic because the secret key would be practically impossible to recover if the smart card made no mistake.

Now, computers may not make mistakes, but they can be induced into making mistakes. Alpha particles are known to flip bits from time to time, although it rarely happens with current designs. But if the number of alpha particles could be increased significantly with either a radioactive source or a microwave, then the errors would become more common.

The approach was extended to other secret-key algorithms by Eli Biham and Adi Shamir, using an extension of their powerful differential cryptanalysis. Although their full paper is not available at the time this book went to press, they provide a strong explanation why it may be possible to extract a DES key by generating about 200 pairs of encrypted data. One part of each pair was encrypted correctly and the

---

[5]It is clear that many in the smart card industry knew of these attacks previously. The FIPS for DES, for instance, insists that any hardware implementation must include checks for mistakes.

other was encrypted incorrectly after a single randomly distributed bit error changed part of the result in the middle of processing. They suggest that the attack could be extended to all DES-like cryptosystems, including ones that generate their own s-boxes from the key material.

Both of these attacks that require random errors can be stopped if the smart card refuses to serve up an encrypted value before checking it. Running the encryption twice or decrypting it can ensure that no mistakes have been made. Anyone who is counting on introducing random errors would need to make sure to introduce the same ones during the second pass when the checking is done. This is a significantly harder step. Generating random errors may be relatively easy or at least conceivable. Repeating the errors is another story.

Another interesting approach to extracting the RSA key is simply timing the process. Paul Kocher [Koc96] showed that it is possible to extract the secret key from an RSA process simply by timing the calculation. A small number of calculations is enough to reveal the key. This attack can be mitigated, to some extent, by adding random padding to the encryption process.

These attacks show that weaknesses can be found in the most unexpected places. A strong encryption system may remain strong while still yielding to a relatively simple attack. These make it more important to distrust the tamper resistance of smart cards and build in additional safeguards.

Smart cards may continue to be valuable because they force someone to attack a particular person's card one at a time. Large-scale, automated attacks that exploit software holes in workstations and PCs are not possible.

Software Weaknesses

The software systems running local workstations are important security barriers and, unfortunately, very weak barriers. The operating system must defend the machine against attacks coming from both inside and outside. Most of the study in the security community involves defending against outside attackers who will try to access data through a network connection. The current TCP/IP system is the result of years of approximation and experimentation.

The OS designers concentrated against outsiders because work against inside attackers is much harder for several reasons. First, many programmers are indistinguishable from attackers. They demand absolute access to all parts of the machine to get things accomplished. Preventing some sorts of access to stop attackers also cripples programmers when they need to fix things.

The second reason is that people lack a good definition for the levels of security. Most common operating systems let programs have the run of the system because that gives the programs the maximum utility to get things done. Macintoshes and PCs running Microsoft Windows operating systems don't even try to stop programs from accessing any part of the disk. So viruses are a common problem.

UNIX systems are more secure, but they have many notorious holes.[6] The system offers a fairly workable definition for segregating system information and allowing only "root" users access. But many users quickly discover that the barrier stops them from doing some useful work and they need "root" access to get the job done. Determining which tasks are permissible for the average user is not an easy chore, and UNIX programmers introduced many security holes when they guessed wrong.

For all of these reasons, software that runs on workstations can't be trusted. All of the software that runs on the workstation alone is vulnerable to some sort of virus attack. In the past, most viruses were relatively benign. The writers had little to gain because there was no network connection. Now, data about accounts, private keys, or actual digital currency can be shipped out through the increasingly common Internet connection.

The range of hypothetical viruses is quite amazing. First Virtual circulated a warning of a potential virus that could attack other financial systems. The virus would lay in wait, watching for 12- to 16-digit strings of numbers, which are often credit card account numbers. The standard credit card numbers also include a check digit to make it easy to verify the accuracy of the numbers immediately. Many people know this checksum, and it would be easy to create a virus that would check the digits to see if they conformed to the standard. Then, the virus could be pretty sure that it had a credit card number in its grip and ship off the number to its master.

---

[6]A good place to begin understanding the UNIX structure is by reading Simson Garfinkle and Gene Spafford's book [GS96].

Each system described in this book would be affected in different ways. The low-level encryption systems like SSL would be the most vulnerable. Stores that required you to type in the credit card number at each transaction would be exposing your credit card number to the virus each time. Other systems like CyberCash's credit card front end would be less susceptible. They require you to type in the number only once, when you establish your account. But a similar virus could watch the screen-drawing code instead of the keyboard. If the number is displayed, it could be grabbed. Other systems like DigiCash don't use credit card account numbers, so they're immune.

The First Virtual system would also be immune to this sort of attack. It replaces the number with a password that would be much harder for any keystroke-sniffing virus to identify. Many of the passwords are dictionary words with a few extra numbers added to the end. It would be difficult if not impossible.

But the First Virtual system would not be immune from a similar attack. If a virus could install itself in the operating system and watch for keystrokes, it might be able to gain access to the mail spool file. The First Virtual system depends heavily on the security of the e-mail system to guard against false transactions. A virus would be able to detect the FV messages asking to confirm transactions and then automatically generate confirmation. The user would not even know that his or her software was automatically responding "Yes" to the question of "Did you spend $150 at Harry's Bar?"

These are just some of the hypothetical viruses that would be easy to write for the current Windows and Macintosh platforms. Other systems are also vulnerable to a lesser extent.

This book cannot be a solid primer on software system security. In fact, the field is still in its infancy. Every new feature added to computers places new requirements on security. The growth in network applications today creates even more potential for security holes. Every company in the software business is trying to make its product "Internet compatible" and that usually means allowing the software to communicate over the Internet. One slight mistake could render any program a wide-open security hole.

Digital cash designers must approach this with trepidation. If absolute security is not possible, there must be mechanisms for detecting aberrant behavior. Credit card companies are already quite well-versed in watching for strange spending patterns with their cards.

These algorithms will be even more important in the digital era. But it is hard to anticipate just how clever these algorithms need to be. For instance, I've received several phone calls from my credit card company to check on some transactions I've made. They usually came on a Saturday when I was out running errands and filling up both cars with gas. The new credit-card-ready gas pumps don't require any face-to-face interaction with a clerk, so thieves often use them to check whether the card has been canceled yet. The person who called to check up on my spending told me that if you use these pumps twice in a day, then it is a major indicator. No one knows what such patterns will look like in cyberspace.

Algorithmic Failures

All of the systems that depend upon encryption are threatened by the possibility that someone will find a way to break the encryption. This can happen in two ways. The most common way is the gradual increase in computer speed, which will eventually produce a machine that can try all possible keys. The 56-bit keys used by DES can be exhaustively searched in about a day by a hypothetical machine that costs about $1 million at the time of this writing. The 40-bit keys used by some algorithms that are exportable from the United States are even more fragile. An average workstation can crack them in a short amount of time.

These attacks are crude and, to some extent, predictable. Computer hardware increases in speed at a reliable rate, doubling in capability every two to three years. But special-purpose hardware can be significantly faster, and it is now easier than ever to design special-purpose hardware. Programmable gate arrays allow someone to simulate any electronic circuit at high speeds. The Supercomputer Research Center in Bowie, Maryland, a public "branch" of the NSA, has built computers around these chips. Others have also explored using them. Determined attackers could do the same.

The greatest danger, however, is mathematical. New insights can yield new attacks that are several orders of magnitude faster. When RSA was published in 1978 [RSA78], Rivest suggested that it could take 40 quadrillion years to crack the sample cipher they included in the paper. This cipher used a 129-digit number that was the product of two prime numbers. Yet, this was cracked in 1994 by a team from Bell

Communications Research using the input of 600 volunteers running software that used spare computing cycles to search for the answer. The process took eight months.

Over the years, the people factoring numbers have found newer and better attacks. Each attack just made the process several times faster, and over the years, these solutions added up to make it possible to factor a 129-digit number. These improvements don't end. For instance, RSA now estimates that the latest techniques would only need two months, not eight months, to crack the 129-digit original key. But none of these attacks led to catastrophic failures in the RSA system. Each new digit added to a key still made it several times harder to break. The basic attacks, however, got significantly faster.

Anyone designing a digital cash system should use two defenses. First, keys should be used that are significantly longer than necessary. Although each new digit slows down the system, the cost of a potential failure is much higher. Many people assume that 1024-bit keys[7] will be sufficient. The RSA corporation maintains a fairly ambitious project to track the results of people attacking their algorithm. In the past, they've done a good job of maintaining a discussion of the state of the art of factoring on their Web pages (www.rsa.com). For information about this algorithm turn there.

The second solution is to make the systems algorithm independent and have replacement algorithms ready to run. Many different public- and private-key algorithms are available. A good digital transaction system should be able to use all of them with ease. The SSL standard, for instance, makes it possible to use many different types of encryption. If one method were to fall victim to clever mathematics, another could easily be substituted.

Other digital transaction systems are not as flexible. Clearly any public-key system with distributed certificates will need to issue new certificates if a new algorithm is introduced. But a good system will be able to anticipate this possibility and make it easy to do.

Unfortunately, there is no good way to anticipate the speed of mathematical insight. The only solution is to watch carefully.

---

[7]To convert digits to bits, multiply by 3.3, which is roughly the $\log_2 10$. That is, $2^{3.3}$ is 10. So 1024 bits is about 310 digits.

Summary

There is no good news about security in a digital cash system. There is only the lack of bad news. To date, no one can offer any absolute guarantees about any of the encryption systems and the nature of mathematics makes it unlikely that any guarantee will be available. The next-best solution is to watch vigorously and be ready to substitute new algorithms and procedures as soon as possible.

This chapter has only touched on several different ways that a digital transaction system could be compromised. Security research is ongoing and incremental. A good place to watch for major announcements about weaknesses in computer systems is the `comp.risks` newsgroup that is edited carefully by Peter Neumann. The computer security groups are also devoted to details of software and hardware architecture, while the cryptography groups (`sci.crypt` and `sci.crypt.research`) cover many of the algorithmic explorations.

Chapter 26

Money Past

Anyone who was raised in the United States with my generation may find it hard to accept the fact that the U.S. dollar is anything but a relatively stable way to hold value. I graduated from high school in the early 1980s, and since then prices have remained fairly constant and inflation has remained low. Many prices are even lower today than they were a decade ago, thanks to the miracles of technological advancement and the pain of brutal global competition. This lack of inflation even occurred despite long-term erosion of the U.S. dollar against the German mark and the Japanese yen. So, except for the higher cost of trips to Berlin or Tokyo, the people who kept their faith in the U.S. dollar were fairly well rewarded. All of this stability and the economic prosperity brought from secure long-term investment is due to the reign of anti-inflation monetarists at the Federal Reserve.

The history of money in the United States, though, is anything but stable. This country has experimented with more systems of managing its money than most. At one time a central bank issuing a central gold-backed currency was in. At another, a free market filled with many banks issuing their own currency dominated the economy. Democracy made it simple for the country to change systems. In one case, the change was decided by the tie-breaking vote of the Vice President acting in the Senate. In many cases, the swift changes of the experiments brought more pain than success as people tried to shift to the new currency endorsed by the latest group of politicians to win an election. It was only recently that the work of the Federal Reserve Bank brought stability to our currency.

The most important lesson for anyone exploring digital cash is that the marketplace can support many different currencies. The history of the United States during the Greenback era after the Civil War shows that it is not only possible but even popular among some groups. The pain and confusion were quickly tamed by efficient marketplaces for exchanging currency that were linked by the new telegraph. This allowed people to analyze the value of their cash and make adequate decisions. The flexibility also allowed the United States to afford the Civil War and pay for expansion across the country. When the country was forced back onto the gold standard, many began to scream from the pain brought by the inflexibility and lack of growth in the amount of currency. Anyone establishing a serious digital cash system should study this era in depth.

The second important lesson is that the choice of money can make winners and losers. Choosing beaver pelts as the currency of choice gives those with access to large tracts of land filled with beavers the ability to mint money. If American states chose, instead, to back a paper currency with tobacco instead of gold, then the tobacco farmers hold a central place in the economy. Gold miners are pushed into the corner of providing luxury items to satisfy people's fancy.

Of course, the choices can have deeper effects. If the currency is backed by gold and the population doubles while the supply of gold remains constant, then a severe shortage of money emerges. Gold practically doubles in value and people become reluctant to spend it because they're making so much holding on to it. The economy begins to freeze up and long-term investment in non-gold industries grinds to a halt as everyone begins to sit on their horde. On the other hand, if a new and prosperous gold mine emerges, then the flood of gold could produce widespread inflation.

Digital currency has the potential to make many winners in cyberspace. Until recently, people could not collect debts over the network. They could exchange information, but they couldn't collect payment for it. Many people gave away data, but it is not clear that it was out of the goodness of their hearts. The academics who ruled the Net at the beginning often traded on reputation. Many cast their opinions onto the Net in the hope that others would find them cool and reward them with letters of recommendation that they could trade with their Deans for higher salaries.

Digital cash will enable people to trade information in return for small payments. It will be possible to charge, say, $.10 to read a page of Web data and this might make many rich. Some Web pages already draw 10,000 visits a day. People who present good and interesting material to the network in easily accessible form will be able to create a good market in trade.

Anyone venturing out into the future of electronic trade will want to look back at the past. Here is a short collection of vignettes from the monetary history of the United States of America that is arranged in roughly chronological order. The information was largely drawn from secondary sources like John Galbraith's *Money* [Gal75], Milton Friedman's *Money Mischief* [Fri94], and many others [Mit03, Ung64, Gal75, Fri94, Hep03, Phi69, Mas68, Spa69, Ber76, Dun60]. Each vignette contains some lessons for the future holders of digital cash, and each offers a good beginning for people interested in that segment of United States history.

Wampum and Beaver Pelts

The early colonists in New England quickly discovered that the Indians placed value on small seashells. The Indians were willing to trade beaver pelts for strings of these shells known as wampum. Once people realized that the Indians were quite willing to supply nice pelts for the shells, the colonists began to trade wampum among themselves as currency to settle other debts. The government of Massachusetts even recognized wampum officially in 1641. It was ideal currency in many ways because it resisted rot. Counterfeiting was a problem because someone had somewhat arbitrarily decided that black shells were worth twice as much as white ones. Apparently, small drops of dye could change one into the other. Wampum dropped from circulation as the beavers were killed off and people realized that the Indians couldn't deliver the pelts anymore. Then the shells reverted to being just shells.

Any digital cash system could evolve in a similar way. Let's say that some company with a large stash of something pretty and universally desirable decides to go into the digital cash business. DeBeers and Co., which maintains an iron grip on the world's supply of diamonds, is one possibility. If this company offers digital cash and promises to give anyone a nice diamond if they turn in 1,000 notes, then these notes can circulate. People who like diamonds may even covet these notes.

Tobacco Reigns

Although smoking tobacco is currently frowned upon by the U.S. government, several tobacco-producing states like Maryland, Virginia and Carolina once recognized the leaf as currency. In 1642, Virginia made tobacco leaves the default currency by banning gold and silver. By 1727, the state recognized paper currency backed by tobacco as legal tender that could be used to settle debts. The tobacco leaves continued to hold sway until the U.S. government assumed power over the currency with the adoption of the Constitution.

The most attractive part of tobacco currency was its flexibility to grow and shrink with the demands of the weather. Most of the people in these colonies raised tobacco, so a man's summer labor rewarded most people fairly equally. In good weather, everyone would have plenty of cash. In bad weather, everyone would have much less. Ordinarily, bumper crops can be a curse for the farmers because the supply can swamp demand and leave the last to market penniless.

Naturally, there were problems with using a leaf for currency. In the early years, a pound of poorly raised and cured tobacco was, in theory, worth the same as a pound of the farmer's best. People often tried to trade their worst grade and horde the best, complicating exchanges and making it difficult to get enough good tobacco for a fine cigar. This problem was smoothed over when the states created tobacco warehouses that graded tobacco for quality. These warehouses would issue paper money that could be exchanged for specified grades of tobacco at any time. This enforced enough discipline to let the tobacco-based currency support solid trade in the other necessary human items.

The Americans didn't stockpile tobacco because it was pretty or shiny; they did it because the Europeans would trade them for the leaves. Ultimately, much of the tobacco went off to Europe where it was enjoyed, not kept in vaults. In some respects, America supplied leaf-based drugs to Europe then in the same way that Colombia supplies leaf-based drugs to America today. The process of physical addiction had a stabilizing effect on the marketplace. Beaver pelts could and did go out of fashion, leaving wampum holders with nothing but shells. A strong human demand for tobacco meant that people were eager to accept tobacco in payment. This addiction also kept the economy booming. There was no danger then that people would wake up one morning and wonder why they were laboring so hard for a pile of shiny metal. When the nicotine craving hit, they were already sweating.

Of course, tobacco continues to play an important role in economies. Cigarettes were a popular currency in the former Soviet Union. The Soviet government tried to stop spending the country's assets on fine-grade tobacco produced by its principle enemy, but it failed. The black market adopted the cigarettes as the currency of choice. This will fade if Russia is able to stabilize the ruble. In prisons, cigarettes are also often the most popular currency because regular U.S. bills can't be spent there.

The experience with tobacco offers digital cash magnates some important lessons. First, a currency that is closely tied to the work of many can be quite effective. If one man can generate a certain amount of cash through an honest day's work, then the economy can grow successfully when more people enter the workforce. Relatively more stable backing like land or gold can fail to provide for most people in times of rapid change.

A Penny Printed Is a Penny Earned

Benjamin Franklin continues to enjoy a reputation for thrift because he coined the expression that a penny saved is a penny earned. In reality, the man was much more pragmatic about the need for money in the colonies. He believed that paper money was a boon to all and he printed plenty of it. One edition of his newspaper even apologized for sporadic publication because the press was busy printing cash. This fact also lends new meaning to the colonialist's belief in the freedom of the press.

Paper money solved two major needs for the colonists. First, it provided a means of exchange because gold was scarce. Rapid immigration and expansion meant that there often wasn't enough gold to go around. Britain demanded payment in gold, so many colonists were pragmatic and made the decision that a bolt of nice English wool was worth more than a shiny coin–especially in the winter.

But paper money's second function was as an instrument of rebellion. At the very least, paper money caused grief for the British occupying forces who didn't want to trade in paper that had no value in England. They couldn't effectively charge taxes when all the people had to offer were piles of colonial paper money. Britain banned new issues of bills in New England in 1751 and in the rest of the colonies in 1764. When war broke out, paper money was the way for the colonies to finance their armies. The states could either impose taxes—the technique that made the British so popular—or they could simply print bills and pay the troops with them. The paper made it possible for the colonies to raise an army. Whenever a shopkeeper, a farmer, or a tradesman honored a note in payment of a debt, they were supporting the revolution.

It is entirely conceivable that someone could choose to use digital cash to try to upset a political order. Currently, printing money requires a large investment in a physical plant. This is the only way to prevent counterfeiting. Digital signatures, however, cost almost nothing to produce and they are, in current practice, impossible to counterfeit. Someone could choose to offer digital currency to the world and could succeed if he or she finds many people who choose to honor the money.

A Brave New Bimetalism

When the United States finally passed the current Constitution in 1787, the country needed to set up a monetary system. The Constitution itself banned the states from creating their own currencies and reserved this right for the federal government.

One of the minor decisions made by the new government was to issue a half-penny coin. Splitting the payment even more allowed merchants to make smaller transactions and price items more accurately. This is even more important given the amount of inflation that has occurred since that day. Micropayments are one of the goals for digital cash because they will allow small amounts to be paid for information. The best systems with the lowest transaction costs for small payments will also enlarge the economy and make it more efficient.

The half-penny was a small detail. The most important decision was to back the U.S. currency with both gold and silver. This bimetalic standard would be grist for endless debates about currency until it was effectively ended after the Civil War. At the beginning, the gold ten-dollar coin contained 247.5 grains of pure gold and the silver one-dollar coin contained 371.25 grains of pure silver. 15 ounces of silver were worth the same as one ounce of gold.

This ratio of 15:1 was enforced by the U.S. Mint, but it did not take into account the laws of nature. As supply and demand fluctuated, the relative ratio of the market prices changed. If silver became in shorter supply, its price might rise so that one ounce of gold might only buy 14.75 ounces of silver. In that case, people with 15 ounces of silver would not take them to the mint. They would trade 14.75 ounces for an ounce of gold and trade that in at the mint for gold $10 pieces.

If the market price was close to the ratio honored by the mint, then both gold and silver would circulate freely. It was too much trouble to melt down the coins for a few extra grains of precious metal. But if the market ratio moved out of line significantly, the coins made out of the expensive metal would disappear from circulation as people melted them down.

The ratio fluctuated rapidly as new gold and silver discoveries came on-line, and the U.S. government would often change the relative weights of the coins to try to bring the ratio in line with the market. This re-alignment process often brought much debate as people would choose sides based upon their interests. The debtors would endorse whatever metal was growing cheaper hoping that they would be able to pay off their debts with less work. The lenders would push for "hard" money that was contracting so as to force people to pay off their debts with more metal.

There were many theoretical arguments about bimetalism. Many economists in the 1800s argued that the constant fluctuation caused plenty of economic hardship by inducing needless coining and recoining of metal as the legal and market ratios shifted relative to each other. David Ricardo, the famous economist, argued for a single metal standard and applied some practical intelligence by investigating the current state of technology in the gold and silver mines. Ricardo thought new techniques were much more applicable to silver and thus silver production should boom bringing an erosion of value in silver. Milton Friedman notes the irony in this analysis and points out that this same technology was used to develop the Comstock lode in the 1860s and bring a flood of gold to the market. Nothing is certain, not even the gold standard.

The economists of the 1800s didn't have Friedman's hindsight, so they pushed successfully for monometalic currency. Britain embraced the gold standard and soon many followed. When the United States ended its experiment with Greenbacks, described in a later section, the

Congress chose to embrace gold but not silver. Thus, the conversion to a monometalic standard was finished.

In retrospect, though, it is easy to see many of the advantages of a bimetalic standard. Many saw the fluctuations brought about by the ebb and flow of metal from the mines as a real problem. First, one metal would be cheaper than the ratio, so people would circulate it. Then another metal would be cheaper, so it would take over the marketplace. These inefficiencies also acted as a buffer and allowed society to easily choose the most expansive currency. This is great in times of growth.

Biddle's Bank

The United States flirted with a national bank in the early years long before the Federal Reserve system emerged. The First Bank of the United States was chartered in 1791 and modeled after the Bank of England. The bank received the U.S. government's funds in deposit and brought some market discipline to the world of paper currencies. If one bank tried to avoid redeeming its paper for gold or silver, the Bank of the United States would stop accepting the rogue bank's paper. The size and political weight of the bank allowed it to enforce a fair amount of discipline.

The bank's sound money policy created two types of enemies: politicians and other banks. Thomas Jefferson argued in a letter to John Adams in 1814 that banks were filled with people "seeking to filch from the public their swindling and barren gains." Paper money, he said, had saved the Republic. Hard money benefitted the quick-witted at the expense of a burgeoning economy.

The other banks also opposed the Bank of the United States because it was such a stern influence over the money supply. Plus, it was a private bank that competed in the marketplace for loans and deposits. Its special relationship with the government made the others green. When the Bank's charter came up for renewal in 1810, the Senate narrowly voted down the bill and forced it to close.

Soon afterward, chaos emerged in the marketplace. Many banks issued currency and people were forced to anticipate the relative values of these currencies. Some banks would try to debase the value of their notes as much as possible, while others would aim for stability and permanence. Telling the difference was often hard, especially when you lived in Baltimore and needed to assess the value of notes drawn on a Pennsylvania bank.

In 1816, the country moved to create the Second Bank of the United States after the War of 1812 taught everyone the advantages of a central bank. This bank became closely associated with the name of Nicholas Biddle, who became the head of the bank in 1823. The man proved to be one of the worst advertisements for hard money. While he apparently did a good job enforcing a sound money policy, he took this job to heart and became almost belligerent. Many portrayed him as a pompous dictator.

One of the most interesting details in the bank's history was a rule in the bank's charter that required all notes to be endorsed by both the president of the bank and the cashier. Only legitimate handwritten signatures were viable. This greatly restricted the amount of paper money that could be issued in a single day, and to this day these hand-endorsed bills are collectors' items. Congress refused to grant Biddle any rest, but failed to rein him in because he simply began ordering his officers to create checks and then endorse the checks in the name of the bank. This made them just as valuable as currency and skirted around the rules.

The bank charter ended in 1836 and Congress passed legislation authorizing an extension in 1832. President Andrew Jackson vetoed the plan and used the action as proof of his populist roots. Many debates followed, but the bank was never reauthorized. Nicholas Biddle felt hurt and fought back with all of his power. He stopped lending money and brought about a recession. Although he considered this revenge, many saw it as proof of the dangerous power concentrated in a central bank. Jackson deposited the government's funds in a collection of pet banks. Soon afterwards, the country established the sub-treasury offices around the nation that acted as de facto national banks.

The most important lessons for digital cash producers from this time period are the effects of a central bank. Many forces conspired against the discipline and argued for less sound money. Even today, the Federal Reserve Bank, the modern central bank, is given plenty of pressure by some members of Congress and critics in the media.

The value of stability became obvious during the interregnum. The American public quickly learned the problems of too much flexibility in the financial system and moved to re-establish a central bank at the earliest convenience.

It is unclear how fast electronic markets could take the place of a central bank like the Banks of the United States. Clearly, the ability to rank the notes of banks and issue advisories when the notes are plummeting in value is something that can be done effectively by a marketplace for exchanging notes. The bond market is a good example of just how effective this is. Try to imagine a central bond agency that would effectively regulate the bond issues, anticipate price shifts, and punish the wrong. Only a free market can work this quickly.

The Greenback Era

Most people interested in the potential for digital cash systems will find the Greenback Era to be one of the most interesting times in U.S. monetary history. The time period began at the end of 1861 at some of the darkest moments of the Civil War. The large war deficits and the prospects for more turmoil started a run at the banks as people brought in their paper money and demanded gold bullion. At the end of the year, the banks and U.S. Treasury stopped honoring the requests.

The Secretary of Treasury, Samuel Chase, replaced the gold-backed money with legal tender treasury notes that were only theoretically redeemable at some unspecified future date. The first issue came in February of 1862 and the value of these notes quickly declined relative to the gold coins and bullion that were still in circulation. Newer batches of notes followed in June 1862 and January 1863.

The nation struggled with the profusion of notes until 1879 when the country once again began trading paper for gold. During these 18 years, the value of the paper relative to gold varied widely and often in reaction to events in the Civil War. When the North was losing, the value of U.S. paper declined in value. When it won, the paper grew closer in value to gold. Daily prices were quoted both nationally and locally and some made money conducting arbitrage between the different markets in different cities.

The resumption of the gold standard was a large political battle led, in part, by a group known as the Honest Money League. Greenback parties opposed their move, extolling the virtue of flexible money. Once the decision was made to return to full convertability, many people worried that there would be a run on gold. It was no small feat to aim the country's hopes and allay its fears of the big change. During December 1878, the value of gold and paper grew steadily closer and by January 2, 1879, few people showed up at the sub-treasury offices in lower Manhattan where the officials had arranged for large quantities of gold coins to be ready. They overprepared; in fact about $132,000 of paper was exchanged for gold, but over $400,000 of gold was converted into paper.

The experiment shows how it may be possible to create different notes that circulate. The key feature is a ready market for conversion. If there is an open and generally accessible market for converting any particular type of currency into another, then people are much more willing to accept the bills. Even if the markets fluctuate wildly according to extraneous events like the course of the war, people are still willing to trust paper currency. The true success, though, is when a large entity like the government is willing to back up the notes with some tangible item.

There was one hidden bombshell waiting in the resumption of the gold standard. The Congress had stopped minting the silver dollar in 1873. This effectively ended bimetalism and gave the loose money forces another target. After they lost out on Greenbacks, they concentrated on the remonetization of silver.

Cross of Gold

William Jennings Bryan was one of the most charismatic politicians to grace the national stage. He earned his ranks in the pantheon of monetary argument by a speech he gave on the way to the Democratic party nomination in 1896. Bryan was the spiritual leader of the prairie populists who had latched onto the demonitization of silver as the cause of all their problems. The hard-money bankers from the East were for gold and the soft-money farmers from the West yearned for the abundance of the silver pouring out of Nevada. Bryan captured the agony in campaign hyperbole:

> ...we will answer their demand for a gold standard by saying to them: You shall not press down upon the brow of labor this crown of thorns, you shall not crucify mankind upon a cross of gold.

The supply of gold was not expanding as rapidly as the economy, forcing deflation and squeezing the farmer. The hard-money supporters in the East were actually supporting deflation that helped the banks and other creditors. The demonetization of silver forced by the Greenback era took the luster off the metal. Suddenly all of the metal used for coins flooded the market. Silver, which only earlier had traded at ratios of 16:1, now was only worth as little as 30:1. Although much of this change was because of the demonetization, Bryan and his cohorts saw this as proof that the East was breaking their wallets.

Bryan won the nomination but lost the election to McKinley. The populist vote was no longer as strong. Soon after, though, the West got everything it demanded as the Treasury loosened reserve requirements on the national banks. New paper currency flowed out and relieved the demand. Currency did what the metal could not.

The emotion of this era shows some of the problems with using metal as currency. People were at the whim of natural forces. The discovery of a large silver or gold mine could shift the price dramatically. If the population surged because of immigration, deflation occurred when the mines could not keep up. Although the hardest of metallic specie seems firm and blessed by some higher standard, the arbitrary nature of mining is problematic. The supply and demand of specie makes its effects upon the economy much more ambiguous than it would appear.

Gold in the 20th Century

The gold standard that began anew in 1879 did not weather the 20th century with much sustained success. At the turn of the century, it functioned well as new mines increased the supply of the metal and cooled the ardor of the loose-money people pushing for silver. But soon the constraint proved to be limiting. When Franklin Roosevelt was elected in 1932, he immediately began arranging for bank holidays to allow the banks to handle the run on their deposits. He also banned the public from owning gold bullion. This did not technically remove the nation from the standard, but it effectively ended it for the average person.

This preserved the gold standard for many years. The U.S. government was able to honor its obligations to those who presented their paper and the other central banks around the globe. The ease changed with economic times. In the 1950s, the booming U.S. economy led the world and that led many to buy into the dollar. In the 1960s, the rest of the world began recovering and this led to an outflow. Soon the markets roiled, ebbed, and flowed with news from around the world. Moving bars of metal was an extremely inefficient way to balance currencies. In 1971, the United States stopped converting its Federal Reserve Notes into gold and free-floating dollars began.

Although many would like to believe that the dollar is not backed by anything real right now, that is far from the truth. There are many very efficient and honest markets for supplying other currencies and commodities. As long as someone can buy, say, 200 metric tons of wheat in several seconds with things called dollars, people will be happy with them.

Conclusions

These descriptions of some of the various experiments with various forms of money are just an indication of how creative the people in the United States have been with money over time. Many of these switches and changes have been the result of battles between different groups and interests. To a large extent, free and efficient markets and the general support of a monetarist Federal Reserve Bank have alleviated much of this turmoil. The markets move so quickly that many farmers, for instance, buy and sell futures in their crops today instead of sitting around growsing about Eastern monetary interests.

But it is best not to forget the anxiety. One of the best examples that conveys the depth of the populist interest in money is the story of *The Wizard of Oz*. Recently, Hugh Rockoff of Rutgers University wrote a long article that drew very interesting parallels between the now classic story and the skirmishes over free silver that roiled the nation at the end of the 19th century [Roc90]. Rockoff makes a very convincing argument that L. Frank Baum's story was a deep allegory about the turmoil.

The equation is simple. Kansas is the center of the heartland and the battle for control of its money is retold as the battle of good Dorothy to survive the slings and arrows of the often outrageous battle over what constitutes a fortune. Here are some of the parallels that Rockoff offers:

Oz Oz is short for Ounce, a reference to the East where "an ounce of gold has almost mystical significance."

Silver Slippers In the book, Dorothy and the Wicked Witch of the West battle for control of silver slippers. They were changed to ruby slippers by Hollywood, perhaps to take advantage of the new color film. (Or was it to cover up the controversy?) Note that all that Dorothy needs to do to return to her native bliss is to click the silver shoes three times.

Dorothy Everything good about America is captured in Dorothy. The evil forces are always trying to keep her, her silver slippers, and her 100-proof goodness from returning to the heartland.

Toto Rockoff suggests that Toto represents the Teetotaling party, which supported free silver and campaigned against free alcohol.

Wicked Witch of the East The Kansas tornado of the free silver movement rises out of nowhere to hold the nation in thrall. The wicked hard-money folks of the East are the first victims of this movement.

Yellow Brick Road Gold is stored as yellow bricks.

Emerald City Naturally, Washington D.C. is the Emerald City. There were some in the 1890s who urged Washington to start public works projects and pay for them with Greenbacks. When Dorothy and her allegories of economic advisors arrive at the city, they must wear green-lensed glasses held onto the head with a gold buckle. Money dominates everything in this city.

Wizard of Oz Marcus Hanna, a Republican party leader, financier, and a major force behind McKinley.

Wicked Witch of the West McKinley himself, who is dominating the West and subjugating all of its people. Note that in the book, the Witch of the West has a gold cap that grants wishes. She uses this to command the Winged Monkeys to go after Dorothy and recover control of the shoes. McKinley ultimately defeated William Jennings Bryan in the election of 1896 and kept America on the gold standard.

The Cowardly Lion William Jennings Bryan, who roared about free silver during the campaign of 1896 and then moved on to other topics.

The allegory is not perfect, and there are some holes in Rockoff's analysis that he notes. But the overall analysis argues that Baum was trying to illustrate the battle over the control over free silver for the people. In the end Dorothy, good Dorothy, keeps the slippers and uses them to carry herself back to Kansas. When she arrives, the shoes are gone but all is well. The Free Silver movement also disappeared after new discoveries of gold brought about the monetary expansion that the populists wanted.

Rockoff also quotes liberally from many of the speeches of William Jennings Bryan that lend much credence to his analysis. Bryan often gave detailed monetary arguments for silver on the campaign trail. The public was obviously very excited about this topic and it clearly dominated the news in the way that health care or Social Security issues permeate the present day. An allegory about bimetalism was as appropriate for a general audience as it would be to create an allegory for genetic engineering for a present-day audience and call it, say, "Jurassic Park."

It is unclear whether monetary discussions will ever inflame America in the same way. But digital cash and the battles of anonymity and government control have the potential to start long battles. Many forces are already agitating for privacy. Other problems may increase if and when stable, convertible elements of currency start floating about the Net outside of the reach of the tax collectors. When this happens, the arguments over what is money, who controls the money supply, and what money people must use may grow more heated than they've ever been. Who knows what literature they will spawn?

Chapter 27

Future Cash

The future of fast-flowing digital money is essentially here. I've already sold materials over the Internet using the First Virtual system. It took me only several minutes to extend my bank and credit card accounts into the digital domain using this system. Others should find it just as easy.

For the near term, most of the commerce on the Internet will be dominated by electronic versions of credit cards and debit cards. Most of the technological work will go into developing the cryptographic infrastructure to support the secure exchange of credit card numbers. The concrete protocols described in this book are excellent solutions to these problems and it won't be long before they dominate the Net.

It is important not to underestimate the advantages that digital signatures offer to create unforgeable signatures and add some real nonrepudiation to the mix. In many ways, digital signatures are better than regular signatures. They can't be forged by someone with skill who uses another signature as a model. They can be forged, though, if someone is able to steal a copy of the person's private key. If good precautions are taken against hackers, then even this avenue should be more secure.

The U.S. government is showing new flexibility in export control by allowing systems like CyberCash to flow out of the country. The officials seem willing to grant an export license to software that doesn't allow arbitrary secret messages. The CyberCash software would only scramble credit card numbers. Smart criminals might see a hole here where information could travel through a covert channel. James Bamford, for instance, tells the story of some criminals who tried to thwart the FBI by sending a message in their weekly cleaning. The data was hidden in the number of shirts and their color.

Token- versus Account-Based Money

As this book has shown, there are two main approaches to digital money. "Account-based" money stores value in the ledger of a trusted third party like a bank. Money is exchanged by subtracting the amount from one entry and adding it to another. "Token-based" money revolves around unforgeable packets of bits that are traded like pieces of paper money or coins. Whoever possesses the packet of bits owns them.

The first wave of systems on the Net will almost certainly be account-based money that is kept by a central computer. The credit card business is already largely computerized, the companies have a presence everywhere in the world, and it is relatively simple for them to embrace the networks.

Digital token-based money may take longer to emerge. There are numerous problems that must be resolved. Double spending is a serious technical problem that can be constrained if complicated cryptographic protocols are used by all parties. The complexity, though, can be solved with a team of programmers. The political problems of token-based cash are even larger. Governments and police departments are growing increasingly fond of tracking the flow of money through the economy. Token-based money seems scary because it is just the digital equivalent of those suitcases full of bills exchanged in drug deals. It seems simpler to have a third party like a bank keeping track of the transactions in their ledger. There is someone for the police to interrogate and subpoena. But the ease of auditing can be an illusion. Many of the Savings and Loans lost a fortune in the late 1980s and it was often difficult to establish who took the money. Accounting systems have loopholes and smart people can mask transactions very successfully. Some accounting systems may be better than nothing, but they are far from perfect.

It is important not to forget the advantages of token-based money. Autonomous software agents are bound to become popular on the network and it would be nice if they could pay their way wherever they go. Sending an agent out with a fixed supply of cash is preferable to sending out an agent with a credit card number. It is just more secure because it limits losses. A credit-card-bearing agent could run into an endless loop that would run the card number up to the limit quickly. A malicious host could replay the incoming agent time and again while taking payment for the action. If it were questioned, it would blame the network's e-mail system for delivering the agent over and over again. Agents bearing Chaumian token-like digital cash would hit their limit when the cash was gone. A replay attack would not work because each bill can only be spent once.

There are some defenses that can be used with an account-based system to prevent these problems. Visa already offers cards with fairly complicated profiles for spending. A card owner might arrange that only x dollars could be spent per day on the account. Or it might prevent y dollars from being spent at a particular merchant over any period. Clearly, these procedures could be made arbitrarily complex and halt many problems with giving a software agent a copy of your credit card number. But it is also clear that there are many limitations. What if suddenly you want your agent to spend more than y dollars at a particular site? You would need to call up the credit card company and adjust the spending profile. This is a pain. Token-based cash is still easier to use in this situation.

In the long run, many companies may begin adopting token-like digital cash technology to issue tickets, coupons, vouchers, and other items that shouldn't be counterfeited. Token cash would be preferable because it would alleviate the problems of maintaining accounts for people. This bookkeeping hassle might reveal some usable marketing data, but it could also drive everyone nuts. It is much easier to broadcast tokens and coupons than it is to open up accounts for everyone.

Anonymity in the Future

The debate over anonymous digital cash does not promise to have the same passion as the debate over encryption. While everyone understands the need for personal secrets, it is not as obvious that the need for encryption extends to the region of commerce. This is largely because the balance is different. Encrypted communications are obviously useful for everyone. They protect both private thoughts and important information with economic value. It's as much a defense against crime as a cover for criminals operating in camera.

Anonymous cash, on the other hand, does not seem to have many legitimate uses. Most business records in this country are kept secret, but they're still kept. Taxpaying imposes extensive recordkeeping requirements. Those who seek to live outside of the country's institutional memory are usually up to something shady.

But even though anonymous cash seems more shady than regular encryption-enhanced privacy, it still has legitimate uses. One of the best examples is in the financial markets, where people are constantly gaming against each other in a complex market.

The Barings Bank collapse in early 1995 is a good example of the danger of a non-anonymous market. Nick Leeson was widely portrayed in the media as the one man who brought the bank to its knees. The one detail, though, that is left out of everyone's calculus of blame is the very non-anonymous feature of the Osaka marketplace. Several people were quoted in the press as saying that they knew that Barings had a huge position and they couldn't figure out what it was up to.

This knowledge can be powerful. The futures and options exchanges are zero-sum games. All of the money that Barings lost was won by someone else. The futures and options exchanges also have margin requirements that force contract holders to put up some fraction of the contract value to guard against loss. If the loss grows, the contract holder often gets a margin call that requires it to pony up even more money to cover the loss. If the holder doesn't have the money, its position is liquidated and it's all over.

Imagine that someone at Barings bet the wrong way and found themselves with a large position that was close to their margin call limit. Now imagine that all of the other big players in the market knew about this position and figured out that they were going to get all of the money if Barings faced a margin call. They could enter the market selling just enough shares to force a margin call. Whammo. All of Barings would be theirs.

While I don't know if this is what happened, it should be obvious that anonymous markets would have been more honest. If the competitors didn't know about a large, open position then they wouldn't be tempted to try to shift the market in a favorable direction.

Another piece of evidence for the value of anonymous markets is the Reuters Instinet. This system matches up buyers and sellers of stocks in much the same way that the specialists do it. The key feature, though, of the system is its anonymity. Large buyers and sellers can cloak their efforts to protect against people ganging up against them. The Wall Street Journal wrote about the system [WSJ94], "Large investors, who wish to keep their long or short positions confidential, especially want to avoid tipping other investors off about their bets in the volatile, mostly small-capitalization over-the-counter market."

The anonymity offered by the system is certainly not complete. A record is kept of all the transactions made at settlement and this record could almost certainly be unwound to track insider trading. But for the most part, this record is kept secret from everyone in the marketplace. The result is a fairer and more reasonable system for everyone participating.

Although most people don't participate in free-floating market-places like the stock market, they often enter into deals where secrecy and anonymity are important. Acquiring large parcels of real estate must be done with stealth because people may raise their price if they know that someone is seeking to build a large parcel out of many contiguous smaller plots.

There are also very personal reasons for anonymous transactions. People often use personal details for political gain. The life of Clarence Thomas is a good example. During his confirmation hearings, baseless rumors circulated freely that people in the media had recovered his video rental records and these records showed a taste for salacious material. Later, some journalists claimed to have a source that saw *Playboy* magazines in his apartment. Despite the fact that this material was legal and probably endorsed and embraced by many of Thomas's enemies, the press entertained these rumors. These actions are good examples of how records of purely legal, above-board transactions could be used against people in the future.

It is important to realize that *Playboy* was more widely circulated during the 1970s than it is during the time when this book is being written. It is entirely plausible that someone arguing about digital cash in the 1970s might not see how a transaction record of *Playboy* magazine purchases might be used against someone. They did not see the future strength of the women's movement or the conservative movement.

There are many other examples of the need for anonymity in the political realm. Abortion is a hot-button issue for many Americans. When one party is in power, it pushes to constrain access to abortion clinics. When the other party is in power, it aims to make access as simple as possible. It is easy to imagine a future where protesting at abortion clinics might be viewed as a sign of instability and dangerous, revolutionary thoughts. It is just as easy to imagine public hearings where people who performed or got abortions were portrayed as being heartless and irresponsible.

There is no easy way to determine how to track many actions in the gray zone. The police may rightly argue that the vast compilation of details about a person are only used against the bad people. Even if we assume that the police will be uniform and perfectly judicious, the problem is that no one can predict what will become "bad" in the future. Tyranny and power require information to suppress people.

What Is Money?

For much of the 20th century, the Federal Reserve Bank tried to estimate the amount of money available to the population. They hoped to use this gauge to indicate the potential for inflation because too much money chasing too few goods drives up prices. The bank created several sophisticated ways of counting the amount of money in the country. First they totaled up all of the money deposited in banks. Then they started adding in credit card debt and other forms of consumer debt. In the '50s, '60s, and '70s, these large numbers seemed very official and certain.

These values are all but worthless today. There are now so many different ways that people store value that the Federal Reserve Bank is practically giving up on estimating the amount of money out there. In a recent set of hearings held before Congress, the Chairman of the Federal Reserve Board, Alan Greenspan, said he was watching the price of gold and other commodities to give him some indication of the direction the winds of the economy were blowing.

I am just an average, middle-class American, but it is easy for me to hold currency that is backed by more than the full faith and credit of the United States government. A quick survey of my assets shows that they're backed by almost anything but. Here's a short list:

Apple Computers One credit card gives me a kickback of 5% that I can apply toward the purchase of Apple Computers. The "dollars" that build up are nontransferable and to some extent I've already paid for them. The merchants pay a premium for clearing the transaction through a credit card and they must pass this cost on to the card holder.

The "dollars" are great for people who are true believers in the MacOS, but they are worthless for MS Windows users in much the same way that books are worthless to people who can't read. But if Microsoft or IBM succeed in driving Apple out of business, then the "dollars" are worthless.

Ford Cars Automobiles are great. Another credit card kicks back 5% of the purchases into an account that can be used to buy a new Ford. If you use the card to purchase Texaco gas, then you get 10% back.

How do you place a value on these assets? Are they better for the car company or the consumer? These "dollars" are a serious incentive to look at Ford cars and trucks when you need a new car. A company can't buy better brand loyalty than this. A consumer, though, is caught holding "dollars" that are backed in Ford cars. This is great if you like the cars, but it could be frustrating if General Motors develops a zippy car that grabs your heart.

Latin American Debt When President Clinton and the Department of the Treasury decided to shore up Mexico by guaranteeing its debt, many people criticized it as a way to bail out Wall Street. While there is no doubt that many white-shoe firms in Manhattan found themselves backing a Mexican economy that wasn't performing up to expectations, there are many Americans on Main Street in a similar bind. The mutual funds allow many average people to join together and buy localized securities. Many invest as little as $500.

To most people, the funds are simply bank accounts. The statements show up with dollar values. They can trade money in and out with ease. But they aren't really holding "dollars," as many investors in Latin American funds discovered. They're holding a mixture of local stocks and bonds that are often valued in local currencies. Their "dollars" weren't backed by the full faith and credit of the U.S. government—that is, until the Department of Treasury stepped in and offered the Mexican government their guarantee.

Frequent Flyer Miles These are emerging as bigger and better currencies with each passing day. The *Wall Street Journal* reported (July

7, 1995, pg B6) that people now launder their miles. Apparently, American Express will give out airline miles to cardholders who participate in their "Membership Miles." But they won't give out miles in American or United. Some people have figured out how to launder the "miles." American Express participates with several hotel chains, including Sheraton, and Sheraton's "miles" are convertable into miles from American or United. Unfortunately, the *Journal* reports that the miles are not directly convertable. 10,000 Sheraton miles buys 5,000 American miles.

Gold Some people actually buy gold coins. Others invest their money in gold mining stocks that rise and fall with the price of gold. There are also different futures contracts that someone can use to invest in gold.

Commodities Many people might subscribe to the standard viewpoint of economists and believe that the salary amount isn't important, it's the buying power. Aside from the pleasure of knowing that you're a millionaire, keeping your money in a basket of goods is a great idea. Who cares if gold goes up to $1,000,000 an ounce if a loaf of bread costs $1,000,000,000?

There are numerous ways that a mutual fund could be created that tracked a basket of basic commodities like wheat, oil, corn, and beef. Goldman Sachs maintains an index of commodity values. Futures contracts can be bought and sold against this index. A mutual fund could create an indexed fund that traded in this market and offered shares that tracked the index. Although I don't know of any fund that does this, there is no reason why it couldn't be done successfully.

Each of these is a good way for someone to hold money that is backed by something else. Although the money may still be denominated in dollars, its value is determined by the underlying asset that provides its foundation. If Latin American debt proves to be valuable, then the shares in a Latin American fund grow in value.

The digital cash algorithms developed in this book are just the beginning. If any of the mutual funds adopted these algorithms, they could begin to offer ways for people to trade the securities over the Internet. There would be no need to move through a broker unless you wanted the accuracy of a market price. Some companies might choose to offer digital cash–based securities simply to open themselves up to a larger market. Corporate financial officers would be less beholden to the investment banks that make markets for their stocks. Companies could issue securities and make their own markets without the services of an investment bank.

The opportunities don't need to be limited to stocks. Imagine, for instance, that Apple allowed people to trade the dollars on their credit card with each other. In one view, this would hurt Apple because they hope to get people to buy their computers, and the credit card "dollars" are just a coupon-like discount program. In another view, the more freely the Apple "dollars" flow, the more people will buy their machines. If they are subsidizing the Apple "dollars" through their promotional budget, then free-flowing cash equivalents of Apple "dollars" are a net loss for them. If they're issuing the Apple "dollars" at cost, then they could care less if people traded them among themselves.

There are big advantages to getting people to trade your currency and hold it as valuable. If people kept their savings in Apple "dollars," then Apple would be able to invest this value in their manufacturing and new product design. The holders of Apple "dollars" would win because they would be able to buy newer, bigger, and better machines with their "dollars." Apple itself would win because it was able to raise capital for less. This is the glorious life of the creator of the reserve currency of choice.

There are downsides. If the reserve currency creator slips, the fall can come faster. In 1995, the U.S. dollar slipped to historic lows against the German mark and the Japanese yen. Many suggested that this was because people were pulling their savings out of dollars and placing it in other currencies. All of the reserves were disappearing and the U.S. dollar faithful paid the price.

In the future, many entities will be able to roll their own currency and push it on the market. For the most successful, it will be an opportunity to raise capital and flourish. For the consumer, it will mean more complicated and difficult decisions. For the future reserve currency king, it will mean a position of unbelievable power. Welcome to the future of free-flowing currencies.

Chapter 28

Card Trader 2010

And now a flash from the future:

Here is the list of top baseball properties offered in the July 2010 catalog of Morgan Stanley Rose, a top financial and memorabilia firm formed when then mere investment bank Morgan Stanley merged with Pete Rose's baseball memorabilia empire. The firm issues a new catalog each day offering some of the latest sports cards and other classic memorabilia on the market. The electronic catalog is read widely by both individual fans and the major industrial-class investors like the California Pension system because investing in memorabilia is one of the preferred ways for people to save for the future.

The boom in trading cards and related memorabilia began in the late 1990s when digital cash technology made it possible for many people to issue digital trading cards that were easy to trade electronically but impossible to counterfeit. Digital marketplaces sprung up on the Internet. The baseball players, sensing another money-making opportunity, cooperated by encouraging the trade and issuing new cards themselves. The novelty, quality, and flexibility of this method of trading quickly encouraged a new burst of trading. Many baseball pundits credit the boom as the final force that erased the bitter ambivalence of the fans that dominated the sport after the 1994 strike.

Many of the early cards were simple TIFF or GIF files that were given individual serial numbers and signed by the player's personal PGP keys. A few forward-thinking, technical players offered them to commemorate spectacular catches, particularly long balls or stunning slides into home plate. These cards emerged largely from the computers of the players' agents who saw this as a chance for the players to emphasize their individual contributions and build their star power without waiting for the media or the team management to recognize them.

One of the first cards issued that now trades for over $1.27 million showed Orville Alsace face in the dirt while somehow catching a ball with an outstretched glove. When Alsace made the catch, he was a rookie stuck on a left-field platoon with three other rookies and one 41-year-old comeback kid. There were only 400 of the initial cards issued and Alsace sold them for only $2.00 a piece, but the stunning picture soon captured the hearts of many. Illicit copies were common but Alsace was smart or lucky enough to create unforgeable copies with the then-nascent digital cash technology.

Soon after the card swept the nation and rose in price to $10,000, the managers smelled a bankable star and gave him a permanent spot in the rotation. Their intuition was correct because Alsace signed endorsement contracts for a major acne-fighting cleanser, a tooth whitener, and a very popular, gross-out bandage firm that printed pictures of infected, festering wounds on the backs of bandages.

The financial community first entered the digital trading card market by accident. Several banks issued mutual funds that invested their cash in digitized trading cards and these proved popular with small-time card traders who didn't feel knowledgeable enough to assess the value of the cards. These funds proved popular, especially after they returned an average yield of over 20% over the years.

The boom began when the investment banks moved in and began to issue sophisticated trading cards that offered much more than just an image. One of the first bundled cards appeared with a picture of Alberto Carmichael and a promise to pay the card holder of record $100 for every home run Carmichael hit during the year. Carmichael financed the card by signing a contract with an incentive clause paying him for each home run. Although the press immediately assumed that the bundled card was a gimmick, they later discovered that Carmichael hit upon the card as a way of buying a 1,500 acre horse farm. He used the proceeds from the card sales to buy the farm at the beginning of the season instead of waiting until the end of the season when the incentive pay was finally granted.

Luckily for him and the bundled card industry, he hit a career-high 52 home runs that year and made everyone happy. At the beginning of the season, the cards were trading at about $3,100, which was in line with his career average 31 home runs over the previous six seasons. The price had jumped to about $3,900 around the all-star break when it became obvious that Carmichael was having a strong year. A bout of tendonitis in August sent the value of the cards plummenting until he recovered after a week and slugged a three-run home run in the first inning after returning to the game. Rumors whispered that the tendonitis had ulterior motives, but no proof was ever offered and the rumors died down after Carmichael hit six home runs in the week before Labor Day.

The bundled card market exploded as players dreamed up new and better ways for cards to be created. The financial markets quickly adapted mathematical tools like the Black-Sholes option model to predict the value of some cards. Soon electronic marketplaces like the one provided by Morgan Stanley Rose emerged and provided the public with a liquid marketplace ready to adapt to quickly changing scores.

Here are some of the most interesting "cards" being offered in the daily electronic tearsheet offered by Morgan Stanley Rose on July 12th, 2010:

Bob Boskins Error-Free Card Boskin created the first "error-free" baseball card in 2004 as a way to emphasize his commitment to the fans. For the last six years, he's issued 10,000 cards that offer to pay the holder $10.00 per error he commits over the year. "When each error costs you $100,000, you're motivated," he says. The 2010 edition of the card features the shortstop leaping high in the air to catch a line drive. Many of the purchasers are fans who are hedging their bets on the performance of the team. The current asking price of $31 shows that the market is expecting two more errors from the man.

Franco "Po" Seiden Clairvoyance Card Seiden is a manager who occasionally gets through a game without getting ejected. Rumor is that the owner was going to fire the man when he realized that the winning percentage went up significantly in the games in which Seiden was ejected. When the team slumped during Seiden's mandatory "vacation" to the Hillary Clinton Clinic for Micromanagers Anonymous, the owner decided not to mess with karma and bought Seiden's explanation that he manages clairvoyantly. The owner hedged his bet, though, by forcing Seiden to issue these cards that pay off two percentage points of his salary for every game that the teams ends up behind the league leader. The card shows a beautiful split illustration of Seiden meditating in the showers while the team star, Boomer Bohanson, blasts a three-run homer into the left bleachers. Current asking prices of $122 reflect a belief that Seiden will keep the team to within six games of the leader.

Johnny Villanell First Birthday Ticket Fans throughout the world cried when Francie Villanell gave birth four months prematurely. The heartache grew as the baby struggled and the hospital bills exploded. After three months, the bills ran to over $2 million, a substantial sum for a second-year outfielder who made only $200,000 a year. When the fans heard that the owner had purchased a health insurance program for the players that stopped paying at $200,000, they cried. Finally, friends issued this ticket for the first birthday party to be held at the stadium. $40.00 buys a gorgeous GIF of the Villanell family as well as admittance to the first birthday party.

Harry "Ha-Ha" Hanrihan Holocard Not a hologram, but a three-dimensional movie of him catching the fly ball that ended the 2009 World Series. You can use the latest extension of the Apple VR technology to view the scene from any angle. Special encryption software limits the use to only machines with proper licenses. A classic collectors item that is sure to increase in value because Hanrihan issued only 5,000. The current asking price of $127 represents a 53% rise from the original price.

Albany Civic Card Set A full set of the 100-card set that Albany issued to merchants to underscore the civic effects of the baseball team. The town gained a major league team in 2006 when the league expanded to an even 128 teams and faced major civic opposition from the beginning. The team tried repeatedly to get the civic government to build a new stadium without ever winning a single vote from the town council. The team threatened to move, but the council wisely realized that there were no cities left without a team.

The team hit upon the idea of issuing digital cards with images of the players and giving them a face value of $10.00. They asked all the restaurant owners, sporting good memorabilia vendors, and the box office to try giving away the cards as change. The team sold the cards to the merchants for $10.00 and offered to redeem the cards for $10.00 or a $12.00 bleacher ticket. Many people were skeptical about accepting the cards, but the fans persisted.

The notes initially circulated rather freely until collectors began snapping up the cards and pulling them from circulation. The team followed up with a second edition. This is a complete collection of the 100 cards in the original set issued. The asking price of $1,500 is supported by the team's outstanding offer to redeem the cards for $10.00 apiece.

Chapter 29

Other Voices

This chapter explores two facets of regulation. Banks are conservative companies regulated by conservative government agencies. Digital transaction mechanisms, however, are new and may face some resistance. The first section explores generic regulation while the second focuses on privacy. Both use interviews to expand the book.

Regulation

Banking in the United States is one of the most heavily regulated industries, in large part because the federal government offers to insure the deposits of many individuals. If a bank goes down, the government makes good on the deposits. In return for this insurance, the banks agree to careful scrutiny of all their activity.

The scope of this banking regulation may turn out to be one of the most important factors for determining what succeeds and what fails in the American marketplace. Each scheme may be subject to different types of regulation, and the openness of the regulators to change may control how quickly a bank will be able to enter into the marketplace.

For instance, the Millicent system (see Chapter 19) only issues merchant-specific scrip, and this may avoid many regulations designed to control the emergence of a secondary currency. Other systems like DigiCash, however, offer electronic dollars that must be controlled by the people who control all bank deposits.

This book is not a book about banking regulation and I know hardly anything about the legal mechanisms in place because I'm not trained as a lawyer. In order to provide some insight into the domain, I've sat down with Tom Vartanian, a lawyer with plenty of experience in banking regulation.

Thomas P. Vartanian is the managing partner of the Washington, DC, office of the law firm of Fried, Frank, Harris, Shriver & Jacobson and the Chairman of its Corporate Department and Financial Institutions Practice. He was formerly General Counsel of the Federal Home Loan Bank Board and the Federal Savings and Loan Insurance Corporation and prior to that was Special Assistant to the Chief Counsel of the Office of the Comptroller of the Currency. He is a member of the Editorial Advisory Board of the Electronic Banking and Commerce Report. He recently testified before the Federal Deposit Insurance Corporation on stored-value cards and other electronic payment systems. He is a member of the Technical Advisory Committee of the Virginia House of Delegates dealing with digital signatures. A collection of his articles on electronic banking and commerce can be found on the World Wide Web at the 21st Century Banking Alert Page at `http://www.ffhsj.com/bancmail/bancpage.html`.

Q.   Banking is one of the most regulated industries in the country. But new technology often means bending or even breaking old patterns. How open are existing U.S. regulations to change?

A.   As technology, the Internet, and the uses and boundaries of cyberspace expand exponentially, the traditional business of financial intermediation will be challenged. Electronic commerce will change the way that money is saved, invested, and transmitted, which in turn, will affect the essence of the payment system. The changes that electronic commerce will impose upon banks will be the most significant and sweeping changes of the 20th century. The current regulatory system in the United States is pervasive, but because so much of what banks can do is in the hands of federal regulators, the system can react to change without the need for Congress to change laws. In that regard, during the last year, both the Office of the Comptroller of the Currency (OCC), which regulates national banks, and the Federal Reserve Board (FRB), which regulates bank holding companies, have invited banks to request on a case-by-case basis a broadening of permissible banking activities, apparently to ensure the banking industry can remain competitive as electronic commerce gains consumer acceptance and as non-banks develop new products that could reduce bank dominance over the payment system. The results so far are encouraging for banks.

In August 1996, the OCC ruled that a subsidiary of a national bank could act as an Internet service provider for persons who were not customers of the bank. In November, it adopted a major change to its rules governing operating subsidiaries of national banks so that such subsidiaries will be able to conduct activities and businesses that are broader than those legally available to a national bank. Similarly, in a series of orders issued during 1996, the FRB has been receptive to bank holding company technology ventures. In September 1996, it proposed to allow non-bank subsidiaries of bank holding companies engaged in data processing or management consulting activities to obtain up to 30 percent of their revenue from activities that were not financial in nature. Currently, federal regulations do not allow any revenue to be derived from such non-financial activities.

In sum, I see the banking regulators encouraging banks and bank holding companies to think outside of the narrow regulatory box that they are so used to and to expand their horizons so that they will remain relevant to the consumers of the 21st century.

Q. What is the official difference between a "bank" and a non-bank company like Fidelity Investments, Merrill Lynch or American Express?

A. The technical difference between these entities is the ability of banks to accept actual deposits that are insured by the Federal Deposit Insurance Corporation (FDIC). In return for FDIC insurance, a bank, its holding company, and its affiliates become subject to extensive federal regulation, examination, and supervision, which do not apply to non-bank organizations and which limit the activities and businesses that the bank may conduct. Unlike regulated banks, non-bank organizations (other than savings institutions and credit unions, which are also generally subject to extensive federal regulation) do not have access to the payment system. Non-bank organizations, such as money market and mutual funds, while operating without the benefit of deposit insurance, have been able to position themselves as effective alternatives to depository institutions for consumers. Non-banks have also become very effective competitors for both consumer and commercial loans. Thus, in the real world, the differences between banks and non-banks are eroding.

Q. Will the distinction between banks and non-banks become even more blurred as technology enhances the nature and delivery systems of financial products and services?

A.   Yes. With, for example, the increased acceptance of stored-value products such as phone cards issued by non-bank entities, and the deployment of smart cards by consortiums of non-bank entities such as transit systems and major retailers, banking consumers may become increasingly comfortable with the absence of banks in their everyday financial transactions. Ultimately, if non-bank firms provide consumers with the capability to move funds by computer and by card in a system that operates independent of and parallel to the existing bank payments system, the line between banks and non-banks will be altered significantly.

Q.   As these lines become blurred, will banking regulations be expanded to include entities that offer bank-like deposit and payment products?

A.   Almost all states have laws prohibiting non-licensed banks from engaging in the business of banking. Many of these states also have laws licensing money transmitters, but it remains to be seen how well these laws correspond to the market-driven development of electronic "banking" and commerce. At the same time, a relatively obscure provision of the Glass Steagall Act generally prohibits non-regulated entities from accepting deposits.

The Payments System Task Force of the American Bankers Association recently issued a report recommending that in order to avoid systemic disruptions of the payment system, the issuance of stored value that is freely transferable among parties beyond the natural limitations of a stored system should be limited to depository institutions. Similar concerns have also been voiced by Federal Reserve System officials.

On the other hand, the FDIC's recent guidance on the deposit insurance treatment of stored-value cards effectively recommends that both insured and non-insured institutions might issue stored-value products when it is determined that insured institutions could structure their stored-value products as either insured deposits or as non-insured instruments. Financial products and services, as well as the mood of regulators and Congress, are generally moving in the direction of a system where companies that are engaged in an expanded range of financial activities are permitted to enjoy the privileges of regulation as long as they submit themselves to the obligations and responsibilities of it. So while this may open up the range of entities that can offer banking-type services and products, it should not expose the new system that develops to greater risk of loss of money or confidence.

Q. Banks often complain about unfair competition by those who lie outside of the reach of the banking regulators. What are the greatest non-bank commercial threats to banks today?

A. This point can be addressed from two different perspectives. As we discussed, banks have largely lost their dominant market position in regard to lending and investments by consumers. Their remaining strongholds are the payment system and the high degree of trust that they hold with consumers. If non-banks can infiltrate the payment system and do so in a way that will establish the same level of trust with consumers, banks may find their last bastion of dominance threatened. The question is whether non-banks who are not pervasively regulated can effectively maintain the public trust that is necessary to the operation of a safe and sound depository and payments system.

The fundamental threat is encompassed by Bill Gates' comment about banks being dinosaurs. His comments suggest that banks will become passive financial intermediaries that merely act as transmitters of technology supplied by non-bank computer companies. But given their privileged role in moving consumers' money, can individual banks or joint ventures controlled by banks control and drive the development and implementation of electronic banking and commerce systems? The answer to this question is likely to have a great impact on what type of business banking becomes in the early part of the next century.

Q. The Stamp Payments Act of 1862 banned the use of private currency under one dollar in value. Was there a good reason for this then? Do any of these reasons apply today?

A. At the time, the issuance of small-denomination paper currency or tokens by merchants was a response to a severe shortage of government-issued coins in circulation. The economists and politicians of the day considered this practice to contribute to inflation and wanted to eliminate it. Whatever the merit of their view at the time, it has little to do with today's economy. Nevertheless, the law, which could raise significant issues in regard to micropayment systems, remains in force today. The Treasury Department appears to agree with our analysis and recently recommended that innovators of electronic money seek guidance from the Attorney General regarding the extent to which the Act may apply to developing electronic payment systems.

Q.   Should the Federal Reserve System issue its own electronic currency or is this something best handled by the private sector?

A.   This question raises an interesting issue. We all accept the Federal Reserve as the sole source of paper currency and the U.S. Mint as the sole source of coins. Yet, it seems likely that private entities will continue to "print" or "mint" electronic money that is transferable in cyberspace. I think that three issues will drive the question of whether a new form of the Stamp Payments Act will impose a new government monopoly over the creation of electronic money.

First, will the government conclude that its ability to influence monetary policy is significantly threatened by the extent to which private entities can create electronic money? Second, will the government and the private sector jointly conclude that security concerns regarding the potential counterfeiting of electronic money are so significant that the safety of the banking and commerce system require government regulation of the creation and transmittal of electronic money? Third, will law enforcement agencies persuade the government that it must control the movement of electronic money and prevent it from becoming a potent and essentially untraceable means of financing criminal activities?

Q.   Deposit insurance is one of the most visible features of banking regulatory policy for consumers. How important do you think it will be to any electronic banking systems?

A.   Where small values are involved, such as with small-denomination stored-value cards, it seems unlikely that deposit insurance will be an important consideration to consumers. Nevertheless, as consumers venture into using electronic payment products either on a card or on a computer, and the amounts and volume of money moved electronically increases, they are likely to be more comfortable doing so through a product that is offered through a bank or that in some way carries deposit insurance. This may be as much a function of the trust factor consumers associate with banks as any application of deposit insurance to electronic value.

Q.   Regulation E places the responsibility for detecting fraud on the bank's shoulders by generally limiting a consumer's exposure to loss to $50. Do you think that this is an effective model for future electronic systems?

A.   The changes that will occur in the banking business will be broad and require a reevaluation of how the business will be conducted in the 21st century. At the same time, it is time for regulators to consider a new approach to financial regulation that does not carry the baggage of traditional financial intermediation in the real world. The regulation of technology in cyberspace, where even the identification of parties presents enormous new challenges, must be zero-based so as to focus on the fundamental public policies that the government will need to foster. Clearly, any new regulatory policies, particularly as they affect the protection of consumers, will initially dovetail the remarkable safety nets that U.S. depositors, savers, and investors have traditionally enjoyed.

The Federal Reserve Board's general approach in its Regulation E proposal to largely limit the applicability of the regulation to small-denomination stored-value cards, those under $100, may be a reasonable compromise between the interests of issuers and consumers.

Privacy

Much of the debate about electronic digital payment systems revolves around the tension over what this will do to the social compact between the government and the people. Some worry that untraceable cash that flows freely through the network will allow illicit lifestyles to flourish. Others are afraid that the state could emerge with too much power to invade our privacy once it is able to track all of our purchases.

In order to expand the scope of the book, I interviewed two people on different sides of the debate. One, Dave Banisar, is a policy analyst for the Electronic Privacy Information Center, a public-interest group devoted to campaigning for privacy rights. He recently co-authored *Spies, Codes and Wiretaps: Documents on the Battle for Privacy on the Information Superhighway* (John Wiley and Sons, 1995) with Bruce Schneier. He has a degree in law from the Catholic University of America in Washington, DC.

On the other side is Stewart Baker, the former general counsel for the National Security Agency, an intelligence agency with the mission to provide electronic intelligence to the government and the military. Now he's a partner at Steptoe and Johnson, a law firm in Washington, DC.

Q & A with Dave Banisar

Q: Why do you think that people need to have privacy? Not just to prevent fraud, but what are the larger reasons?

A: I think privacy is necessary for both personal and economic reasons. They're intertwined. People are generally uncomfortable about being completely accountable for everything they do. They want to feel that they have a little space in which they can exist and learn and experiment without having to justify everything they say, do, and think. Justice Louis Brandeis described it in 1928 as "The right to be left alone, the most comprehensive of rights, and the right most cherished by civilized men."

Financial privacy enters into this in a number of ways. You can go into a bookstore today and buy a controversial book, a *Playboy*, or whatever you want to read and then hand the clerk a $20 bill and walk away. Nobody knows except you and the clerk that you've purchased this, and the clerk probably doesn't know your identity. If you were forced to disclose your identity for each and every transaction, it would discourage a lot of more innovative or nonconformist thinking. People would be concerned about that knowledge coming out.

Q: One recent book about Clarence Thomas alleged that he purchased *Playboy*. In the past, the magazine was more generally accepted. It certainly was one of the first to publish major black journalists.

A: Sometime things are accepted now and in ten years from now they'll be looked at with horror. In the 60s, everyone smoked pot. Now it's looked at as a flaw in your character.

Imagine that one of the anti-abortion groups got ahold of the credit card records of abortion clinics? I can see the same thing happening with other issues. How about Salman Rushdie's book? Wouldn't it be useful for Muslim extremists to know who bought the book? You could target one person and make an example of them. Small segments of the population could really kill off the publishing industry or any other kind of group supporting a view that they oppose. Controversial books generate profits and animosity, but people buy them because they do not generally believe there will be any chance of retribution. That is all changing in the electronic era.

Q: Do you think the credit card companies can protect people's privacy?

A: Even the NSA admits that there is no such thing as perfect security in any computer database. The best they can do is minimize the risks to an acceptable level. But in large distributed databases with large numbers of authorized users, it is extremely hard to do. In the last few years, they caught a number of individuals making a living off of selling data from some of the most sensitive databases, including those run by the FBI, IRS, and Social Security administration. Countless others were never caught.

Credit card companies certainly should be concerned about their customer's privacy. If they fail to protect it, they stand to lose a lot of business to someone who can or to straight cash sales. American Express had made a big deal out of hiring away a senior person at the U.S. Office of Consumer affairs two years ago to create a privacy project. After a year, they closed the office and she became another lobbyist for Amex and quit. It doesn't appear that they learned much from her. They certainly didn't do a good job when they were subpoenaed by the Philip Morris Tobacco company and they turned over the records of ABC reporters—without even challenging the subpoena like all the other organizations that received the same notice did. They then provided records on spending going back seven years—well beyond what the subpoena required. They also gave the records of six other reporters who were not even involved in the subpoena, including some at other newspapers such as the *Wall Street Journal*. If I were ABC, I would cancel all my Amex accounts and move them somewhere else.

Since that incident, Mastercard has started a large survey on customer privacy. I expect that it will show a large interest in privacy among card holders [PT95].

Q: Have there been instances when banks have released information about their clients?

A: Bank confidentiality is almost nonexistent these days. The release of information happens all the time. If you read Jeff Rothfeder's *Privacy for Sale*, he talks about how police and private detectives have access to records through friends, shared passwords, or other loose systems. Many laws require the disclosure of info.

Q: So it's not like a phone tap with a warrant?

A: In the Right to Financial Privacy Act, the threshold is extremely low. The banks rarely challenge the requests. They respond to several thousand each year and that number has increased sharply in the last five years.

Banks are also required to collect and routinely provide a large amount of information on transactions under the Bank Secrecy Act, a

very misnamed law. They have to report large cash transactions to the
Treasury Department.

Plus, there's a blurring line between banks, mutual funds companies, and information-providing businesses. Banks want to get into the
information-providing business. They see a real market for credit analysis and marketing data about their clients. Now Bankers Trust also
wants to get into the key escrow business and hold your encryption
keys in case you or the federal government needs them.

Q: They're getting plenty of information right now?

A: Plenty, and the danger is that a lot of financial information is not
really in any kind of context that can be used to properly evaluate
it. If you go to a grocery store and buy a pack of cigarettes, then an
insurance company might interpret this to mean that you're a smoker
and raise your rates. But you could have bought them for a neighbor
or a friend.

Q: And the laws don't stop them?

A: The law has done a poor job at keeping up with new technologies. The marketers have been very effective at only allowing laws
that cover very small segments, such as video records, from passing
and preventing the enactment of broad privacy principles such as the
Europeans and Canadians have enacted.

In addition, the bars to some behavior just are not that efficient.
That's why systems like Chaum's are important to provide anonymity
from the beginning.

Q: What about money laundering?

A: I find the whole money-laundering argument to be a real red
herring. It seems to be driven by law enforcement officials with an
insatiable desire for information about everyone. Certainly the number
of money launderers out there cannot be that high. Should it justify
that everyone's privacy be wiped out?

I also don't believe that it will wire out the tax system. The fact
is that almost all money that is collected for taxes is done from an
employer before you get your paycheck. Organizations of all sizes have
to keep transaction records describing payments. This only leaves the
underground economy, which will find new ways of payment, such
as diamonds, gold, etc., that don't have serial numbers.

In addition, the proposed system attempts to balance many of
these concerns. The basic Chaum system only provides anonymity of
the purchase. The money starts out in the bank account of the customer

and ends up in the bank account of the merchant. Both have names. They just don't know who bought the widget or what the money was for.

Q: Let's say that they have complete transaction trails of everything you've done. What could they do?

A: Anybody could compile very detailed dossiers about people at very low cost. You could compile such a file today, but it wouldn't be worth it in most cases. I see them developing routine dossiers on people and who knows how someone would use them to gain power. Someone might watch dirty movies. Someone might read nonconformist books that your boss might not like.

Q: Imagine all of this power in the hands of the characters of *Melrose Place*. Think of the schemes that they could work out.

A: That might be a bit extreme. But who knows how the information could be taken out of context. Just knowing who smokes cigarettes could keep health insurance costs down.

Q: What do you think about Al Capone? They couldn't get him for what he did, but they got him for tax evasion. The movie *The Untouchables* embellished the actual record. The books weren't encrypted. How would they get him in a world of digital cash?

A: He ran a cash business back then. They followed him around then and they could send someone around to watch him today. They would probably get more information that way, too.

Q & A with Stewart Baker

Q: What is the great danger of anonymous cash?

A: Anonymous digital cash poses the same dangers as ordinary cash, but it adds to those dangers by giving criminals the convenience of digital payment systems. Right now, cash allows drug dealers to move large amounts of money around without the police being able to trace the organization and its customers. It allows people to carry on illegal businesses and to conduct illegal transactions anonymously.

But physical cash poses problems for really big criminal enterprises. It's unwieldy. Bills over $100 are rare, and even $100 bills are not that common. Doing a $1 million illicit transaction in twenties is awkward. Some drug rings have had to fill plastic garbage bags with bills and weigh them rather than count them in order to conduct cash transactions quickly and conveniently. Today, few legitimate businesses deal in cash in that quantity, so the difficulty of using physical cash for big money transfers does help the police identify criminal activity.

If digital anonymous cash catches on for large transfers, many of the problems crooks have faced in using physical cash will disappear. Even enormous sums can be put on smart cards or other digital forms and carried in a shirt pocket. So some investigative tools now used to identify criminal activities will be eliminated by the advent of digital anonymous cash.

Q: Gangsters have been dealing in cash for ages. What peace will we gain from total transaction records?

A: While anonymous digital cash poses some risks to law enforcement, traceable digital payment systems could have real law enforcement benefits. If all transactions can be traced, it will be possible to identify everyone who had dealings with, say, a Cali cartel kingpin or a terrorist.

At the same time, we have to recognize that this kind of total enforcement opportunity may make it possible to enforce laws that the community may not really want enforced that strictly. In some communities, small marijuana purchases or discreet prostitution may not be pursued as a practical matter even though they remain illegal. If all payments can be traced, however, it will be possible to identify all the customers of a small-time dealer or prostitute. How can society deal with this issue? Not by trying to destroy government's ability to trace all transactions, I would suggest, but by taking a second look at its enforcement policy more generally.

To understand this point, just imagine a world in which a speeding ticket is issued automatically every time your car exceeds the speed limit. If it were deployed, such a technology would probably lead both to more tickets and to an increase in the speed limit. The same thing could happen with respect to other minor crimes that can be traced through payment records. We will be forced to ask whether we really want to enforce all of the laws we have on the books.

Q: Encryption is obviously a very useful way for people to protect their interests from criminal elements. Is there any similar advantage for anonymous financial transactions?

A: The case for completely anonymous cash is much weaker than the case for good encryption, in my view. Anonymous digital cash is not necessarily a protection against crime. While you might be mugged for real cash and even for anonymous digital cash, you aren't likely to be mugged for your credit card or for traceable cash, so a lack of anonymity can prevent criminal attacks on law-abiding citizens.

Similarly, traceable cash will provide a receipt and cash flow record that could protect users against defective merchandise and fraud. It's true, however, that anonymity may protect the privacy of certain purchases, and some law-abiding citizens will want that privacy protected at all costs. We don't want crooks to be able to guess our income or competitors to be able to guess our business strategy by getting easy access to our expenditure records.

Probably the answer to this concern is legal protection for the privacy of expenditure records, or a technical fix that makes tracing payments difficult for private actors but not impossible for the government acting with a warrant.

Q: Money is very fungible. Can we really expect to trace cash flows successfully? Fairly?

A: In many cases, some kind of tracking will be essential to detect double spending. There's nothing easier to duplicate than bits (just ask the Software Publishers Association and their piracy hotline). If such a tracking system must be maintained to prevent forgery, tracing for law enforcement purposes can be accomplished with similar expense.

Q: Can we convince a jury?

A: Sure. Especially once ordinary people get used to the idea that they dont need to keep receipts anymore because they can track purchases electronically. Today the government regularly builds criminal tax evasion cases by showing that the defendant's purchases exceeded his declared income for prolonged periods. If juries accept that kind of accounting analysis, using the results of digital payment records will be a piece of cake.

Q: Tax law is notoriously complex and many major companies are practically in constant audit. Figuring out what happened with the money and determining if the transactions are fair is often close to impossible—even when accurate audit trails exist. Will we be able to detect money laundering and show something illegal "beyond a shadow of a doubt?"

A: Tax audits are often not the same as financial audits, in which the question is where the money went. Tax audits are often about whether the claimed tax treatment of expenses or income is justified by supporting evidence (not whether you had lunch with your brother-in-law, but whether you discussed business; not whether you went to Hawaii, but whether the trip had a business purpose, etc.).

Payment tracing may not help resolve such disputes. There may even be sophisticated money-laundering schemes that escape prosecution because bare payment records don't reveal the purpose of the scheme. But remember that money laundering becomes much harder as records get better. The point of laundering is to give cash received in criminal activities a new and apparently legitimate origin. Businesses that take in a lot of cash are great laundering opportunities. But if the cash can be traced, it is much harder to get away with such simple laundering tactics as doubling a business's actual daily revenue.

Finally, don't assume that traceable cash will only be used to crack financial crimes. Imagine the value to the FBI of being able to quickly determine whose cash was used to rent the Oklahoma City bombing truck and to trace other payments from the same card or person both backward and forward in time, or to look for other purchases by other persons that follow the same geographic and chronological pattern as Timothy McVeigh's.

Q: Do the money transaction laws place seductive pressures on the banking and securities industry? The drug trade and its enormous profits have often corrupted some parts of the police force. Is the corrupting influence of money laundering a problem for the banking industry?

A: There have certainly been prosecutions of members of the financial industry for money laundering. No profession is immune from temptation.

Q: Right now, there are stories that the police apply a certain amount of financial intelligence against the drug trade. For instance, it's been said that they gain access to the sales records of grow lamps and then set out after the best customers. This is certainly clever detective work, but do imperfect transactions records implicate too many innocent people?

A: I have yet to hear of an illegal or unwarranted arrest of some honest but enthusiastic indoor gardener based on such information-gathering. At best, such detective work can only provide leads. No one is likely to be convicted based on such evidence alone. Since the police and prosecutors want convictions, not just arrests, they are almost certain to use such information mainly to help them focus their investigations and to begin the process of looking for more evidence. And while no one is enthusiastic about the idea that buying too many grow lights could attract the attention of the authorities, it's easy to think of situations where we'd be glad to have the police follow up on legitimate purchases. (Wouldn't you feel better knowing that someone was taking a look at non-farmers who buy tons of fertilizer and fuel oil, to take one example?)

Appendix A

Digital Cash Patents

This is a sample of the abstracts of some U.S. patents that might affect the plans of some creators of digital cash. The collection was created by searching through several of the major U.S. classes of interest (380/23, 380/25, and 380/30). The selection should not be viewed as comprehensive nor as a substitute for a directed search.

3938095 Computer responsive postage meter

Frank T. Check, Jr. and Alton B. Eckert, Jr. and Bruce E. Hinman and Howell A. Jones, Jr. and Raymond R. Lupkas and Robert B. McFiggans

A high-volume mailing installation is disclosed in which the output of a programmable high-speed electronic digital computer provides destination and postage amount information, a high-speed chain printer driven by the computer prints the destination information on address labels, and an authorized postage printing meter is mounted piggyback fashion on the chain printer and responds to the same computer for automatic printing of authorized postage impressions of the calculated amount on the same mailing labels. The meter includes a fast, rugged solenoid-actuated segmented flat bed postage printer unit and fixed-program electronic digital postal accounting circuitry, with appropriate security features to prevent or detect postal fraud.

3990558 Method and apparatus for preparing and assessing payment documents
Kurt Ehrat

A method and apparatus is described for preparing and assessing machine-readable payment documents such as bank or postal checks to avoid fraud. The checks are prepared by enciphering the serial number and the amount for which the check is made out with secret code data to provide a crypto number which is printed on the check with the serial number and the amount. The check is assessed as valid by reading out the printed data and enciphering the amount and serial number with the same secret code data as used when preparing the check to provide a crypto number which is compared with the crypto number read from the check. If the two crypto numbers are the same, the check is assessed as valid.

The crypto number can be derived from additional data such as the credit card number of the person making out the check, the time and date, and the number of the machine preparing the document.

4253158 System for securing postage printing transactions
Robert B. McFiggans

A postage meter includes printing and accounting stations interconnected through an insecure communications link. Each time the meter is tripped, a number generator at the printing station is activated to generate a number signal, which is encrypted to provide an unpredictable result. The number signal is also transmitted to the accounting station. At the accounting station the postage to be printed is accounted for and the number signal is encrypted to provide a reply signal. The reply signal is transmitted to the printing station where a comparator compares it with the encryption result generated at the printing station. An equality of the encryption result and the reply signal indicates that the postage to be printed has been accounted for and the printer is activated.

4376299 Data center for remote postage meter recharging system having physically secure encrypting apparatus and employing encrypted seed number signals
Ronald L. Rivest

A data center for remote postage meter recharging receives resetting signal information to reset a remotely located postage meter. The remotely located postage meter has signal information stored therein for use in recharging the meter with additional postage in conjunction with a signal information received from the data center and entered into the meter. The data center includes a sealed unit for processing received resetting signal information and encrypted signal information stored at the data center outside of the sealed unit. The stored encrypted signal information at the data center is equivalent to the signal information stored in the remotely located postage meter. The sealed unit includes a decrypter for decrypting the encrypted signal information so that it may be combined with the resetting signal information to generate a signal for use in resetting the remotely located postage meter. The sealed unit also includes an encrypter for encrypting information to provide updated encrypted signal information to be stored at the data center outside of the sealed unit for use when the remotely located postage meter is again to be reset with additional postage.

4423415 Non-counterfeitable document system
Robert N. Goldman

A system is disclosed for authenticating an object on the basis of certain physical phenomena or character, specifically, measurable, but not practicably duplicable random variations in the object. In one form, the object (authenticator (T)) is a paper tag having a reference space (14), the varying translucency pattern of which is a measurable but practicably unduplicable characteristic of the paper. The reference space (14) is sensed to provide reference signals indicative of the varying translucency. A reference numeral (10) is then provided from some registered form, as on the tag or in a list. If the numeral (10) is readily accessible, it likely will be cryptographically encoded. Note the value of putting encoded information on the tag to avoid the need for large reference files.

  For verification, freshly sensed reference signals, as from the tag (T) (actually characteristic of the tag) are compared with signals that previously were sensed as characteristic of the tag (T). Structures are disclosed as specific forms of the authenticator (T), along with apparatus for authenticator production, detection and manipulation. Different forms of tags (210) are disclosed, the measurable characteristic of which involves light transmissivity and reflectivity. Apparatus (111) for spectrographic confirmation of tag material is also disclosed. In an illustrative form of a tag (T) as an identification means, tags and processing apparatus utilize magnetic medium (218) and printed images (214). The magnetic medium is also disclosed to be recorded as for developing information on shelf life and sales channels.

4757537 System for detecting unaccounted for printing in a value printing system
George B. Edelmann and Arno Muller

A system for detecting fraudulent imprints on documents is disclosed. The system comprises a metering device, a host, and a verifying facility. The metering device provides a validation signal to the host and its associated printer. Thereafter, the printer prints information which includes information from the validation signal. Thereafter the information printed on a mailpiece can be validated at the verifying facility by detecting the validation information provided by the metering device. The system provides a method to make a secure metering device without an integral printer. This value printing system provides for a secure system that will allow for the detection of fraudulent imprints at a verifying facility.

4759064 Blind unanticipated signature systems
David L. Chaum

An improved blind signature system not requiring computation during blinding for anticipating which of a plurality of possible signatures will be made during signing, while still allowing the blinding party to unblind and recover the unanticipated kind of signature on what was blinded. An exemplary embodiment blinds by forming a product including a plurality of generators raised to powers normally secret from the signing party, and unblinds by forming a product with the multiplicative inverse of a signed form of the generators raised to the original powers. Re-blinding allows a signature on a value to be transformed into a signature on a particular blinded form of the value.

4775246 System for detecting unaccounted for printing in a value printing system
George B. Edelmann and Kevin D. Hunter and Arno Muller and Alfred C. Schmidt, Jr.

A system for detecting fraudulent imprints on documents is disclosed. The system comprises a metering device, a host, and a verifying facility. The metering device provides a validation signal to the host and its associated printer. Thereafter, the printer prints information which includes information from the validation signal. Thereafter the information printed on a mailpiece can be validated at the verifying facility by detecting the validation information provided by the metering device. The system provides a method to make a secure metering device without an integral printer. This value printing system provides for a secure system that will allow for the detection of fraudulent imprints at a verifying facility.

4796193 Postage payment system where accounting for postage payment occurs at a time subsequent to the printing of the postage and employing a visual marking imprinted on the mailpiece to show that accounting has occurred
David E. Pitchenik

A system for maintaining the security of user postal funding charges and allowing accurate accounting of delivery charges includes the step of an apparatus for printing on a mailpiece or type at the originating station value to cover delivery charges along with encrypted validation information which is later employed to account for postage funds, particularly at the time of delivery. A visual marking is imprinted on the mailpiece at the time of accounting to show that accounting has occurred. The mail deliverer can rely on the visual indication for assurance that processing and accounting has occurred.

4802218 Automated transaction system
Christopher B. Wright and Stephen Bristow

An automated transaction system employs a card maintaining an account balance and a terminal for dispensing an article of value and debiting the card's balance. The card has a secure, resident microprocessor which executes an interactive handshake recognition procedure with a secure, resident microprocessor in the value-dispensing section of the terminal prior to actuating a requested transaction. In the preferred form, the handshake procedure operates by an exchange of encrypted words between the card microprocessor and the dispenser microprocessor using corresponding encryption algorithms and a secret key number, and the card microprocessor providing a command signal to the dispenser microprocessor only upon successful completion of the procedure.

The automated transaction system is particularly suitable as a postage metering terminal having a postmark printer as the value-dispensing section. Postage is printed only if the handshake procedure is executed between the card microprocessor and the printer microprocessor. The postal terminal also receives a rate card for computing postage automatically, and prints an invisible authentication mark along with the postmark to discourage counterfeiting. The terminal can be configured to print standard form waybills for postal and private carrier services by loading waybill information from an IC ROM services card. The balance in the user card is refilled in a refilling terminal using a master card which maintains a master account balance and a supervisor card which is in the custody of an authorized person.

4873645 Secure postage dispensing system
Kevin D. Hunter and Robert T. Durst, Jr. and Jose Pastor

A secure postage dispensing system is provided, which comprises: apparatus for receiving mailing information including a list of addresses, wherein the list is associated with a number of mail pieces to be sent and information indicative of the postage due for the mail pieces; structure for calculating the total postage required for the mail pieces; and structure for establishing communication with a funds control center, which is adapted to receive the total postage and the total number of mail pieces to be mailed and includes instrumentalities for effecting a funds transfer in the amount of the total postage to a carrier service and, upon completion of such funds transfer, returning a cryptographic key and a batch identifier. In addition, the dispensing system includes apparatus for using said cryptographic key to provide a unique encrypted number for each address in the list of addresses, and apparatus for outputting the list of addresses with each address having the unique encrypted number appended thereto.

4885777 Electronic transaction system
Kazuo Takaragi and Ryoichi Sasaki and Takayoshi Shiraishi and Nobuhiro Kurashiki

An electronic transaction in which in order to improve a reliability of message certification by digital signature and enable the use of the digital signature in a formal transaction in place of conventional signature or seal, the following procedures are implemented utilizing the fact that, in a public-key cryptograph system represented by an RSA system, a first encoded message derived by encoding a first decoded message by using a public key of a first transacting party is equal to a second encoded message derived by encoding a second decoded message by using a public key of a second transacting party: (a) Check sender/receiver; (b) Add content certification function; (c) Double check the person by the possession of a secret key and the response by a terminal; (d) Add a grace period to the electronic seal; and (e) Send back a tally impression from the receiver to the sender.

4914698 One-show blind signature systems
David Chaum

Numbers standing for cash money can be spent only one time each, otherwise the account from which they were withdrawn would be revealed. More generally, a technique for issuing and showing blind digital signatures ensures that if they are shown responsive to different challanges, then certain information their signer ensures they contain will be revealed and can be recovered efficiently. Some embodiments allow the signatures to be unconditionally untraceable if shown no more than once. Extensions allow values to be encoded in the signatures when they are shown, and for change on unshown value to be obtained in a form that is aggregated and untraceable.

4926480 Card-computer moderated systems
David Chaum

A user controlled card computer C and communicating tamper-resistant part T are disclosed that conduct secure transactions with an external system S. All communication between T and S is moderated by C, who is able to prevent T and S from leaking any message or pre-arranged signals to each other. Additionally, S can verify that T is in immediate physical proximity. Even though S receives public-key digital signatures through C that are checkable using public keys whose corresponding private keys are known only to a unique T, S is unable to learn which transactions involve which T. It is also possible for S to allow strictly limited messages to be communicated securely between S and T.

4934846 Franking system
Dennis T. Gilham

A method of franking mail items is disclosed in which the franking impression includes a machine-readable portion and a visually readable portion. The machine-readable portion comprises a data block including at least a postage charge and a pseudo-random number, and the data block is encrypted prior to printing. During printing of the franking impression, at least a part of the machine-readable portion is read and compared with the data block intended to be printed. If the comparison is satisfactory, the printing operation is continued to print the visually readable portion. The pseudo-random number is changed for each franking transaction, which may be each item or batch of items. The machine-readable portion is read at a mail handling centre to provide an input to a postage charging and accounting function.

04947430 Undeniable signature systems
David L. Chaum

Cryptographic methods and apparatus for forming, checking, blinding, and unblinding of undeniable signatures are disclosed. The validity of such signatures is based on public keys and they are formed by a signing party with access to a corresponding private key, much as with public-key digital signatures. A difference is that whereas public-key digital signatures can be checked by anyone using the corresponding public key, the validity of undeniable signatures is in general checked by a protocol conducted between a checking party and the signing party. During such a protocol, the signing party may improperly try to deny the validity of a valid signature, but the checking party will be able to detect this with substantially high probability. In case the signing party is not improperly performing the protocol, the checking party is further able to determine with high probability whether or not the signature validly corresponds to the intended message and public key. Blinding can be used while obtaining undeniable signatures, while providing them to other parties, and while checking their validity.

4949380 Returned-value blind signature systems
David Chaum

A payer party obtains from a signer party by a blind signature system a first public-key digital signature having a first value in a withdrawal transaction; the payer reduces the value of the first signature obtained from the first value to a second value and provides this reduced-value form of the signature to the signer in a payment transaction; the signer returns a second digital signature to the payer by a blind signature system in online consummation of the payment transaction; the payer derives from the first and the second signature a third signature having a value increased corresponding to the magnitude of the difference between the first and the second values. Furthermore, the following additional features are provided: payments are unlinkable to withdrawals; a shop between the payer and signer can be kept from obtaining more value than desired by the payer; the first value need not be revealed to the signer or intermediary in the payment transaction; the returned difference can be accumulated across multiple payment transactions; and the returned difference can be divided between a plurality of payment transactions.

4962531 Transaction system comprising one or more host exchanges and a number of distributed terminal stations
Wilhelmus H. M. Sipman and Lambertus Snel

A transaction system comprises terminal stations which can communicate with a host exchange. In order to improve the communication, concentrators are arranged between the host exchange and the terminal stations. Given functions can be accommodated within the concentrators so that they need not be provided in the terminal station. The concentrators as well as the terminal stations are provided with a security box in order to realize encryption/decryption of the data transport; for the terminal station this box is preferably realized in the form of a smart card which acts as an operator identification element. A customer can identify himself by means of a user identification element, for example, a magstripe card or a further smart card. The encryption mechanism is preferably DES.

4984270 Method and system for transmission of financial data
Jack LaBounty

An improved system for transmission of financial data includes, in preferred embodiments, an encryption key stored on a bank card and used to encrypt preselected data prior to transmission. Encrypted data is then transmitted through all intermediate computers without decryption and reencryption. Decryption occurs only at the final destination, where the encryption key has been stored. In preferred embodiments, the encryption key is combined with a terminal identification value to provide further security.

4991210 Unpredictable blind signature systems
David L. Chaum

Blind signature systems secure against chosen message attack are disclosed. Multiple candidate original messages can be accommodated. Each of plural candidates in the final signature can be marked by the party issuing the signature in a way that is unmodifiable by the party receiving the signatures. The exponents on the candidates in the final signature need not be predictable by either party. In some embodiments, these exponents are not at all or are only partly determined by the candidates in the signature shown. Single candidate signatures are also accommodated.

5017766 Portable electronic apparatus capable of confirming validity of transaction data
Masuo Tamada and Tsutomu Tanaka and Hideo Matsuoka

In an IC card having an update function, transaction data, account type, supplementary amount, and valid date are input to the IC card. The IC card adds a renewal number data held therein to the input transaction data, and the data is encrypted using key data, thus generating reference confirmation data. Input confirmation data is generated using the identical encryption generation algorithm by a host system of a credit company. The input confirmation data is supplied to the IC card. A comparison means in the IC card compares the input confirmation data with the generated reference confirmation data. As a result of the comparison, if these data coincide each other, the input data is stored in the memory in the IC card as new transaction data and update processing is executed.

5018196 Method for electronic transaction with digital signature
Kazuo Takaragi and Ryoichi Sasaki

A mediation can be requested to a computer connected to a communications network when transacting parties A and B effect an electronic transaction and trouble takes place during the transaction. The transaction is effected by a procedure where the transacting party B transmits its preliminary digital signature to the transacting party A. When the transacting party B agrees with the contract document M transacting part A has submitted, the transacting parties A and B exchange their formal signature with each other. These signatures are obtained by coding data including a hash total h(M) obtained by transforming the contract document M, identifiers of the transacting parties A and B, and a data identifier indicating whether the data are prepared for the preliminary or the formal signature by the public-key cryptosystem using a secret key for one of the transaction parties. When trouble takes place, the mediation organization decodes the signatures submitted by the transacting parties as evidence by using a public key and checks as the basic of h(M) and the identifiers of the transacting parties whether the evidence data concern the same transaction or not. Finally, it decides the sort of the signatures based on the data identifiers and deduces a conclusion of the mediation.

5048085 Transaction system security method and apparatus
Dennis G. Abraham and Steven G. Aden and Todd W. Arnold and Steven W. Neckyfarow and William S. Rohland

An improved security system is disclosed which uses an IC card to enhance the security functions involving component authentication, user verification, user authorization and access control, protection of message secrecy and integrity, management of cryptographic keys, and auditability. Both the security method and the apparatus for embodying these functions across a total system or network using a common cryptographic architecture are disclosed. Authorization to perform these functions in the various security component device nodes in the network can be distributed to the various nodes at which they will be executed in order to personalize the use of the components.

5131039 Optionally moderated transaction systems
David Chaum

A tamper-resistant part is disclosed that can conduct transactions with an external system through a moderating user-controlled computer or that can on other occasions be brought into direct connection with the external system. In the moderated configuration, the moderating computer is able to ensure that certain transactions with the external system are unlinkable to each other. In the unmoderated configuration, the tamper-resistant part can also ensure the unlinkability of certain transactions. Also testing configurations are disclosed that allow improper functioning of the tamper-resistant part, such as that which could link transactions, to be detected by user-controlled equipment. Another testing configuration can detect improper functioning of an external system that could, for instance, obtain linking information from a tamper-resistant part.

5181786 Method and apparatus for producing admission tickets
Hendrik W. Hujink

Method and apparatus for producing admission tickets that feature electromagnetically stored and detectable information and also visual information that contains, at least partly, identification data of the holder of the admission ticket, wherein the electromagnetically detectable information and the visual information are provided on separate carriers and wherein the separate carriers are placed in an, at least, partly transparent completely sealed sleeve. Admission tickets (14") are produced by a central processing unit (1), a video camera (2) linked with the central processing unit, and a dispenser (3) linked with the central processing unit. The dispenser has a printer for printing an image, recorded by the video camera (2), on a suitable carrier (17), which image has been converted by the central processing unit (1) into electric control signals. A magazine (4) holes a number of electromagnetically programmable responders (14), and a programming device is controlled by the processing unit (1). The dispenser (3) further places a transparent, completely sealed sleeve (8, 30) around a responder (14) and a carrier (17) featuring a printed image together.

5233657 Method for franking postal matter and device for carrying out the method

Stephan Gunther

A method for franking postal matter uses an apparatus of a postage user having franking functions and being coupled through telecommunication devices with a remote data processing center for recording and releasing postage. A terminal device of a telecommunication system installed at a location of a user is coupled with a data processing center associated with a postage service for settling postage through telecommunications connections. Data is transmitted to the data processing center in one direction for requesting a central recordation of postage and for generating franking data. At least essential portions of a franking image corresponding to the requested franking are transmitted in another direction. The franking image is completed in the terminal device with stored image portions. A device for franking postal matter includes a terminal device of a postage user. The terminal device performs franking functions. A two-way telecommunication input device couples the terminal device with a remote data processing center for recording and releasing postage. The terminal device has a printer, a coding device for securing the two-way communication with cryptographic encoding, and a safety device for preventing counterfeiting of a franking imprint.

5241600 Verification system for credit or bank card or the like

W. Daniel Hillis

A verification system for verifying authorized use of a credit or bank card or other identification card. The verification system makes use of an image embossed on or laminated onto a card, and information stored on a magnetic strip or other storage arrangement laminated onto or otherwise affixed to the card. The information stored on the card is related to the image embossed on the card. A card reader reads the image and generates information defining the image. In addition, the card reader reads the information and compares it to the image signature to determine if they conform. Further use of the card may be based on the degree of comparison between the information read from the card and the image signature.

5267314 **Secure transaction system and method utilized therein**
Leon Stambler

A transaction system is disclosed wherein, when a transaction, document, or thing needs to be authenticated, information associated with one or more of the parties involved is coded together to produce a joint code. This joint code is then utilized to code information relevant to the transaction, document, or record, in order to produce a variable authentication number (VAN) at the initiation of the transaction. This VAN is thereafter associated with the transaction and is recorded on the document or thing, along with the original information that was coded. During subsequent stages of the transaction, only parties capable of reconstructing the joint code will be able to uncode the VAN properly in order to re-derive the information. The joint code serves to authenticate the parties, and the comparison of the re-derived information against the information recorded on the document serves to authenticate the accuracy of that information.

5276737 **Fair cryptosystems and methods of use**
Silvio Micali

A method, using a public-key cryptosystem, for enabling a predetermined entity to monitor communications of users suspected of unlawful activities while protecting the privacy of law-abiding users, wherein each user is assigned a pair of matching secret and public keys. According to the method, each user's secret key is broken into shares. Then, each user provides a plurality of "trustees" pieces of information. The pieces of information provided to each trustee enable that trustee to verify that such information includes a "share" of a secret key of some given public key. Each trustee can verify that the pieces of information provided include a share of the secret key without interaction with any other trustee or by sending messages to the user. Upon a predetermined request or condition, e.g., a court order authorizing the entity to monitor the communications of a user suspected of unlawful activity, the trustees reveal to the entity the shares of the secret key of such user. This enables the entity to reconstruct the secret key and monitor the suspect user's communications.

5310999 Secure toll collection system for moving vehicles
David M. Claus and Kevin D. Murphy and Marjorie E. Taylor

A secure toll payment system is realized by transmitting a changeable encryption code from roadside equipment at a toll plaza to a moving vehicle. Thereafter, the moving vehicle uses it to encrypt payment information according to the Data Encryption Standard algorithm. The moving vehicle transmits the encrypted payment information to the roadside equipment, which performs a credit or debit transaction. Because the encryption code changes from time to time, so too does the nature of the signal which is transmitted by the vehicle; and fraud, based on electronic eavesdropping, is substantially eliminated. The encryption code comprises an 8-bit random number and a time/date number. Vehicle-mounted apparatus includes a transponder unit and a portable smart card which inserts therein. The roadside equipment includes a pair of spaced-apart antennas that are sequentially located along an express payment lane at a toll plaza and a computer (Plaza Server) which controls them.

5311594 Fraud protection for card transactions
Arno A. Penzias

The problems of fraud in card transactions can be reduced by, after requiring the person engaged in the card transaction to initially identify himself, such as by supplying a card number, a) requesting, the person to supply as authentication information either 1) a randomly selected piece of prestored information or 2) information derived from a randomly selected piece of prestored information; and b) completing the transaction only if the authentication information requested is correctly supplied. The authentication information requested is described in terms of its nature, i.e., what it represents, so that one cannot deduce from the request the correct response without knowing the selected prestored piece of information. Since the authentication information is randomly determined for each card transaction, a thief will rarely, if ever, be able to successfully complete a card transaction simply by supplying, in response to a request, the same piece of authentication information last supplied by the authorized person. Each authorized person already knows the particular pieces of information that are prestored for him, e.g., birthdate of spouse, year of school graduation, and mother's telephone number. Thus, he need exert no extra effort to remember them. If the pieces of prestored authentication information are various numbers, they may be transmitted over a telephone network from a caller to the authorization system using currently available dial pads and DTMF signaling.

5317636 Method and apparatus for securing credit card transactions
Gerardo Vizcaino

This disclosure relates to a method and apparatus for improving the security of credit card transactions. It involves a so-called "smart" credit card, which includes a processor, a memory, and a display window. When used, the card produces a verification number, which is based on a transaction sequence number and an encryption algorithm stored in the memory of the card. The verification number produced by the card is read in the display window and transmitted to a verification computer. The computer uses the verification number, together with a de-encryption algorithm, to produce a computed transaction sequence number. If the computed transaction sequence number corresponds to a transaction sequence number stored in the memory of the computer, then the computer will authorize the transaction; otherwise, it will not. Both the card and computer change their respective transaction sequence numbers, such as by incrementation, so that different transaction sequence numbers are stored in the respective memories, for the production of a different verification number for the next transaction.

5321751 Method and apparatus for credit card verification
Lawrence A. Ray and Richard N. Ellson

Techniques for multiple verification of credit cards incorporating digital image information and authorization data onto a credit card to assist in the card verification process. This technique requires the authorized card holder to have a picture identification accompany the application for the card. Picture information is converted to a digital image that is stored and used in one or a plurality of means for verifying that the presenter of the card, at the point of the transaction, is the authorized user. Such means include visual comparison of card presenter and extracted digital image information and verification that the data has not been altered. Encryption of the data, as it is read from the card, at the point of origin is used to formulate encoded authorization data that is then compared against like encoded authorized card holder data stored at a centrally located database.

5325431 Looking and listening fee collection system for pay broadcasting

Kazuaki Naruse

A looking and listening fee collection system for satellite broadcasting of this invention is designed to collect looking and listening fees for satellite broadcasting by using balances prestored in an IC card. More specifically, looking and listening fee information and a scrambled broadcast signal of a pay broadcast are received. The received scrambled broadcast signal is descrambled. The broadcast corresponding to the descrambled broadcast signal is televised on a TV receiver. An IC card reader/writer receives the IC card in which a monetary value is stored, and reads/updates the monetary value stored in the IC card. When a pay broadcast is televised by the TV receiver, the IC card reader/writer is used to update the monetary value stored in the IC card to a monetary value obtained by subtracting the looking and listening fee for the pay broadcast from the monetary value stored in the IC card. With this system, looking and listening fees for satellite broadcasting can be collected in units of programs or on a time basis.

5343529 Transaction authentication using a centrally generated transaction identifier

Milton Goldfine and Marvin Perlman and Robert A. Montgomery

Each access attempt transmitted to an authentication agency causes the agency to produce a request identifier unique to that request. The request identifier is transmitted back to the authentication code generator of the user initiating the access attempt, and to an authentication code generator in the agency. The agency also retrieves a user identifier from a database and sends it to its authentication code generator. Both the user's authentication code generator and the agency's authentication code generator independently combine, through identical or complementary transformations, the user identifier and the request identifier to form a user authentication code and an agency authentication code. The two authentication codes are presented by a comparator, which issues a permit signal only if the comparison indicates a match between the two authentication codes. The permit signal is transmitted to a transaction control device to permit the transaction to proceed. Since the authentication code is unique to each transaction attempt, interception of an authentication code will not permit an unauthorized user to successfully initiate another transaction. As an additional security feature, the user of irreversible transformations in the authentication code generator would prevent decoding of an intercepted authentication code and would not allow an unauthorized user to derive the user identifier associated with the transaction. As required by a particular application, additional levels of security can be achieved by using encryption steps in combination with the irreversible transformations at selected points in the process.

5373558 Designated-confirmer signature systems
David Chaum

Cryptographic methods and apparatus for signing (101), receiving (102), verifying (103), and confirming (104) designated-confirmer signatures are disclosed. Such a signature (11) convinces the receiver that the confirmer can convince others that the signer issued the signature. Thus, more protection is provided to the recipient of a signature than with prior art zero-knowledge or undeniable signature techniques, and more protection is provided to the signer than with prior art self-authenticating signatures.

A designated-confirmer signature is formed in a setting where the signer creates and issues a public key (201) and the confirmer also creates and issues a public key (202). Should the confirmer offer a confirmation (13), the verifier is convinced that the signature was issued by the signer. Such confirmation can itself be, for example, self-authenticating, unconvincing to other parties, or designated confirmer. With plural confirmers, various combinations may be realized, some even including confirmer anonymity.

5375172 Postage payment system employing encryption techniques and accounting for postage payment at a time subsequent to the printing of postage
Wojciech M. Chrosny

The postage system employs encryption techniques to verify that a user has printed postage. The postage at the time of printing is not accounted for by the meter. Accounting occurs at a time subsequent to the printing of postage. The user is provided with a postage validating device which provides an indication on the mailpiece of the validity of the imprint to identify the user and a user account number. Charges for the postage thus printed occur at a subsequent time. The imprint is read, preferably by scanning techniques, to determine validity, amount to be charged, and an account number which is charged for the delivery.

5381478 Cipher communication system for transaction data
Yasuo Iijima

A cipher communication system for communicating transaction data between a host computer and a portable electronic device, wherein the host computer includes a first memory for storing a master key data, a generator for generating a transaction key data which is used for enciphering the transaction data, a data converter for enciphering the transaction key data according to the transaction key data, and a first interface for transferring the transaction key data enciphered by the data converter; and wherein the portable electronic device includes a second interface for receiving the enciphered transaction key data transferred from the host computer, a second memory for storing the master key data, a second data converter for deciphering the enciphered transaction key data received by the second interface, and a third memory for storing the transaction key data deciphered by the second data converter, in the manner causing the stored transaction key to be eliminated at a completion of the communication.

5379344 Smart card validation device and method
Stig B. Larsson and Christoph T. Hoffmann and Phillip C. Dimond

A validation device (2) for a smart card (1) of the kind having unprotected data storage memory (4) and protected data storage memory (5) selectively accessible by means of a user access code. The device (2) performs an encryption upon identification data to produce the user access code and reads identification data from the unprotected memory (4) for further encryption. The access code is supplied to the smart card (1) and selected data from said protected memory (5) is read for encryption to produce validating data. A comparator (8) compares the identification data with the validating data and rejects the smart card (1) if the data do not agree and establishes access to said protected memory (5) if the data do agree.

Appendix B

Internet Sources

Here are some URLs that might prove useful for people exploring digital cash systems.

http://www.cnri.reston.va.us:3000/XIWT/documents/dig_cash_doc/ ToC.html *The html page of a "white paper" by the Cross-Industry Working Team (XIWT), a coalition of U.S. industry that is trying to supply its vision for the Net.*

http://www.zurich.ibm.ch/Technology/Security/sirene/ outsideworld/ecommerce.html *A thorough collection of pointers to other data sites containing information on electronic commerce.*

Commercial Providers WWW Pages

http://www.fv.com/ *The home page of the First Virtual system.*

http://www.commerce.net/ *The home page of CommerceNet, a non-profit consortium that is creating protocols for secure Web usage.*

http://www.digicash.com/ecash/ecash-home.html *DigiCash maintains this home page for its ecash project.*

http://www.zurich.ibm.ch/Technology/Security/sirene/projects/ cafe/index.html *CAFE (Conditional Access For Europe) is a European coalition of companies and universities developing portable electronic wallets.*

http://cybercash.com/ *CyberCash is a Virginia-based company developing protocols to link cyberspace with banks and allow payment.*

http://www.ini.cmu.edu:80/netbill/ *The NetBill is a project of the Information Networking Institute at Carnegie-Mellon University.*

http://nii-server.isi.edu/info/NetCheque/ *The home page of the Net-Cheque system developed at the Information Sciences Institute and the University of Southern California.*

http://www.openmarket.com/about/technical/payment/ *Open Market page describing its payment system.*

http://www.u-net.com/gmlets/ *The home page of LETSystem that runs Manchester Money.*

http://www.netchex.com/ *NetChex's home page.*

Other Important Sources

ftp://ftp.psy.uq.oz.au/pub/Crypto/SSL/SSLeay-x.xx.tar.gz *The location for the SSLeay source code, a free version of SSL produced by Eric Young.*

http://www.awa.com/softlock/slhome.html *The home page for SoftLock Services, a company that offers a way to encrypt information so people can pay for it a bit at a time.*

http://www.surety.com/ *The home page for Surety Technologies, a company that is building very neat software for timestamping documents.*

Places to Buy

Here is a collection of Web pages that offer items to buy.

http://www.cts.com/ *CTSNET's Marketplace offers more than 100 different small and varied businesses. Some examples include "Kids at Heart Software," a company that markets its own kid-oriented software, and the "Unarius Academy of Science," which offers monographs on UFOs and interdimensional things. No special payment systems are evident.*

http://www.industry.net/cgi/main/guest *The IndustryNet Marketplace contains more than 300 businesses that mainly make tools, machines, and stuff for other industrial clients. They offer, for instance, the Vulcan water cannon that is a bit too much for your kids looking to up the pool arms war. Some use it to shape bulletproof glass. There are more catalogs than buying opportunities here.*

http://www.shopping2000.com/ *A collection of about 60 of the top catalog names in the business including Marshall Field's, REI Coop, and Barnes and Noble. Most of the catalogs, though, just describe some of their best merchandise and ask people to call their 800 numbers.*

http://marketplace.com/obs/obshome.html *The Online Bookstore offers books that will be shipped to you. There are long descriptions and plenty of pictures. Many of the books are well presented. You order by filling out a HTML form with a credit card number.*

http://www.vpm.com/ *The Village Potpourri Mall (VPM) offers a variety of Web options. Several companies operate storefronts where you can purchase items, and others maintain catalogs. The VPM maintains its own credit card numbers and you can obtain one by filling out a form with your standard credit card number. The VPM uses this as a simple security shell. They immediately pass on any charges made on the VPM card to your normal card.*

Bibliography

This book covers a great deal of ground and it often skims over many technical details that are important, illustrative, and informative. Here is a list of some other texts that many people interested in the deeper issues at hand might want to visit.

[And93]   R. Anderson. Why cryptosystems fail. In *Proceedings of the First ACM Conference on Computer and Communications Security*, pp. 215–227, 1993.

[AMS95]   R. Anderson, H. Manifavas, and C. Sutherland. A practical electronic cash system. Technical report, Cambridge University, 1995.

[APR83]   L.M. Adleman, C. Pomerance, and R.S. Rumley. On distinguishing prime numbers from composite numbers. *Annals of Mathematics*, 117(1), 1983.

[Bau91]   Michael S. Baum. *Electronic Contracting and EDI Law*. Wiley Law Publications, New York, 1991.

[BBC+88]   P. Beauchemin, G. Brassard, C. Crépeau, C. Goutier, and C. Pomerance. The generation of random numbers that are probably prime. *Journal of Cryptology*, 1(1), 1988.

[Ber76]   William A. Berkey. *The Legal Tender Paper Monetary System of the United States*. W.W. Hart, Steam Book and Job Printers, Grand Rapids, Michigan, 1876.

[BFK93]   A. Blum, M. Furst, M. Kearns, and R. Lipton. Cryptographic primitives based on hard learning problems. In *Proceedings of Crypto 93*. Springer-Verlag, 1993.

[Bra93]   S.A. Brands. An efficient off-line electronic cash system based on the representation problem. Technical Report CSR9323, Computer Science Department, CWI, Mar 1993.

[Bra94]   S. Brands. Untracable off-line cash in wallet with observers. In *Advances in Cryptology–CRYPTO '93*. Springer-Verlag, 1994. *Stefan Brand's description of untraceable, off-line cash.*

[Bra95a]   Stefan A. Brands. More restrictive blinding issuing of secret-key certificates in parallel mode. Technical Report CS-R9534,Centrum voor Wiskunde en Informatica, Amsterdam, 1995. *A sequence of papers describing how to use secret-key certificates to increase the security of certificates and the electronic cash that depends upon them for accuracy. The process works by having the certificate-granting authority sign the private key instead of the public key. This adds another level of security.*

[Bra95b]   Stefan A. Brands. Restrictive blinding issuing of secret-key certificates in parallel mode. Technical Report CS-R9523, Centrum voor Wiskunde en Informatica, Amsterdam, 1995.

[Bra95c]   Stefan A. Brands. Restrictive blinding of secret-key certificates. Technical Report CS-R9509, Centrum voor Wiskunde en Informatica, Amsterdam, 1995.

[Bra95d]   Stefan A. Brands. Secret-key certificates. Technical Report CS-R9510, Centrum voor Wiskunde en Informatica, Amsterdam, 1995.

[BS91a]   E. Biham and A. Shamir. Differential cryptanalysis of DES-like cryptosystems. In *Advances in Cryptology–CRYPTO '90 Proceedings*. Springer-Verlag, 1991.

[BS91b]   E. Biham and A. Shamir. Differential cryptanalysis of DES-like cryptosystems. *Journal of Cryptology*, 4(1):3–72, 1991.

[BS91c]   E. Biham and A. Shamir. Differential cryptanalysis of feal and n-hash. In *Advances in Cryptology-EUROCRYPT '91 Proceedings*. Springer-Verlag, 1991.

[BS92]   E. Biham and A. Shamir. Differential cryptanalysis of snefru, khafre, redoc-ii, loki, and lucifer. In *Advances in Cryptology–CRYPTO '91 Proceedings*, 1992.

[BS93a]   E. Biham and A. Shamir. *Differential Cryptanalysis of the Data Encryption Standard.* Springer-Verlag, 1993.

[BS93b]   E. Biham and A. Shamir. Differential cryptanalysis of the full 16-round DES. In *Advances in Cryptology–CRYPTO '92 Proceedings*, pages 487–496. Springer-Verlag, 1993.

[CEvdG88] D. Chaum, J.H. Evertse, and J. van de Graff. Demonstrating possessionof a discrete logarithm without revealing it. In *Advances in Cryptology—EUROCRYPT 87*, pages 127–141, Berlin, 1988. Springer-Verlag.

[CFN93]   David Chaum, Amos Fiat, and Moni Naor. Untraceable electronic cash. In *Proceedings of Crypto 88*, New York, Berlin, Heidelberg, London, Paris, Tokyo, 1993. Springer-Verlag. *The classic work on untraceable cash written by David Chaum, Amos Fiat, and Moni Naor.*[1]

[Cha83]   D. Chaum. Blind signatures for untraceable payments. In *Advances in Cryptology: Proceedings of Crypto 82*. Plenum Press, 1983.

[Cha85]   D. Chaum. Security without identification: Transaction systems to make big brother obsolete. *Communications of the ACM*, 28(10), Oct 1985.

[Cha88a] D. Chaum. Blind signature systems. U.S. Patent #4,759,063, Jul 1988.

[Cha88b] D. Chaum. Blinding for unanticipated signatures. In *Advances in Cryptology–EUROCRYPT '87 Proceedings*. Springer-Verlag, 1988.

[Cha92]   D. Chaum. Achieving electronic privacy. *Scientific American*, Aug 1992. *A classic popularized summary of David Chaum's work that is more conceptual than mathematical.*

---

[1]Also interesting because *Fiat Money* is a term of art in economics.

[DLP93]   I.B. Damgaurd, P. Landrock, and C. Pomerance. Average
           case error estimates for the strong probable prime test.
           Mathematics of Computation, 61(203), Jul 1993.

[Dun60]   Gerald T. Dunne. *Monetary Decisions of the Supreme Court*.
           Rutgers University Press, New Brunswick, New Jersey,
           1960.

[ElG85a]   T. ElGamal. A public-key cryptosystem and a signature
           scheme based on discrete logarithms. In *Advances in Cryp-
           tology: Proceedings of CRYPTO 84*. Springer-Verlag, 1985.

[ElG85b]   T. ElGamal. A public-key cryptosystem and a signature
           scheme based on discrete logarithms. *IEEE Transactions on
           Information Theory*, IT-31(4), 1985.

[Emm90]   Margaret A. Emmelhainz. *Electronic data interchange : a to-
           tal management guide*. Van Nostrand Reinhold, New York,
           1990.

[EO95]   T. Eng and T. Okamoto. Single-term divisible electronic
           coins. In *Advances in Cryptology–EUROCRYPT '94 Pro-
           ceedings*. Springer-Verlag, to appear, 1995. *T. Eng and T.
           Okamoto elaborate on splitting up coins.*

[Fri94]   Milton Friedman. *Money Mischief*. Harvest Books of Har-
           court Brace, San Diego, 1994. *Milton Friedman's* Money
           Mischief *is an excellent survey of U.S. monetary history.*

[Gal75]   John Kenneth Galbraith. *Money: Whence It Came, Where It
           Went*. Houghton Mifflin, Boston, 1975.

[GJ79]   M.R. Garey and D.S. Johnson. *Computers and Intractability:
           A Guide to the Theory of NP-Completeness*. W.H. Freeman
           and Co., 1979.

[GMR82]   Shafi Goldwasser, Silvio Micali, and Charles Rackoff. The
           knowledge complexity of interactive proof systems. In
           *Proceedings of the 17th ACM Symposium on the Theory of
           Computing*, pages 270–299, 1982.

[GS96]   S. Garfinkle and G. Spafford. *Practical Unix Security*.
           O'Reilly & Associates, 1996.

[GW96]   D. Goldberg and D. Wagner. Randomness and the Netscape browser: How secure is the World Wide Web? *Dr. Dobbs Journal*, January, 1996.

[Hal94]   N. Haller. The S/KEY one-time password system. In *Procedings of ISOC 94*, 1994.

[Hay76]   Friedrich Hayek. *Denationalisation of Money*. Institute for Economic Affairs, Westminster, London, 1976. *The* Denationalisation of Money *by Friedrich Hayek is a favorite source for deep thinking about competing currencies.*

[Hay90]   B. Hayes. Anonymous one-time signatures and flexible untraceable electronic cash. In *Advances in Cryptology-AUSCRYPT '90 Proceedings*. Springer-Verlag, 1990. *Barry Hayes describes how to prevent against theft of digital cash using one-time signatures. The paper elaborates on how to use aliases to further guard anonymity.*

[Hep03]   Alonzo Barton Hepburn. *History of Coinage, Currency in the United States, and the Perennial Contest for Sound Money*. The MacMillan Company, New York City, 1903.

[Ish96]   C. Ishikawa. Re: TILT! Counterfeit pachinko cards send $588M down the chute. *RISKS*, 18(16), 1996.

[Kal92]   B.S. Kaliski. The MD2 message digest algorithm. Technical report, RSA Laboratories, Inc., Apr 1992.

[Kob87]   Neal Koblitz. *A Course in Number Theory and Cryptography*. Springer-Verlag, New York, Berlin, Heidelberg, London, Paris, Tokyo, 1987.

[Koc96]   P. Kocher. Timing attacks on implementations of Diffie-Hellman, RSA, DSS, and other systems. In *Proceedings of Crypto 96*. Springer-Verlag, 1996.

[Kur93]   Joel Kurtzman. *The Death of Money*. Back Bay Books, Little Brown and Company, Boston, New York, Toronto and London, 1993. *Joel Kurtzman's popular exploration of the coming electronic marketplace is called* Death of Money. *I think he plays up the potential for destabilization brought about by lightening-fast markets and avoids reveling in their ability to adapt faster and more continuously.*

[Lam81]   L. Lamport. Password authentication with insecure communication. *Communication of the ACM*, 24(11), Nov 1981.

[Ley93]   Valerie A. Leyland. *Electronic Data Interchange: a Management View*. Prentice Hall, New York, 1993.

[Man95]   M. Manasse. The Millicent protocols for electronic commerce. First USENIX Workshop on Electronic Commerce, July, 1995.

[Mas68]   Joseph Earl Massey. *America's Money: The Story of our Coins and Currency*. Thomas Y. Crowell, New York City, 1968.

[Mit03]   Wesley Clair Mitchell. *A History of the Greenbacks*. University of Chicago Press, Chicago, 1903.

[NIS92]   NIST. Proposed Federal Information Processing Standard for Secure Hash Standard. *Federal Register*, 57(21), Jan 31 1992.

[Oka95]   T. Okamoto. An efficient divisible electronic cash scheme. In *Proceedings of Crypto 95*, New York, Berlin, Heidelberg, London, Paris, Tokyo, 1995. Springer-Verlag. *The latest sequel from T. Okamoto describing how to further exploit the binary tree hierarchy to build even more efficient versions of transferable and subdividable cash.*

[OO90]   T. Okamoto and K. Ohta. Disposable zero-knowledge authentication and their applications to untraceable electronic cash. In *Advances in Cryptology–CRYPTO '89 Proceedings*. Springer-Verlag, 1990. *An earlier scheme for Okamoto and Ohta that provides transferability and subdividability without the binary tree hierarchy.*

[OO92]   T. Okamoto and K. Ohta. Universal electronic cash. In *Advances in Cryptology–CRYPTO '91 Proceedings*. Springer-Verlag, 1992. *One of the major papers by T. Okamoto and K. Ohta to describe how to provide cash that can be respent and split apart.*

[Pai93] J.C. Pailles. New protocols for electronic money. In *Proceedings of Auscrypt 92*, pages 263–274, New York, Berlin, Heidelberg, London, Paris, Tokyo, 1993. Springer-Verlag. *An extension of the hierarchical splitting scheme that uses Schnorr's signatures by J.C. Pailles.*

[Ped95] T. P. Pedersen. Electronic payments of small amounts. Technical Report PB-495, Aarhus University, Denmark, August 1995.

[Phi69] Henry Phillips Jr. *Historical Sketches of the Paper Currency of the American Colonies*. Burt Franklin, New York, 1969.

[PT95] Amex blunder: Leaving home without it a plus for privacy? *Privacy Times*, March 1995.

[Riv91] R. Rivest. The MD4 message digest algorithm. In *Advances in Cryptology–CRYPTO '90 Proceedings*. Springer-Verlag, 1991.

[Riv92] R. Rivest. The MD5 message digest algorithm. Technical Report RFC 1321, RSA Data Security, Inc., Apr 1992.

[RS96] Ron Rivest and Adi Shamir. PayWord and MicroMint: Two simple micropayment schemes. Technical report, Massachusetts Institute of Technology, Cambridge, Massachusetts, 1996.

[RSA78] R. Rivest, A. Shamir, and L. Adleman. A method for obtaining digital signatures and public-key cryptosystems. *Communications of the ACM*, 21(11), 1978.

[Rob94] M.J.B. Robshaw. MD2, MD4, MD5, SHA, and other hash functions. Technical Report TR-101, RSA Laboratories, Jul 1994.

[Roc90] Hugh Rockoff. The Wizard of Oz as a monetary allegory. *Journal of Political Economy*, 98(4):739, 1990.

[Sch90] C.P. Schnorr. Efficient signature generation for smart cards. In *Advances in Cryptology–CRYPTO '89 Proceedings*. Springer-Verlag, 1990.

[Sch91a]   C.P. Schnorr. Efficient signature generation for smart cards. *Journal of Cryptology*, 4(3), 1991.

[Sch91b]   C.P. Schnorr. Method for identifying subscribers and for generating and verifying electronic signatures in a data exchange systen. U.S. Patent #4,995,082, Feb 1991.

[Sch94]   Bruce Schneier. *Applied Cryptography*. John Wiley and Sons, New York, 1994.

[Sim84]   G.J. Simmons. The prisoner's problem and the subliminal channel. In *Advances in Cryptology: Proceedings of CRYPTO '83*. Plenum Press, 1984.

[Sim85]   G.J. Simmons. The subliminal channel and digital signatures. In *Advances in Cryptology: Proceedings of EUROCRYPT 84*. Springer-Verlag, 1985.

[Sim86]   G.J. Simmons. A secure subliminal channel. In *Advances in Cryptology–CRYPTO '85 Proceedings*. Springer-Verlag, 1986.

[Sim93]   G.J. Simmons. The subliminal channels of the U.S. Digital Signature Algorithm (DSA). In *Proceedings of the Third Symposium on: State and Progress of Research in Cryptography*, Fondazone Ugo Bordoni, Rome, 1993.

[Sim94]   G.J. Simmons. Subliminal communication is easy using the DSA. In *Advances in Cryptology–EUROCRYPT '93 Proceedings*. Springer-Verlag, 1994.

[Spa69]   E.G. Spaulding. *History of the Legal Tender Paper Money Issued During the Great Rebellion Being a Loan Without Interest and a National Currency*. Express Printing, Buffalo, New York, 1869.

[SS78]   R. Solovay and V. Strassen. A fast monte-carlo test for primality. *SIAM Journal on Computing*, 7, Mar 1978.

[Ung64]   Irwin Unger. *The Greenback Era*. Princeton University Press, Princeton, New Jersey, 1964.

[Way92]   P. C. Wayner. Content-addressable search engines and DES-like systems. In *Advances in Cryptology: CRYPTO '92*

Lecture Notes in Computer Science, Vol. 740, pages 575–580. Springer-Verlag, 1992.

[Whi]   Lawrence H. White. *Competition and Currency: Essays on Free Banking and Money*. Laissez Faire. *Lawrence White produced this collection of essays on how competitive currencies can operate.*

[Win84a] R.S. Winternitz. Producing one-way hash functions from DES. In *Advances in Cryptology: Proceedings of Crypto 83*. Plenum Press, 1984.

[Win84b] R.S. Winternitz. A secure one-way hash function built from DES. *Proceedings of the 1984 IEEE Symposium on Security and Privacy*, 1984.

[WSJ94]   Reuter's instinet is biting off chunks of nasdaq's territory. *Wall Street Journal*, October 1994.

[WSJ96a] Article on pachinko losses. *Wall Street Journal*, May 26, 1996.

[WSJ96b] Second article on pachinko losses. *Wall Street Journal*, July 24, 1996.

Index

About AP Professional

AP PROFESSIONAL, an imprint of Academic Press, a division of Harcourt Brace & Company, was founded in 1993 to provide high-quality, innovative products for the computer community. For over 50 years, Academic Press has been a world leader in documenting scientific and technical research.

AP PROFESSIONAL continues this tradition by providing its readers with exemplary publications that bring new topics to light and offer fresh views on prominent topics. Often, today's computer books are underdeveloped clones, published in haste and promoted in series. Readers tend to be neglected by the lack of commitment from other publishers to produce quality products. It is our business to provide you with clearly written, educational publications that contain valuable information you will find truly useful. AP PROFESSIONAL has grown quickly and has established a reputation for fine products because of this commitment to excellence.

Through our strong reputation at Academic Press, and one of the most experienced editorial boards in computer publishing, AP PROFESSIONAL has also contracted many of the best writers in the computer community. Each book undergoes three stages of editing—technical, developmental, and copyediting—before going through the traditional book publishing production process. These extensive measures ensure clear, informative, and accurate publications.

It is our hope that you will be pleased with your decision to purchase this book, and that it will exceed your expectations. We are committed to making the AP PROFESSIONAL logo a sign of excellence for all computer users and hope that you will come to rely on the quality of our publications.

Enjoy!

Jeffrey M. Pepper
Vice President, Editorial Director

Related Titles from AP PROFESSIONAL

Ahuja: *Network and Internet Security*

Ahuja: *Secure Commerce on the Internet*

Campbell/Campbell: *World Wide Web Pocket Directory*

Casey: *The Hill on the Net*

Crane: *Mutual Fund Investing on the Internet*

Feiler: *Cyberdog*

Fisher: *CD-ROM Guide to Multimedia Authoring*

Foley: *The Microsoft Exchange Guide*

Graham: *TCP/IP Addressing*

Keogh: *Webmaster's Guide to VB Script*

Levine: *Live Java*

Levitus/Evans: *Cheap and Easy Internet Access (Macintosh Version)*

LeVitus/Evans: *Cheap and Easy Internet Access (Windows Version)*

Loshin: *TCP/IP for Everyone*

Murray/Pappas: *Visual J++ Handbook*

Ozer: *Publishing Digital Video*

Ozer: *Video Compression for Multimedia*

Pappas/Murray: *Java with Borland C++*

Pfaffenberger: *Netscape Navigator 3.0 (Mac Version)*

Pfaffenberger: *Netscape Navigator 3.0 (Windows Version)*

Pfaffenberger: *Publish it on the Web! (Mac Version)*

Pfaffenberger: *Publish It on the Web! (Windows Version)*

Pfaffenberger: *Netscape Navigator Gold*

Pfaffenberger: *The Elements of Hypertext Style*

Ribar: *The Internet with Windows 95*

Schengili-Roberts: *The Advanced HTML Companion*

Sinclair/Hale: *Intranets vs. Lotus Notes*

Sullivan: *Using Internet Explorer to Browse the Internet*

Testa: *Graphical Treasures on the Internet*

Tittel/Robbins: *E-mail Essentials*

Tittel/Robbins: *Internet Access Essentials*

Vacca: *JavaScript Development*

Vacca: *VRML: Bringing Virtual Reality to the Internet*

Vaughan-Nichols: *Intranets*

Watkins/Marenka: *The Internet Edge in Business*

Wayner: *Agents at Large*

Wayner: *Disappearing Cryptography*

Wayner: *Java and JavaScript Programming*

Ordering Information

AP PROFESSIONAL
An Imprint of ACADEMIC PRESS
A Division of HARCOURT BRACE & COMPANY

Orders (USA and Canada): 1-800-3131-APP or APP@ACAD.COM
AP PROFESSIONAL Orders: 6277 Sea Harbor Dr., Orlando, FL 32821-9816

Europe/Middle East/Africa: 0-11-44 (0) 181-300-3322
Orders: AP Professional 24–28 Oval Rd., London NW1 7DX

Japan/Korea: 03-3234-3911-5
Orders: Harcourt Brace Japan, Inc., Ichibunan

Australia: 02-517-8999
Orders: Harcourt Brace & Co. Australia, Locked Bag 16, Marrickville, NSW 2204, Australia

Other International: (407) 345-3800
AP Professional Orders: 6277 Sea Harbor Dr., Orlando FL 32821-9816

Editorial: 1300 Boylston St., Chestnut Hill, MA 02167; (617) 232-0500

Web: http://www.apnet.com/